# THE ENTERPRISING BARRISTER

What is it like working as a barrister in the twenty-first century? The independent Bar has undergone a transformation in the last 30 years and evolved into a commercialised, enterprising profession. Based on interviews with and observation of barristers and chambers' staff, this book identifies key changes that have taken place at the Bar and how these are reshaping barristers' professionalism and working culture. This is the first empirical overview of the depth, scope and effects of multiple reforms that have been imposed on the profession and explores how practitioners have responded. It analyses how this once-unified profession has fragmented, as the lived experiences of barristers in different practice areas have diverged. Highly specialised sets of chambers now operate like businesses, whilst others, dependent on legal aid funding, struggle to survive. This book offers a unique examination of different sites of change: how the chambers model has evolved, how entrepreneurial barristers market themselves, how aspirant law students prepare to enter the profession and how regulatory and procedural reforms have imposed managerial constraints on practitioners. The conclusion considers what these far-reaching changes mean for the future of the Bar in England and Wales.

# The Enterprising Barrister

*Organisation, Culture and Changing Professionalism*

Atalanta Goulandris

•HART•

OXFORD • LONDON • NEW YORK • NEW DELHI • SYDNEY

HART PUBLISHING

Bloomsbury Publishing Plc

Kemp House, Chawley Park, Cumnor Hill, Oxford, OX2 9PH, UK

1385 Broadway, New York, NY 10018, USA

HART PUBLISHING, the Hart/Stag logo, BLOOMSBURY and the Diana logo are trademarks of Bloomsbury Publishing Plc

First published in Great Britain 2020



A catalogue record for this book is available from the British Library.

Library of Congress Cataloging-in-Publication data

Names: Goulandris, Atalanta, author.

Title: The enterprising barrister : organisation, culture and changing professionalism / Atalanta Goulandris.

Description: Oxford ; New York : Hart, 2020. | Based on author's thesis (doctoral – City, University of London, Department of Sociology, 2017) issued under title: Continuity and change : the professional lives and culture of self-employed barristers in England and Wales. | Includes bibliographical references and index.

Identifiers: LCCN 2020004873 (print) | LCCN 2020004874 (ebook) | ISBN 9781509928767 (hardcover) | ISBN 9781509928774 (Epub)

Subjects: LCSH: Practice of law—England. | Lawyers—England—Marketing. | Practice of law—Economic aspects—England.

Classification: LCC KD463 .G68 2020 (print) | LCC KD463 (ebook) | DDC 340.068—dc23

LC record available at https://lccn.loc.gov/2020004873

LC ebook record available at https://lccn.loc.gov/2020004874

ISBN: HB: 978-1-50992-876-7
ePDF: 978-1-50992-908-5
ePub: 978-1-50992-877-4

Typeset by Compuscript Ltd, Shannon

To find out more about our authors and books visit www.hartpublishing.co.uk. Here you will find extracts, author information, details of forthcoming events and the option to sign up for our newsletters.

# ACKNOWLEDGEMENTS

I give heartfelt thanks to all the barristers, chambers staff and other participants, without whom this book would not have been possible. They were generous with their time and knowledge, and many shared some of the difficulties they are facing in their professional lives, during a time of great change at the Bar. Particular thanks to the barrister (and his family) who housed me for a week and whom I shadowed throughout his working days in that period. Special thanks also to the two barristers who read an early draft of the research findings – feedback from practitioners was hugely valuable and very much appreciated.

I am especially grateful to Eugene McLaughlin for his years of support, wisdom and encouragement, and to Andy Boon for his helpful guidance and for permitting me to air and share some of my preliminary research findings at two consecutive annual Socio-Legal Studies Association conferences. I would also like to thank Steven Vaughan and John Flood, who urged me to write this book, and to Hart Publishing, in particular Kate Whetter, for commissioning it, and to her and all the others at Hart who gave production, editorial and marketing support.

Last, enormous thanks to Stephane, Dimitri and Sophia, to whom I dedicate this book.

## Note

This book draws, in part, on the research and findings that formed the basis of my PhD:

'Continuity and Change: The Professional Lives and Culture of Self-Employed Barristers in England and Wales', Department of Sociology, City, University of London, awarded in 2017.

An earlier and different version of Chapters 3 and 5 appeared in:

Goulandris, A (2015) 'Reshaping Professionalism: Branding, Marketing and the New Entrepreneurial Barrister' *International Journal of the Legal Profession* 22(3): 272–98.

CONTENTS

*Acknowledgements* ........ *v*
*List of Abbreviations* ........ *xi*

**1. The Enterprising Barrister** ........ **1**
I. The Research ........ 1
II. Ethnographic (Re)Immersion ........ 3
III. Observation ........ 5
IV. Research Context: A Period of Crisis ........ 5
V. Theoretical Framing of the Legal Profession ........ 6
VI. Early Perspectives ........ 7
VII. Professional Jurisdictions ........ 8
VIII. The Neoliberal Profession ........ 10
IX. New Modes of Governance ........ 13
X. The Structure of the Book ........ 14

**2. Old Bar, New Bar: Reforming the Profession** ........ **16**
I. The Early Origins of the Bar ........ 16
II. The Inns of Court: Influence, Control and Training ........ 18
III. A Gentleman's Profession: Status and Distinction ........ 19
IV. Lawyer Monopolies and Jurisdictional Disputes ........ 20
V. Representation and Regulation ........ 22
VI. Legal Aid and the Growth of the Bar ........ 23
VII. Calls for Reform ........ 23
VIII. Loss of Monopolies and Internal Reforms ........ 25
IX. The End of an Era: The Courts and Legal Services Act 1990 ........ 26
X. Solicitor Advocates ........ 27
XI. State Withdrawal: Reduction of Legal Aid – Civil Work ........ 28
XII. *Transforming Legal Aid* ........ 29
XIII. The Neoliberal Bar: Independent Regulation and the Legal Services Act 2007 ........ 31

**3. The Business of Chambers** ........ **34**
I. The Traditional Chambers Model ........ 35
II. The Growth of Chambers and the Rise of Specialist Teams ........ 38
III. Location: Front Stage, Backstage and Chambers as a Virtual Space ........ 41
IV. The New Commercialism: Business and Management ........ 43

V. The New 'Super Clerk' ........ 47
VI. Chambers as a Business ........ 48
VII. Chambers' Branding ........ 50
VIII. ABS and Going 'Global' ........ 52
IX. Online/Virtual Chambers ........ 55
X. A Traditional Chambers Model or Something New? ........ 55

**4. Getting in, Fitting in: The Enterprising Aspiring Barrister ........ 58**
I. Pupillage Places ........ 60
II. The 'Special' CV ........ 61
III. Mini-pupillages ........ 62
IV. Further Educational Qualifications ........ 63
V. Other Work Experience ........ 64
VI. The Implications of these New Trends ........ 65
VII. Pupillage Selection Processes ........ 67
VIII. The Sifting Stage ........ 68
IX. The Interview Stage ........ 71
X. Discussion ........ 73

**5. Getting Work: The New Marketeers ........ 75**
I. Barristers and Solicitors ........ 77
II. The Self-Promoting Barrister ........ 78
III. Online Branding, High Visibility and Social Media ........ 79
IV. Marketing in Groups/Teams ........ 83
V. Individual Initiatives: Specialism, New Practice Areas and Diversification ........ 85
VI. Relationship Building ........ 88
VII. Attitudes to Marketing ........ 90

**6. Direct Access ........ 94**
I. Fees ........ 96
II. Suitability ........ 97
III. Client Contact: 'I Don't Want to be a Solicitor' ........ 100
IV. Offending Solicitors: Biting the Hand that Feeds You? ........ 102
V. Public Awareness ........ 103
VI. What Next? ........ 105

**7. Bar Culture ........ 107**
I. The Development of Bar Ideology ........ 108
II. Excellence, Commitment and Integrity ........ 109
III. Independence and Self-Employment ........ 112
IV. Independence and Excellence Constrained ........ 116
V. The Loss of State Support ........ 116

VI. Powerful Clients ..... 118
VII. Conditional Fee Agreements ..... 120
VIII. Managerial Reforms and Independent Regulation ..... 121
IX. Civil Procedure and Costs Rules ..... 124
X. Public Service and Pro Bono ..... 125
XI. Discussion ..... 126

**8. Community, Unity and Fragmentation ..... 130**
I. The Inns of Court and Circuits ..... 131
II. Specialist Bar Associations ..... 134
III. Chambers ..... 135
IV. A United Bar or an 'Imagined Community'? ..... 138
V. The 'Private/Public Divide' ..... 139
VI. Changing Chambers ..... 142
VII. Women at the Bar ..... 143
VIII. Discussion ..... 147

**9. Conclusion: A New Bar, with a New Kind of Barrister? ..... 149**

*Appendix ..... 155*
*Bibliography ..... 158*
*Index ..... 169*

# LIST OF ABBREVIATIONS

| | |
|---|---|
| ABS | Alternative Business Structure |
| AGFS | Advocates' Graduated Fee Scheme |
| BPTC | Bar Professional Training Course |
| BSB | Bar Standards Board |
| CAB | Citizens Advice Bureau |
| CBA | Criminal Bar Association |
| CFA | Conditional Fee Agreement |
| COMBAR | Commercial Bar Association |
| CPD | Continuing Professional Development |
| CPS | Crown Prosecution Service |
| DBA | Damages Based Agreement |
| FRU | Free Representation Unit |
| GDL | Graduate Diploma in Law |
| HMCTS | Her Majesty's Courts and Tribunals Service |
| IBC | Institute of Barristers' Clerks |
| LETR | Legal Education and Training Review |
| LLP | Limited Liability Partnership |
| LPMA | Legal Practice Management Association |
| LSB | Legal Services Board |
| MOJ | Ministry of Justice |
| PCT | Price Competitive Tendering |
| QASA | Quality Assurance Scheme for Advocates |
| QC | Queen's Counsel |
| SRA | Solicitors Regulation Authority |
| VHCC | Very High Cost Case |

*Statutes:*

| | |
|---|---|
| AJA | Access to Justice Act 1999 |
| CLSA | Courts and Legal Services Act 1990 |
| LASPO | Legal Aid, Sentencing and Punishment of Offenders Act 2012 |
| LSA | Legal Services Act 2007 |

# 1

# The Enterprising Barrister

This book is an account of how self-employed barristers have adapted to the changes the independent Bar of England and Wales (the Bar) has undergone in the last 30 years. The externally imposed reforms have been significant, wide in range and, in some cases, deeply felt and have prompted a radical shift in how self-employed barristers (barristers) organise themselves, seek work, perceive and present their professional function. I argue that four key external changes and their consequences have triggered this shift: the Bar's loss of monopoly on higher court audience rights; the imposition of independent regulation; the liberalising rules concerning organisational structure; and, finally, the withdrawal or reduction of public funding in many areas of practice. The focus of the book is not to review arguments for or against the reforms. Instead, it examines the dynamics and the consequences of the reform process from the perspective of different barristers and how they are negotiating a rapidly changing working landscape.

The qualities now needed to be a successful barrister have evolved. Legal qualifications, together with analytical and advocacy skills, are no longer enough. The contemporary barrister must be innovative, resourceful, self-promoting, commercially astute and accountable, attributes that contrast sharply with how traditional professionalism has been perceived both by practitioners and academics (Evetts 2011). This book advances the argument that a career at the Bar is now an enterprising undertaking, by which I mean, it is market and customer focused and shaped by managerial concerns. Barristers' professional relationships within their organisational structures and with their clients have changed. The enterprise culture has seeped into many aspects of their working lives, as they are required to be more flexible, client-facing, competitive and efficient. Practitioners now sometimes bid for work, are often paid by results and have had to develop sophisticated marketing strategies to survive. A striking new, entrepreneurial rhetoric dominates their professional lives. All of the above are at odds with their traditional ideology and ways of working (Evetts 2015).

## I. The Research

The Bar remains an under-researched profession. The last in-depth empirical overview of barristers' organisational structures and professional culture was

Morison and Leith's (1992) comparative study of barristers in Great Britain, which pre-dated most of the reforms or was written before they had any significant effect. Richard Abel's (2004a, 2004b) political analysis thoroughly investigated, via secondary sources, the Bar's resistance to these changes before they were introduced and, more recently, Justine Rogers' (2011, 2014; Pirie and Rogers 2013) account of pupillage yields rich data on early professional identity formation. Her research, carried out in 2007, charts the path of pupils in their year-long training period during some of the earlier changes explored in this book. In the last decade, the profession's regulator, the Bar Standards Board (BSB) has initiated its own research agenda and in addition there is some research on specific aspects of or changes to the profession (eg, Harris and Piercy (1998) on early marketing; Flood and Whyte (2008) on direct access; Maclean and Eekelaar (2009) on the nature and impact of barristers' advocacy in family cases; Mason and Vaughan (2017) on the experiences of LBGT+ practitioners; and Freer (2018) on attempts to increase the prospects of non-traditional entrants coming into the profession). Despite the valuable insights of this body of research, this study is the first analysis of the overall effects of the reforms on the Bar's organisational, working and cultural life.

This book is derived from qualitative empirical data and analysis of other, extensive data sources. In-depth, face-to-face interviews were carried out with 63 participants. Most were barristers and the rest comprised barristers' clerks, chambers staff, solicitors and others. The research was carried out during a 19-month period between March 2013 and September 2014. There were further follow-up interviews with a third of the participants during a seven-month period between October 2018 and April 2019. The sample is fully broken down in the Appendix, where it appears as a complete, anonymised list in the order in which the interviews took place. Each participant has been given an identifying code and is classified by gender, practice area and year of call for the barristers and experience for the others. In summary, of the 63 interview participants:

- A total of 51 were barristers, 20 of whom practised on circuit.
- They worked from 19 sets of chambers, across three of the six different circuits in England, in addition to those in London.
- All worked within a set of chambers, save one, who was a sole practitioner and another who had set up a Limited Liability Partnership (LLP), which employs other barristers and paralegals.
- From the barrister sample, 34 were men and 17 were women. A third of them were under 15 years' call, the remainder being more experienced, 10 of whom were Queen's Counsel (QC). Four were heads of their chambers.
- There was an even spread of practitioners doing criminal (13), general civil (13) and specialist civil work (14), slightly fewer family practitioners (9), one barrister who did a crime/family mix and one general common law practitioner who did both criminal and civil work.

- The rest of the participants were chambers staff (four senior and second clerks, one chambers director, two managers and one marketing consultant), two solicitors, an academic legal blogger and a Bar Council employee.

Interviews were transcribed onto time-coded software and then transposed onto MAXqda, compatible specialist software, which was used to code, manage and retrieve the data. Analysis was based on a grounded theory approach, whereby insights were explored and developed from themes that emerged during this process (Strauss and Corbin 2015). The sample size is relatively small, does not include barristers practising in Wales and can in no way be representative of all practitioners' opinions or experiences. There were inevitably multiple personal perspectives or realities. However, enough common material or patterns emerged to form a picture of some of the effects of the reforms and the ways in which certain chambers and barristers have responded.

A wide selection of Ministry of Justice (MOJ) and policy documents, select committee and other government reports and Green Papers were used, as were Bar Council and BSB research and reports. Twitter, legal blogs and the trade press provided further access to a variety of relevant issues and developments. Analysis of official Bar statements or newsletters, mediated through some of the professional bodies, was also invaluable, revealing the rhetoric and discursive transformation of the Bar, which facilitated a wider understanding of the changes in the field beyond the immediate dataset.

## II. Ethnographic (Re)Immersion

I practised at the Bar from 1985 to 1993 and was a tenant in a common law set of chambers based in the Temple, with an annexe on one of the circuits. My re-immersion 20 years later as a researcher, Rip van Winkle-like, was double-edged (Wilkinson and Kitzinger 2013). On the one hand, there was considerable familiarity, as I had previous knowledge and professional experience as a young practitioner. On the other, I was struck by how many things were different, some radically so. There were obvious advantages. I was able to access barristers more easily with the help of former colleagues, who were instrumental in facilitating introductions to participants of all ages and practice areas, who in turn led me to others. My insider (albeit out-of dater) status made communication with all the participants smooth. Many spoke to me as if I was one of them, even though I had made my position clear and I felt no power imbalance, as is often noted when researchers interview an elite group (Smith 2006; Mikecz 2012). The Inns of Court, chambers environment and courtrooms were all familiar territory, causing no in-the-field anxiety. All, save one, were happy to be audio-recorded during interviews, releasing me from manic note taking and giving the exchanges a more conversational flavour. My pre-existing knowledge meant that interviews elicited richer material, beyond stock answers and window dressing, and I was able to challenge responses that seemed too glib or superficial.

But there were drawbacks too. I was sometimes less detached than an independent researcher and had to guard against a tendency to be over-sympathetic. It was difficult not to bristle at the 'fat cat' portrayals that were appearing in the press and to over-identify with the challenges some practitioners faced. What surprised me was just how socialised I had *remained* after 20 years. It seems that once a barrister, always a barrister. However, my insider status was fluid. Some changes were so great they were completely beyond my experience, so there was an ongoing dynamic of refamiliarisation, de-familiarisation and re-assessment of what I thought I knew. I found myself making mistaken assumptions because I thought I understood the terrain. Below are a couple of examples (there were more) of how this impacted on my line of questioning in some of the interviews.

## A. Interview Extract 1

> Barrister: I've not had a brief from chambers this century and probably 10 years before that. I mean I've always made my own work.
>
> AG: Do most people, after a certain level, generate their own work?
>
> Barrister: I would say so, if they're being successful.
>
> AG: So your new work is coming from your connections and relationships with solicitors, rather than the clerks drumming up new business for you?
>
> Barrister: Yes, absolutely.

Later in the interview, I discovered that this participant generated work by publishing a book, going to conferences, chairing a specialist committee on the Bar Council and speaking on panels. Barristers are allowed to be far more proactive, enterprising and inventive in their search for new custom since my time. My leading question was not just very bad interviewing technique, but reveals mistaken suppositions. In a subsequent interview, I remedied this:

> Barrister: I get all my own work.
>
> AG: How do you get your work?

## B. Interview Extract 2

> AG: So the management committee does the daily stuff?
>
> Barrister: Yes.
>
> AG: But for the big decisions you will have a chambers meeting?
>
> Barrister: Yes.

I assume I know the division of labour between committees and the distinction between what they do and what happens in a general chambers meeting. I do not ask what the 'daily stuff' consists of, but presume to know. It is very probable that it had changed considerably in 20 years. I transcribed each interview soon after the event, so was alerted to these basic mistakes. On a more prosaic level, I also misjudged more superficial matters. I dressed in black trousers and jacket for the interviews, thinking I would blend in. I was often over-dressed. Many barristers now wear casual clothes in chambers. Quite a few turned up in shorts or tracksuits and jumpers; one was in tennis whites. Further, I was concerned that participants would be reluctant to meet me in chambers, as it was almost unheard of for people to give interviews or participate in research studies whilst I was in practice. Aside from one, all invited me into their chambers, many introduced me to their clerks and colleagues and told them of my study. No one seemed remotely put out that I was researching the Bar, in contrast to suspicions noted by two previous ethnographers (Flood 1981; Rogers 2010).

## III. Observation

The interviews were complemented by ethnographic observation during multiple visits to chambers and courts, as well as attendance at formal and informal Bar events. The periods of observation were varied and included: one week shadowing a criminal barrister, eating on numerous occasions as a guest in hall in the Inns, attending an annual Bar conference and an advocacy instructors' training session in the Inner Temple, repeated marshalling at the Crown Court and other varied court visits, as well as attending a legal aid consultation meeting between barristers and MOJ representatives, a legal aid protest meeting in Lincoln's Inn and both strike action days in January and March 2014. Many interviewees gave me physical tours of their chambers: the clerks' and support staff rooms, meeting/conference/hot desk areas and their own rooms. On four occasions, I spent full days in different sets, interviewing, chatting informally and observing. The most sustained period was when I shadowed a circuit criminal barrister for a week. I stayed with him and his family, commuted to court and chambers with him, inhabited his workplace and watched him work at home in the evenings and early mornings. I shadowed him in the robing rooms and at court. In all these locations, he introduced me to other barristers, to solicitors and Crown Prosecution Service (CPS) lawyers, as well as to the judges hearing the cases, explained what I was doing and why I was there. I read the briefs, listened to him talk about cases, sat behind him in court and had to make a conscious effort not to take notes of evidence as if I were his junior or pupil.

## IV. Research Context: A Period of Crisis

Just as the research began, the Legal Aid, Sentencing and Punishment of Offenders Act 2012 (LASPO) came into force, reducing the scope and amount of public funding for a wide range of civil, family and tribunal cases. All of the first part of the fieldwork took place during the heated dispute between the Bar and the MOJ over the proposed and actual reforms and cuts to legal aid in criminal and public law cases, introduced in a consultation paper *Transforming Legal Aid* in April 2013. The interviews were carried out in what was (and is still) perceived to be a time of unprecedented crisis for parts of the profession and in some cases participants were upset, angry and worried about their income levels and the general state of the Bar as they saw it. This was especially so in the case of publicly funded practitioners. During the research period, almost a third of the participants moved chambers, some more than once. Some left the profession altogether. One set of chambers, which I observed and interviewed members of, dissolved completely. These were, for some, very stressful and emotional times, yet the participants were still willing to be interviewed and talk about these dramatic changes in their professional lives, the ramifications of which were obviously inextricably linked to their personal lives. Whilst I was in some ways familiar with aspects of barristers' working lives, this kind of uncertainty and unhappiness had not been part of my experience. Many spoke fondly of the era when I had been in practice, when work was plentiful and well remunerated, and told me that I was lucky to have left when I did. Perhaps not surprisingly, I felt that the profession had become more politicised and its members more self-aware of their relationship with the outside world and how the Bar was perceived. There is very little research on the emotional response of professionals to changes in their working lives (for doctors' reactions to change, see McDonald et al (2006); Watt et al (2008)). Although the performance of and fees charged by barristers are under constant scrutiny and the profession has undergone significant reforms, there is very little understanding of what and how practitioners feel about them.

## V. Theoretical Framing of the Legal Profession

This research was influenced by existing theorising about how professions develop and evolve, what constitutes professionalism, how professional culture and ideology develop and how neoliberal practices are reshaping professional life. It draws mainly on the Anglo-American-centred literature because of the very different nature of Continental professional development. The latter involved far greater state involvement and lacked the relative independence of professionals from market and hierarchical pressures, a feature prominent in Anglo-American modes of professionalism (Kritzer 1999; Muzio and Kirkpatrick 2011). With regard to theorising the triggers of change, this study's analysis draws, inter alia, on the work of Andrew Abbott (1988), whose focus is on the jurisdictional battles between professions over control of particular areas of work, which he sees as central to understanding professional development and organisational change. However, the Bar has to be seen in the wider political and economic world in which lawyers operate and in the context of technological advances that have reshaped practitioners' working lives. Thus, a broader literature and set of perspectives has also been considered to test its applicability and relevance to the Bar. There has been much debate on the general causes and effects of neoliberal practices on professional life (eg, Miller and Rose 1990; Arthurs and Kreklewich 1996; Rose 1999; Dent and Whitehead 2002; Clarke 2004; Peck 2008, 2010; Gane 2012; Reed 2018). The thinking underlying this study draws mainly on such literature that focuses on the changing nature of professionalism (eg, Freidson 2001; Evetts 2011, 2012, 2013, 2015; Muzio and Kirkpatrick 2011), in the context of the legal profession in particular (eg, Abel 1986, 1987, 1988, 2004a; Sommerlad 1995, 2007, 2011; Paterson 1996; Flood 1996; Hanlon 1997; Flood et al 1998; Kritzer 1999; Muzio 2004; Boon et al 2005; Ackroyd and Muzio 2007; Boon 2010; Muzio and Flood 2012).

## VI. Early Perspectives

Two main sociological conceptualisations of professions were first developed in the early part of the twentieth century. Carr-Saunders and Wilson (1933) and Parsons (1939), inspired by Durkheim, are examples of those who took a structural functionalist approach, linking the professions with social structure and the division of labour, highlighting the traits and positive functions and achievements of occupational groups. Their interpretation is that professions are organised groups of experts who have undertaken elaborate training to acquire esoteric knowledge, which they apply in a manner that is shaped and guided by codes of behaviour to ensure ethical practice. These are moral communities, self-regulating and collegiate, with uniform interests, whose function is to serve and mediate between the needs of the individual and state power. Their cultures are strong and essential in order to socialise new recruits into uniform ways of working, impose ethical norms and maintain legitimacy. Critical studies from the 1960s onwards debunked this approach, claiming it unquestioningly followed professionals' ideology, which presented an altruistic, public service image. Instead, these later studies focused on professions' exercise of power to gain market monopolies and control over who entered their ranks (Johnson 1972; Larson 1977; Abel 1986, 1987, 1988). This 'power literature' was less interested in what professionals actually did and the expertise used to do it, and focused more on the structures used to control and extort rents (Abbott 1988). Many of these studies were theoretical, with little empirical examination, and took a largely critical view of professional groups, focusing mainly on self-interested motivations and distinct professional ideologies, which were very resistant to fundamental change (Saks 2012). Not all agreed. Lamenting the assaults on professions, which frame monopoly and social closure as modes of domination and exploitation, Freidson (2001) draws attention to the fact that they are, instead, mechanisms for supporting growth and refinement of disciplines and the quality of their application. This book explores the Bar's professional ideology in later chapters and, whilst not seeking to prefer any particular perspective, is interested in exploring how barristers themselves perceive their culture and why it affects their decisions, before then critically interrogating its nature and extent of uniformity, and whether it has been eroded and/or reshaped in the last three decades of change.

The second method of conceptualising the professions arose from the Chicago School of Sociology's teachings, under the inspiration of Everett Hughes, and adopted a quasi-anthropological approach, rooted in observation and first-hand experience of the professions. This research was carried out in that same spirit. These earlier studies paid more attention to the organisational features and 'the outcome of everyday battles over the use of resources, the limits of task ownership' and the interdependence and cooperation between professional groups, who divided work up into tasks, which changed in an evolutionary process that depended on competing others (Dingwall 2014 [1983]: 5). Hughes observed that professions sought monopolies, but at the same time deliberately limited their areas of work and responsibilities, delegating associated tasks to other occupations or groups. He felt that competition between groups was less concerned with financial gain, being driven more by characteristics of status (Dingwall 1983/2014; Hughes 1994), supporting Burrage's (2006) later interpretation of professional development. Abbott (1988) attributed his own conceptualisation of professional development to the Hughes tradition (1988: 112, 326). He adopted and developed it, extending his model to include not just the workplace but also the wider public and legal environments.

With the implementation of neoliberal economic policies, there has been a shift away from concerns about market closure and control, which had been evident in those earlier critical studies. Solicitors and barristers have largely lost their monopolies and restrictive practices and they no longer have control over qualification and regulation. Moreover, there is much differentiation within and across these and other professions, which challenges the universal applicability of one theory (Suddaby and Muzio 2015). A more recent body of literature considers how different aspects of professional life, structure, organisation and culture have changed because of commercialisation, whereby professions have taken on a more competitive and managerial approach. This has given rise to debates about what this means in terms of understanding professionalism (Dent and Whitehead 2002; Evetts 2011, 2013, 2014, 2015).

## VII. Professional Jurisdictions

Abbott (1988) asserts that control of work brings professions into conflict with each other, making their histories interdependent. Each profession is bound to a set of tasks by ties of jurisdiction, which are never absolute or permanent, and within this interactive system, or ecology, professions compete and from time to time tasks are created, abolished or reshaped by external forces. The attendant re-adjustments create disturbances that filter through the system, thereby linking structure with professional tasks. The first step in professional development is for a professional group to construct work or a particular task into a known professional problem and then ask society to recognise that group's (preferably exclusive) right to solve it (Abbott 1988: 59–60). This right can be acknowledged formally, by legislation or by custom, but must amount to a legitimate claim to control particular tasks or work. A good example with reference to the Bar dates back to the profession's earliest manifestation, when it had a monopoly on higher court audience rights, a claim established by judicial custom rather than legislation. This claim was deeply embedded and durable. Shifting it had eluded solicitors and attorneys for centuries, until its displacement in 1990. A claim's robustness depends on the organisation of the professional group and its ability to mobilise members, influence media support and public opinion (Abbott 1988: 82). As Abel (2004a) so thoroughly showed in his political analysis of the Bar's fight to preserve its monopoly in the late 1980s, the profession failed to muster support for its cause either in the press or from the public and was ultimately unsuccessful. For an earlier example, Burrage (1997, 2006) and Osiel (1989/90) both illustrate how the Bar failed to exclude solicitors and attorneys from being advocates in the county courts in the mid-nineteenth century, in some respects because at that stage (and unlike solicitors), the profession had no representative body to assist in that particular jurisdictional fight.

For Abbott, the development of professions is dependent on a mass of contingent forces, which can 'unsettle' previously agreed jurisdictional claims. Challenges to jurisdiction can come from other professions, for instance, solicitors challenging the Bar's advocacy monopoly, or external forces can change the status quo. The ongoing withdrawal of state funding for many types of legal work as well as the recent liberalisation of the legal services market have triggered the disturbances within the system that Abbot envisages, sparking new boundary shifts between the two branches and other professions, as well as within the Bar itself. Francis (2011) explores the notion of boundary in depth, noting that it relates not simply to jurisdictional claims and work tasks, but also to professional identity and emotion. The knock-on effects of these shifts are still unfolding, in terms of the Bar's internal organisational structures, modes of working and practitioners seeking to reshape their practices and identities. New knowledge, areas of expertise and tasks are being sought, identified and developed in an attempt to extend barristers' jurisdiction in new directions and to compensate for work lost. These attempts to create new, distinct and self-contained areas of knowledge, which in turn are translated into new areas of practice, have been central to the creation of the professions (Fournier 2000). For Abbott, these strategies involve professionals' 'abstracting ability to define old problems in a new way' or seizing new problems so as to survive (Abbott 1988: 30). Within this framework, professionalism is a dynamic that results from conflict (Boon and Flood 1999; Francis 2011). Many of the findings discussed in later chapters support Abbott's system of claims, unsettlement, disturbances, adaptation and development or loss of jurisdiction.[1] It is precisely how practitioners resist, negotiate, adapt and compete during periods of flux and conflict that gives insight into professional development and decline (Suddaby and Muzio 2015).

## VIII. The Neoliberal Profession

Consideration of the broader forces at play is also required so as to situate the reforms and internal changes that followed. Developing Abbott's thesis, Freidson (2001) argues that the state has the power to officially recognise, define and classify particular kinds of work in the labour force and permit or support the division of labour and jurisdictional disputes. Neoliberal policies have been unrolled in the last few decades that reduce constraints on commercialism, break open restrictive practices and promote consumerism, factors which all oppose ideal-type professionalism. Theorising about and research into how this has affected the legal profession address features such as self-regulation, independence and autonomy, organisational structure, discretion and professional culture, even if little of it touches on barristers specifically (except Abel 1986, 1987, 2004a) and is more concerned with the solicitor branch (eg, Stanley 1991; Sommerlad 1995; Ackroyd 1996; Flood 1996; Paterson 1996; Hanlon 1998; Flood 2011).

Traditional forms of collegial governance within the solicitor profession are being displaced by a more commercial approach (Sommerlad 1995; Muzio and Kirkpatrick 2011). Customer services, generating new work and efficiency reign supreme, monitored by the ongoing measuring of performance (Ackroyd and Muzio 2007; Sommerlad 2011). Studies have variously noted that professional services have become more specialised and more global, and that lawyers are sometimes constrained by the entrepreneurial demands of their employers. Firms are restructuring, or branching out into multi-disciplinary practices, breaking the previously established boundaries of the tasks undertaken. The professional–client relationship has radically changed, with the latter becoming more demanding and powerful (Kritzer 1999; Hanlon 2001; Webb 2004; Ackroyd and Muzio 2007).

Legal aid, introduced in 1949, enlarged lawyers' client pool, necessitating a growth of the profession, but as a result of the state's recent unwillingness to fund it, many are now unable to maintain levels of work and struggle to make a reasonable living. Hanlon (2001) notes the emergence of two 'hemispheres' or markets within the legal profession, a concept taken from Heinz and Laumann's study (1994)

[1] Although this study embraces Abbott's approach, it is worth noting that Bourdieu similarly places lawyers in a social universe, which he terms the 'juridical field', and argues that the social practices of law are a product of its functioning, by which he means the power relations within it, which determine its structure and which order the competitive struggles within it. His juridical field, like Abbott's jurisdictions, are sites of struggle, where actors compete for monopolies or control over certain tasks and acquire or preserve their social, cultural and economic capital (Bourdieu 1986/1987).

on Chicago lawyers: the publicly funded branch, to which the state is hostile, evidenced by successive governments' reduction in legal aid and the accompanying justifications for it; and the more 'efficient' or profitable, commercial branch, which Hanlon nonetheless perceives to also be in peril, due to increased consumer power and commercialisation. Ackroyd and Muzio (2007), writing about the solicitor branch, also note the ideological and economic hostility towards lawyers, manifested in the deregulation of their monopolies, and their commercialisation and managerialisation. If the Bar also has two such hemispheres, how has this impacted on the profession's uniformity? Over 30 years ago, Abel noted that publicly funded practitioners comprise a weak community at the Bar because of their work and income insecurity (Abel 1986). Levels of pay are now so low in some areas of practice that one journalist was prompted to ask whether barristers could earn more working in McDonald's (Schraer 2019). Has the increased differentiation and stratification in practitioners' practice areas, clients and income fragmented the profession? How might this impact on, for example, the application and oversight of a uniform ethical code? After the recent celebrations of the Bar Council's 125th anniversary, another journalist asked: 'Is the profession thriving or flailing? It depends on your perspective' (Ames 2019b). Whilst the profession's representative bodies are keen to portray an image of unity through the rhetoric of 'one Bar', Ames noted the marked differences in income and lifestyle of commercial and criminal practitioners.

This assault on the professions comes not just from government policy, but reflects a wider shift in attitudes. Professionals no longer attract the trust and unquestioning faith of clients, can no more claim to have exclusive stock of specialised knowledge, as their monopolies and markets have opened up to competition from others, and the once respected educational, training and socialisation processes are now no longer sufficient qualifications to guarantee a professional's legitimacy. Professionals must now increasingly adapt and learn with continuing professional development (CPD). A professional's claims of altruism and working for the common good at best fall on deaf ears and at worst are seen as self-interested political strategies. Self-regulation has been replaced by external oversight and supervision. In essence, there has been an '[e]rosion of normative superiority' within the professional classes, a shift from the trusting, if asymmetric, relationship of the modern professional to a very different kind of alliance between '[a] reflexive and insecure expertise producer and a self-confident and critical expertise consumer' (Pfadenhauer 2006: 565, 571; Evetts 2015). For Freidson (2001: 208), the critics of professionalism have succeeded in undermining the credibility of the professional service ethos and has 'strengthened the power and increased the legitimacy of ideologies of consumerism and managerialism that underlie the activities of both capital and the state'. In his view, this has freed professionals up 'to devote themselves to single-minded efforts to maximize their own incomes'.

Abbott noted that changing social values can recast the legitimation of professions, even if nothing else had changed (1988: 177), so professions need to constantly revise their validation systems. Whereas barristers used to be legitimised by, for example, their social status or 'gentlemanliness' (1988: 191), different attributes are now sought and promoted to invite acceptance and respect. Independent and collegiate professions, such as the Bar, are obliged to justify their very existence as their traditional modes of working are viewed by some as anachronistic (Reed 2018). The findings in this book show that efforts to be more open and transparent, to provide a customer-centred service and have a representative body that creates an image of a modern, diverse, expert and merit-based profession are all designed to legitimate the Bar in the new economic, cultural and regulatory climate. Barristers and their associations have engaged in sophisticated marketing exercises via Twitter, websites, newsletters and other platforms to make the profession more accessible and visible. Yet the very utility of lawyers is, in many areas, being challenged by technological developments and the current reform programme of Her Majesty's Courts and Tribunals Service (HMCTS). It is forecast that many smaller tasks or hearings previously done by junior practitioners will be automated, carried out online, via video-link or over the telephone without any lawyer assistance at all (Susskind 2000, 2010, 2013; Rozenberg 2019). This new professionalism, or 'post-professionalism', recognises a professional's loss of exclusivity, the increasing segmentation, through specialisation and the growing use of technology to access information resources, so that services previously provided by professionals can now be given by others or can be automated (Kritzer 1999; Susskind 2000, 2010).

Thus, the liberalisation and injection of competition into the legal services market, the globalisation of legal services and the effects of managerial reforms have reshaped professionalism, creating debates about whether or not it truly exists as previously conceptualised (Boon 2010). Some posit that professionalism is at an end or has at least been reconfigured in a new hybrid form, where the principles of professionalism, enterprise and managerialism have blurred (Abel 1986; Dent and Whitehead 2002; Ackroyd and Muzio 2007; Evetts 2012, 2015). Others assert that legal professionalism was always only a construct, contingent, dynamic and always open to renegotiation, and is now evolving again to accommodate these new developments without letting them undermine core professional values (Paterson 1996; Faulconbridge and Muzio 2008). Professionalism has now adopted two different forms, one with organisational features (commercialisation, managerial control, standardised procedures and accountability in the form of external regulation) and, second, occupational professionalism, which emphasises the traditional features (collegial authority, discretion and control over work, practitioner trust, professional ethics and internal control) (Evetts 2015). As Muzio and Flood (2012: 372) point out, these distinctions or categorisations fail 'to capture the messiness, elusiveness and contested character of empirical reality'. Rather than running parallel, organisational logics and traditional occupational professionalism often overlap and, depending on the work setting and employment status of those involved, affect the practitioners in different ways. For example, the extent of managerial control and assessment is different for employed barristers and those working at the independent Bar. Similarly, collegial relations within chambers depend on the governance, staffing, size and geographical spread of any given set. Thus, the layering of new organisational features over traditional professionalism will always vary in both substance and effect. To what extent the Bar's traditional characteristics have been reshaped by commercial and organisational logics is key to this enquiry, as are the variations of such influences. These matters are explored in later chapters, though it is the only profession that hitherto resembled anything like its original occupational form, possibly because of the self-employed status, and therefore relative independence, of its practitioners (Ackroyd 1996).

## IX. New Modes of Governance

Apparently competing but intersecting forces have emerged in the last few decades, which seek to radically alter the legal profession. On the one hand, as discussed above, it has become more commercially oriented, with liberalising rules regarding working structures and practices to promote competition and entrepreneurship. Such liberalisation is framed in terms of market 'freedoms'. On the other hand, there is increased state control and constraint via imposed legal aid cuts, outside regulation and managerial measures. Gane (2012) posits that it is precisely this combination that Foucault had in mind when speaking of neoliberal forms of governance (see also Sommerlad 1995). Using Peck's terms (2010: 22), it is both 'roll back' and 'roll out' – market freedom and increased surveillance and regulation, with competition at its core. According to Peck, neoliberalism was never about the state completely deferring to the market, but more 'associated with rolling programs of market-oriented reform, a kind of permanent revolution … an open-ended and contradictory process of regulatory restructuring' (Peck 2010: 7). So the marketisation of the Bar, its structures and the liberalising rules that free the profession to work in any number of different ways or combinations is framed as emancipating barristers from rigid, traditional and constraining rules about how to work, permitting them to compete in a no longer sheltered market. However, the profession now faces increased constraints, imposed on it by outside regulation, which demand new modes of accountability in relation to chambers organisation, recruitment, training and case management, costs and court procedures and customer service. Peck (2010: 22) argues that these 'restructuring projects' typically focus on dismantling institutions, upsetting centres of power and attacking systems by, for example, funding cuts and are examples of Abbott's (1988) disruptions of jurisdictional settlements, all of which can be seen in the recent reforms to the Bar and which will be exemplified in this book.

Moreover, a new form of individual autonomy lies at the heart of this disciplinary control, exercised through responsible self-management (Miller and Rose 1990, Grey 1994; McNay 2009). Miller and Rose call it 'government of the internal world', where behaviours are shaped and normalised by malleable, self-regulating subjects (Miller and Rose 1990: 2). How new entrants succeed in getting into the profession and how practitioners compete for work is considered in the empirical chapters in the light of this new, enterprising and responsibilised professional, who is 'an individual actively seeking to shape and manage his or her own life in order to maximise its returns in terms of success and achievement' (Miller and Rose 1990: 26). These indirect mechanisms of (self)-government, which envision a neoliberal citizen who makes rational personal choices to seek self-fulfilment, disguise the fact that social and structural inequalities can be the cause of lack of success (Miller and Rose 2008). Most barristers do not have any significant training in business development, marketing or management, are generally risk-averse and hitherto have only had to focus on providing an individual service to a client, factors that are also considered in the empirical chapters.

## X. The Structure of the Book

In sum, this book considers the relevance and applicability of Abbott's concept of professional development when looking at the causes and processes of change at the Bar. It further draws on the shifting analyses of professionalism and the intersecting effects of neoliberal forms of governance – marketisation, managerialisation and responsiblisation – and interrogates the applicability of that literature to the Bar, given that its structure and ways of operating are quite different from any other legal professional and are guided by quite distinct ideologies and cultural references. Specifically, Chapter 2 gives a short historical overview of the development of the Bar and then identifies what market, state and regulatory pressures have driven the reforms. The subsequent chapters consider how the Bar has adjusted its own internal organisation, structure and outlook in response and how these have, in turn, reshaped its traditional professional culture and identity. Chapter 3 analyses the more commercial and customer-oriented chambers model and the organisational structures and hierarchies within which barristers operate, whilst Chapter 4 investigates the recruitment process, in an era of increasing numbers of qualifying students and intense competition. What skills do aspiring entrants to the profession need to have? What selection criteria do recruiting committees apply when deciding whom to invite for an interview and offer a pupillage to? Chapters 5 and 6 explore how barristers get and maintain work, focusing especially on the two relatively recent phenomena of marketing at the Bar and direct/public access, both of which are the very antithesis to the profession's traditional culture. Barristers are compelled to specialise and undertake considerable marketing and self-promotion in order to get work, much of which is now being done by solicitors or litigants in person. Chapter 7 explores how practitioners perceive their professional culture and why this matters in a period of great change, and the penultimate Chapter 8 considers how all these modifications have affected the unity and cohesion of the profession. The final chapter summarises the research findings and reflects on their significance in the context of the Bar's future and the broader debates on the concept of professionalism.

How might this book contribute to the discussion about evolving professionalism? Abbott's theory is applied and tested in the context of the Bar and elaborated upon. Whilst many features of his professional development thesis are evidenced in the changing ecosystem of the Bar, this book interrogates it further by examining how professional change, growth or decline are also inextricably linked to internal professional culture. It argues that previous theorists have, to some extent, underestimated the strength of the Bar's ideology and practitioners' self-identity and perceived status or function. Many are quick to dismiss it at self-serving, without in-depth consideration of how, from barristers' perspectives, it influences choices made in times of change. In the Hughes tradition, drawing from interview and ethnographic data, this book examines how this relatively small, self-employed group distinguishes itself from other employed lawyers. How has professionalism at the Bar evolved? How have elements of enterprise and commercialism changed the profession? Traditional professionalism at the Bar has evolved, but in its own, idiosyncratic and distinct way.

# 2

# Old Bar, New Bar

## *Reforming the Profession*

What follows is a selective history of the profession and an outline of the reforms that have reconfigured it in the last 30 years. The intention is to provide a framework within which to locate the subsequent empirical chapters. The Bar, as an institution, has a strong sense of identity and distinct professional culture, so an understanding of its development and traditional, idiosyncratic ways of working will help to contextualise practitioners' perceptions of and reactions to these changes. Despite the various shifts that the profession has undergone, a constant and central aspect of barristers' identity is their role as independent advocates, and the sections below seek to highlight that this distinct function appeared from their first emergence, even before they were recognised as a professional group. The social status attached to this role and the demographic make-up of the early Bar go some way towards explaining how this small, homogeneous profession developed almost unaltered during a period of vast social and economic change from the late eighteenth century onwards. Barristers sought not to expand their markets, or to take advantage of new areas of work, but instead fought with the solicitor/attorney branch over jurisdictional boundaries in order to maintain their independence and role as specialist advocates (Burrage 2006; cf. Abel-Smith and Stevens 1967; Abel 1988).

## I. The Early Origins of the Bar

The common law, shaped by earlier customary law, emerged after the royal courts were established and continued to develop and expand through decisions and precedents made by judges. As oral proceedings became more technical and since they were conducted in French, it became necessary for expert advocacy. From the earliest appearance of legal professionals in the non-clerical courts, there was a division of labour, based on the separation of functions of advocacy on the one hand and representation on the other, so the split evident in today's two branches was not the result of a schism, as the division of labour pre-dates professional formation. The 'advocatus' stood by a litigant and spoke for him, whereas the 'procurator' or representative stood in for a litigant who was absent

(Baker 2000). These advocates (also called pleaders or narrators) became known as Serjeants-at-Law (serjeants) during the thirteenth century, when they acquired a monopoly of advocacy in the Court of Common Pleas, the court most often used for civil litigation. Serjeants were selected by the king, wore a distinctive coif and were perceived to be a professional group (Prest 1986; Burrage 2006). It was not just a professional qualification, but a public honour, with a status on a par with knighthood. By the fifteenth century, they were the natural leaders of the Bar and it was from this group that the common law judges were chosen (Baker 2000; Boon and Levin 2008).

Apprentices to the serjeants, later known as barristers, were in evidence by the late thirteenth century, attached to the court where they were installed in galleries or 'pecunes' specially built for them. Although not all became serjeants, more senior ones became the junior branch of the Bar, with rights of audience in the King's Bench, Chancery, the lesser courts and on circuit. The term 'utter' or 'outer' barrister first appears in the mid-fifteenth-century records of Lincoln's Inn. 'Inner' barristers were students. Barristers only emerged as fully fledged advocates during the sixteenth century, when the volume of litigation increased and the serjeants could not meet the demand (Prest 1986; Burrage 2006). Further, the King's Bench court, which travelled around the country, developed a group of lawyers of its own and it was these peripatetic lawyers, who were senior apprentices to the serjeants, who evolved into modern barristers (Abel-Smith and Stevens 1967). Unlike serjeants, barristers were not appointed by the Crown. A third category of counsel, the King's Counsel, was created under the Stuarts. These were barristers upon whose services the king had a prior claim and they were obliged to assist the Attorney General and the Solicitor General if called upon to do so. Barristers' rights of advocacy were not conferred by statute, but by judicial discretion.

By 1300, the second group, comprised of attorneys or procurators, appeared so often in the Common Bench that it too had become an occupation. Attorneys spoke in court on behalf of non-attending litigants, set the procedures in motion, managed suits and could challenge what a serjeant said on behalf of his client. They were selected by judges and sworn in to do their duty as officers of the court. In the fifteenth century, the work of attorneys was paralleled by solicitors in the Chancery Court. At that time, and in an early example of interprofessional competition, judges campaigned to exclude attorneys so that young barristers could carry out their work. They were unsuccessful, as the latter were too busy with court appearances, advisory and drafting work.

There were no less than seven classes of legal practitioner in the common law courts by the end of the seventeenth century. The senior branch comprised serjeants (the most senior advocates), King's Counsel and utter or outer barristers (juniors). The junior branch was made up of solicitors, attorneys, conveyancers (or scriveners) and pleaders, who drafted the documents to initiate litigation. In the ecclesiastical and admiralty courts, a parallel group of lawyers had evolved, with proctors carrying out a similar task to that of attorneys/solicitors and a group of advocates in Doctors' Commons, or College of Civilians, who had a monopoly on the court work. In due course, pleaders were to be absorbed by barristers, scriveners by solicitors, and under the Judicature Act 1873, solicitors and attorneys merged and serjeants were abolished, leaving the two-branch division of barristers and solicitors that exists today (Zander 1968; Warren 1978). What is clear from the brief outline above is that from the outset, there was a clear difference in function between the two branches, with advocacy being the defining feature of a barrister. Barristers were not officers of the court (like attorneys) and nor were they selected by the King (like serjeants). Their specialist status was reinforced by the common law judges, who themselves came from that branch of the profession and at whose discretion rights of advocacy were conferred, thus leaving them with a peculiar and unique independence.

## II. The Inns of Court: Influence, Control and Training

Initially there were about 20 Inns around the Holborn and Fleet Street areas, housing mainly apprentices and clerks. By the middle of the fifteenth century, barrister apprentices were based in the four Inns of Court, which were founded in the fourteenth century, initially established as lodging houses for those attending the Westminster courts (Lemmings 2004). Serjeants had their own Inns, in which they remained after appointment to the bench, and attorneys gathered in the Inns of Chancery (Baker 2000). A fairly long and elaborate apprenticeship was the sole form of legal education, as common law was not regarded as an academic subject that could be taught at university. By the Tudor period, the Inns of Court had developed into significant educational centres, providing a chapel, library and dining hall, which hosted mock trials (moots), debates and readings or extended lectures delivered by senior practitioners. Aspiring lawyers had to spend eight years there before being called and a further five before fully qualifying to practise (Warren 1978). The Inns were the centre of social, political and cultural life, with an intricate hierarchy and much symbolic ritual, which promoted solidarity, collegiality and an established order of rank, within which a young lawyer would be socialised into the profession's ways and ethos, and could locate his standing and progress (Boon 2014).

As more cases reached the courts, the Bar opened up to junior members of the Inns and numbers swelled as it further transformed itself into communities of masters and pupils, united by institutional loyalty and divided from the solicitor/attorney branch by rank and wealth (Lemmings 2004). However, the Inns went into rapid decline in the late seventeenth century, around the same time as the confrontation between the municipal and chartered bodies within the City of London and Charles II and then James II, who sought to limit the power of these 'little commonwealths' or 'republics' and have royal control over them. The Bar, whose autonomy rested not on charter, but on custom, fiercely resisted, and the incoming William of Orange restored the liberties and privileges of the chartered bodies, including those of the Bar, which remained an institution of self-government. It controlled admission, training and certification and the right to defend and regulate its work jurisdictions, a situation that remained largely unchallenged and unchanged until the late twentieth century (Burrage 1997: 149). This long history of independence and self-governance remains ingrained in Bar culture and contrasts sharply with the new regime of external regulation and oversight, something that will be explored in Chapter 7.

The programmes of education at the Inns were gradually abandoned and benchers focused their efforts on the organisation of dinners, building maintenance and rent collection. A common view asserts that until the nineteenth century, the Inns failed to have much influence over entry or professional life. However, there is evidence from minutes of meetings in the Inns that the internal control exercised over those who challenged the status quo remained constant. Although practitioners may have been insulated from the influence of patronage, private corruption or state coercion, their freedom was very much curtailed by the internal powers of the Inns, which proactively policed all who were admitted, disciplining those affiliated with political radicals or showing any signs of cultural unorthodoxy (Wesley Pue 1997). Given the small size of this professional group, its limited geographical spread and the homogeneity of its members, this type of formal and informal control was very effective. There have been many critics during the history of the Bar of barristers' training, entry requirements and self-government, but, as Burrage states, 'the absence of criticism of their honesty and integrity stands in sharp relief' (2006: 517). High levels of compliance with the rules of etiquette are attributable to the informal, collegial disciplinary authority within the profession itself and the oversight of judges within the courtroom (Abel-Smith and Stevens 1967; Burrage 2006). Whether these controls are still effective as the profession becomes larger, more spread out, diverse and fragmented is explored in Chapter 8.

## III. A Gentleman's Profession: Status and Distinction

Although there had been a decline in recruitment of aristocratic students since the Glorious Revolution, the Bar remained an effective route into the aristocracy. Its status gradually became related less to social associations and more to the performance of a specific task. It became important for practitioners to reinforce their difference, to separate themselves and their work from attorneys, who dealt with clients and client money and were thus considered to be engaged in trade, so the latter group were excluded from the Inns, distancing the Bar from their consumers (Lemmings 2004). Collective life at the eighteenth-century Bar was an exclusive preserve of the rich and something of a gentleman's club. From 1798, members were obliged to dine a minimum amount of times in hall, and circuit messes sprung up for those moving around the provinces.

In the eighteenth century and under pressure of too much work, barristers began to delegate the preparation of briefs and evidence gathering to solicitors and attorneys (a move that was widely viewed at the time as a lowering of standards). Formal regulation of solicitors and attorneys was enacted in 1729, controlling the costs they charged, formalising training and giving them a monopoly on initiating litigation. A decade later, their first professional association, the Society of Gentleman Practisers in the Courts of Law and Equity, was formed. Although there were no sanctions on breaking this monopoly, solicitors and attorneys, supported by their professional association, extended the scope of their work, bringing in barristers only when they wished, thus reducing the latter's contact with clients, whilst at the same time seeking to keep advisory and pleading work for themselves. Barristers were, at this stage, still permitted to be briefed directly by the lay client. Nonetheless, this system of 'referral' for much work began and barristers were complicit in distancing themselves from the original sources of work. To avoid unprofessional touting, barristers were discouraged from currying favour with attorneys and solicitors, except at arm's length, and from socialising with them (including travelling together on public transport). This function was left to the clerk, who acted as intermediary, and in developing this role, barristers surrendered control over their own working lives and the fees they charged (Abel-Smith and Stevens 1967). Therefore, the introduction of the barrister's clerk was not driven by business innovation, but more by a professional logic, a desire to maintain status, difference and distance (Burrage 2006). Strict rules of etiquette governed the way in which the two branches interacted: a barrister would never go to a solicitor's office; barristers' court dress affiliated them with the bench, excluding solicitors, who had to sit behind them and were referred to as 'my friend', not 'my learned friend', the way in which fellow counsel called one another. By the mid-nineteenth century, the separation of status between the two branches was complete, with solicitors using the tradesmen's entrance when calling at barristers' homes (Burrage 2006).

## IV. Lawyer Monopolies and Jurisdictional Disputes

Armed with a monopoly on the initiation of proceedings, attorneys sought to take over the monopoly of conveyancing in the City of London from the scriveners, succeeding in 1760 and acquiring a national monopoly in 1804. Towards the middle of the nineteenth century, solicitors increased their advocacy work. The creation of the county courts (about 500 nationwide) under the County Courts Act 1846 forbade lay clients from instructing barristers directly in cases within its jurisdiction and enabled solicitors to do much of the advocacy, taking a sizeable chunk of the junior Bar's work. At the same time, the numbers at the Bar had doubled and losing work in the superior courts to the county courts, and in turn to solicitors, gave cause for concern. In language reminiscent of today's anxieties, the *Law Times* reported the gloomy prospects of the Bar, concluding that the common law Bar's days were numbered: 'One fiftieth part of the present race of Barristers will suffice for all the work for which, in a few years, Barristers will be required' (*Law Times*, 11 August 1849: 438, cited in Abel-Smith and Stevens 1967: 55).

In response, the Bar sought, unsuccessfully, to exclude solicitors from acting as advocates in courts in which they were traditionally allowed to appear: Compensation Courts, Bankruptcy Courts, Magistrates and Quarter Sessions. Without the support of a representative body, the Bar failed to mobilise any collective protest or action. It achieved some success when the County Courts Act was amended in 1852, permitting direct lay access to barristers. Further, whilst maintaining the audience rights of attorneys, the Act forbade them from instructing other attorneys to appear as advocates when they themselves chose not to, obliging them to instruct the Bar in those cases (which were common as it was more profitable for them to spend the day in the office rather than at court). It remained the custom that in all other courts, a client could instruct a barrister direct, but this was altered in 1888 by the new representative body, the Bar Committee, later called the Bar Council. Thereafter, in contentious matters, a barrister could not see a lay client without the intervention of a solicitor and even in non-contentious matters direct contact became restricted, causing one newspaper to wonder if the Bar Council had 'entered into a conspiracy with the solicitors to compass its own destruction' (*Saturday Review*, 6 May 1905, cited in Abel-Smith and Stevens 1967: 222). In fact, during this period, barristers showed remarkable indifference to potential markets, losing opportunities for work under the Arbitration Act 1889 to newly formed arbitrators and leaving accountants to do bankruptcy and insolvency work, even though there was much less work available, particularly for the junior Bar (Abel-Smith and Stevens 1967).

Muzio and Flood's historical account (2012) of lawyers' intrinsic commercialism and entrepreneurship charts their involvement in industrial and commercial enterprise from the mid-nineteenth century. Yet, their examples focus mainly on the behaviour of solicitors and attorneys rather than barristers. Whilst Abel-Smith and Stevens (1967) and Abel (1988, 2004a) assert that the Bar was driven by market concerns and the desire to defend its economic self-interest, Burrage offers an alternative explanation. In his view, the Bar was never in the least market-oriented, but was more concerned 'to define and defend a principled division of labour between the two professions. It was a matter of honour and status rather than of money and markets' (Burrage 2006: 484–85). Burrage asserts that this is the only plausible reason why barristers voluntarily surrendered tasks such as conveyancing and why they agreed to referral. It was an attempted exchange for what they believed was their function, which was to have a monopoly over advocacy in all courts. So whilst numbers at the Bar increased by 50 per cent from 1835 to 1885, reflecting a demand caused by demographic changes (redistribution of the population to the manufacturing cities), little else within its professional organisation changed. Newer forms of business structure did not seem to affect the profession, which remained largely centralised in London, and by 1900, only six per cent of practitioners worked full time in the provinces (Burrage 2006). Despite these inroads into the Bar's work in the late nineteenth century, solicitors and attorneys themselves faced stiff competition from the growing professions of accountants, who began drawing up documents required in bankruptcy cases, auctioneers who drafted leases and agreements for sale, debt collectors and unqualified people posing as lawyers (Abel-Smith and Stevens 1967).

Thus, the interprofessional push and pull for control over certain types of work is nothing new, although the jurisdictional status quo remained relatively unchanged for the next 100 years. It is these core monopolies across both professions that have been broken in the last 30 years. The removal of market protection, together with the imposition of independent regulation, drastic cuts to legal aid funding and the liberalisation of the rules governing how legal services can be provided, has triggered many of the internal reforms and the reconfiguration of the Bar. It is the effects of such changes that form the essence of this book.

## V. Representation and Regulation

Barristers did not form a professional association until 1883. Until then, admission, discipline and dismissal were controlled by 'self-perpetuating oligarchies of benchers' in each Inn and the Attorney General (as leader of the Bar) rather than a representative or elected body (Abel-Smith and Stevens 1968: 47). The four Inns consolidated their regulations regarding admission and 'keeping terms' (eating dinners in hall) in 1863. Following significant reforms in a series of Judicature Acts in the 1870s, which changed the structure of the profession and deprived the junior Bar of much of its work, a Bar Committee was established in 1883, initially as a consultative body, but transforming into the Bar Council in 1894, when it acquired powers of representation, discipline and etiquette from the Inns. The Bar's distinctive, traditional and professional characteristics remained virtually unchanged for the next 100 years. It emerged after the Second World War as a 'pre-modern profession', small, homogeneous and in the main geographically concentrated within the four Inns of Court around the Royal Courts of Justice, whose governance, together with that of the circuits and of the Bar Council, was largely informal and invisible (Abel 1986: 38). The Bar's structure of governance changed in 1966 with the creation of the Senate, which centralised the disciplinary powers previously held by the Inns. Laypersons were appointed on some of the committees but this did little to satisfy outsiders that the Senate continued to protect practitioners from criticism, and until 1987 the Bar Council and the Senate shared the responsibility of the Inns and of the Bar Council. This reverted to the Bar Council alone in 1987 until January 2006, when the representative and regulatory functions were split. A year later, the MOJ created a separate and independent body under the Bar Council's umbrella, the BSB, which became the profession's regulator. Thus, after centuries of self-regulation, the profession became subject to external governance. Central to the profession's newly formulated objectives, pronounced by its new regulator, is a priority to serve the public interest and to place the consumer at the heart of the system.

## VI. Legal Aid and the Growth of the Bar

The two most significant changes in the post-Second World War years were linked – the growth of the profession and its increasing dependence on public funds. With an increased demand for services, particularly in the fields of criminal and family law work, funded largely under the new legal aid provisions, the Bar attracted a larger and more diverse membership in terms of race and gender, as a result of an increased and broader university graduate demographic. A new type of barrister evolved, a social service professional, to cater for a new type of client (Hanlon 2001). No longer linked to an elite clientele, these barristers were committed to helping the disadvantaged. A measure of the Bar's independence was diminished, as large numbers of practitioners became dependent on state funding for significant portions of their practice. Fees, which had remained stagnant, doubled or tripled between 1957 and 1962, and there was a sharp revival of work. It was during this prosperous period that the Bar shed some of its restrictive practices: kite briefs, extra fees for practising on a different circuit and an erosion of the two-thirds rule, whereby a junior barrister on a case automatically received that ratio of the leading silk's fee. At the same time, surplus work was given to pupils (Abel-Smith and Stevens 1968). Numbers continued to swell to cope with the increase in legal aid work. In 1960, there were 1,919 practitioners, by 1979, there were 4,263, and in 1987, 5,642 barristers were in self-employed practice and the state was key to this expansion and prosperity (Zander 1988; Hanlon 2001). The dependence on state funding was not initially seen as a challenge to a barrister's independence, which was considered more a matter of professional values and conduct and, as Hazell stated, 'the independence of the Bar will last just as long as its capacity to withstand improper pressures, from whatever source' (Hazell 1978b: 169). Chapter 7 explores whether practitioners think that the cuts to legal aid have given rise to outside pressures that constrain what work they do and how they do it.

## VII. Calls for Reform

As indicated in Chapter 1, early analysis of the professions rested on structural functional assumptions, rooted in Durkheim, where social order was of critical importance and the professions were seen to act as an antidote to the unconstrained self-interest of individuals. Professionals, motivated by altruism, provided mastery in a specialised field and maintained high standards through self-regulation, with high client trust and respect of professional expertise in a relationship that was necessarily uneven (Carr-Saunders and Wilson 1933; Parsons 1939). From the 1960s onwards, new theorists, influenced by Marx and Weber, rejected this perspective for uncritically adopting professional ideologies and claimed that the structures of professionalism were solely concerned with retaining monopolies, economic gain and power. Professional associations were accused of being unrepresentative, biased (or at any rate ineffective) regulators, and admission criteria were simply a method of social closure, evidencing no link between the extensive and expensive education and credentials received and the actual work done (Johnson 1972; Larson 1977; Abel 1986, 1988).

The first critical studies on the Bar challenged its structure, governance and restrictive practices (Abel-Smith and Stevens 1967, 1968; Zander 1968; Hazell 1978a). Although these studies conceded that 'there is little essentially wrong with the standards of competence or integrity' (Zander 1968: 8) and that lawyers in England probably had more integrity than anywhere else in the world (Abel-Smith and Stevens 1968), their critique of the profession was part of a wider concern about the provision of legal services generally, evidenced by three reports by the Monopolies Commission and a report on legal aid within a 15-year period, culminating in a Royal Commission in 1979 (Zander 1988). The Bar's monopoly on advocacy in the higher courts was deemed anti-competitive and potentially exploitative in terms of fees; the governing bodies (the Senate, the Bar Council and the Inns of Court) were almost entirely made up of members of the profession and were unaccountable to anyone, having control over entry and the creation and enforcement of ethical codes; the split professional structure precluded direct access to barristers and led to problems of continuity in cases, and clients often met their counsel for the first time outside the doors of the court. The profession was peppered with restrictive practices, which were based on antiquated rules and clearly were not in the public interest. As one MP commented in the *Daily Mirror* in 1966, these practices were so 'lucrative and so effectively enforced that they would make the most passionate demarcationists in the trade unions turn green with envy' (cited in Zander 1968: 9). The Bar Council rigorously defended these practices to the Monopolies Commission, asserting that they were necessary to maintain the highest standards, but critics remained unconvinced that there was a link between the two. As Zander observed: 'A chastity belt is not the only way of preserving a wife's virtue' (1968: 12).

In 1976, a Royal Commission (the Benson Commission) was asked to review all aspects of the legal profession and to examine, in particular, three issues: the Bar's monopoly over rights of audience in the higher courts; solicitors' monopoly over conveyancing work; and, lastly, the division of the profession. In 1979, the Benson Commission decided to maintain the status quo on all three fronts and Margaret Thatcher, the incoming Prime Minister, accepted these findings. Therefore, it was something of a shock when at the end of 1983, a private member's bill, backed by the Consumers' Association, was introduced to abolish solicitors' conveyancing monopoly and received unexpected support in the House of Commons at its second reading. By agreement, the private bill was withdrawn and the government introduced its own bill in the same terms, which later formed the basis of the Administration of Justice Act 1985, permitting licensed conveyancers to compete with solicitors from early 1987 (Zander 1988, 1990).

## VIII. Loss of Monopolies and Internal Reforms

The solicitors' loss of their conveyancing monopoly provoked a whole raft of legislative and internal reforms of both branches of the profession. In anticipation of competition for and loss of this work, the Law Society had already relaxed the ban on individual solicitors advertising (excluding television) and reduced the level of conveyancing fees. In early 1984, solicitors directly challenged the Bar's monopoly of advocacy in the higher courts, even though they had not exercised their rights in the lower courts as much as they might have, as it was not economic to do so (Flood et al 1998; Boon and Flood 1999). The Legal Aid Efficiency Scrutiny Committee reported in June 1986 that there was no reason why solicitors should not have rights of audience in the Crown Courts where a guilty plea was being entered, as it would save £1 million in legal aid. A Joint Committee (the Marre Committee), made up of five barristers, five solicitors and five independents, was set up in 1986 to consider the Bar's higher court advocacy monopoly once again. They failed to reach agreement. In 1986, the state decoupled the market rate for legal services and legal aid costs, and in 1988, the legal aid budget was removed from the Law Society's control and was given to the newly formed Legal Aid Board, under the Legal Aid Act 1988 (Zander 1988; Hanlon 2001). The Bar's Chairman, Robert Alexander QC, brought an action against the Lord Chancellor over the low levels of criminal legal aid fees. The Bar further responded by introducing a number of internal reforms. First, it created the General Council of the Bar in January 1987 (the Bar Council), an elected body which replaced the Senate, reduced the powers of the Inns and made membership compulsory so as to fund it. Second, it lifted its own professional ban on advertising in its Code of Conduct on 31 March 1990 (Hill 2003), permitting barristers to list their qualifications and specialisations in a Bar directory and chambers to publish and distribute their own brochures. It further changed its policy of chambers having to be within the Inns of Court in order to alleviate the shortage of space and provide more comfortable premises for clients (Zander 1988, 1990).

Barristers were now part of a wider shake-up of professional services across the public sector. The Department of Trade and Industry published the Review of Restrictive Trade Practices Policy (CM No 311) in 1988, revealing the government's clear intention to end such practices enjoyed by professions. Thatcher's government believed that a competitive economy needed to be unregulated and open, with limited government spending, ending the social democratic consensus that had been in place since the end of the war (Crouch 2011). The 'public interest' was redefined as the market allocation of resources, not access to services based on citizenship, and professional ideology did not sit well with this, as it was deemed to be self-interested and parasitic, especially in areas of practice that relied on the public purse (Hanlon and Jackson 1999; Lane et al 2002). The social and cultural assumptions surrounding a professional as someone to trust and respect, to safeguard a client's wellbeing in the application of his or her professional judgement, were being questioned by the instrumental logic of the market (Dent and Whitehead 2002). The notions of entrepreneurship and competition on the one hand, and accountability and new managerialism on the other, were to form the basis of widespread reforms across the implementation of social policy, the teaching, medical and accountancy professions, as well as within the police forces and civil service, irrespective of whether or not they undermined the ideal of a professional dedicated to her or his client and indifference to financial gain (Clarke et al 1994; Newman and Clarke 1994; Abel 2004a; McLaughlin 2007).

## IX. The End of an Era: The Courts and Legal Services Act 1990

In October 1987, Lord Mackay of Clashfern was appointed Lord Chancellor and actively sought to divide the professions on the issue of audience rights (Abel 2004a). In October 1988, without warning, he announced three new Green Papers on the legal profession,[1] publishing them in January 1989, with a three-month consultation period. His stated overall intention was to provide the public with the most efficient and cost-effective network of legal services, subject to assurances of quality and competence. The key proposals that affected the Bar were: to end its monopoly on higher court advocacy rights, to permit advertising, to re-introduce direct access to the Bar, to let barristers work from anywhere and not be tied to a set of chambers, to allow partnerships, corporate structures and multi-disciplinary partnerships, to consider contingency fees and to set up a Legal Ombudsman to handle complaints. Moreover, the government sought the right to oversee, through an Advisory Body, which had the rights to grant advocacy licences, to establish professional codes of practice, to recognise specialisms and to determine education and training of the profession.

The reaction of the Bar and the judiciary was predictably negative and forceful, and caused some to note the apparent contradiction between the government's stated laissez-faire ideology and the proposed heavy state control in the actual proposals (Zander 1990; Abel 2004a). Solicitors were, in the main, supportive of the proposals, as were the press and the consumer lobby. The Bar raised a £1 million 'fighting fund' and began a long campaign that was to be somewhat

[1] *The Work and Organization of the Legal Profession* (Cm 570, 1989); *Contingency Fees* (Cm 571, 1989); *Conveyancing by Authorized Practitioners* (Cm 572, 1989).

successful in the short term, in that the proposals were watered down in the White Papers released in July 1989 (Zander 1990). However, the Bar failed to preserve its monopoly on higher court audience rights. After years of resisting challenges to remove it, the profession was no longer able to persuade the state (the public or the media) to preserve it. Solicitors (but at this stage, not employed barristers or Crown Prosecution lawyers) could take up advocacy rights in the higher courts if they had satisfied the training requirements. The impact of the Courts and Legal Services Act 1990 (CLSA) was relatively gentle for much of the 1990s, but, at the time of writing, all of the initial proposals in the Green Papers have come about, some initiated internally by the Bar itself, under the powers awarded to it under the CLSA, the later Access to Justice Act 1999 (AJA) and the Legal Services Act 2007 (LSA).

## X. Solicitor Advocates

By June 1996, there were 409 qualified Solicitor Advocates, 338 of whom had become so by exemption, out of a total of over 66,000 solicitors in the jurisdiction. In a qualitative study, Flood et al (1998) explored what factors influenced solicitors to take up this right and found that it was artificial to view the market for advocacy as a single one, but rather a series of markets related to particular areas of work. Although there were differences in attitude, overall their study felt that it was unlikely that solicitors would develop their in-house advocacy services in the near future, but it did find that solicitors were keeping more drafting and advisory work to themselves (Flood et al 1998; Boon and Flood 1999). Since their study, there has been a drastic reduction in the scope and extent of legal aid funds, and solicitor advocates and/or employed barristers are much more likely in some cases to carry out the advocacy themselves. Irrespective of ability, training or experience, many criminal law solicitors now have a financial incentive to keep work in-house (Fitzgibbon 2015). Boon (2016) reports that in August 2015, there were 6,651 solicitor advocates. By July 2019, this had risen to 6,918 (2,372 for civil work, 3,129 in the criminal courts and 1,417 for both (Solicitors Regulation Authority (SRA) 2019)). This figure represents over half the number of barristers at the independent Bar. In terms of work lost, the most recent figures available indicate that, in a five-year period, the level of cases conducted by solicitor advocates in the Crown Courts rose by 24 per cent in contested trials and by 40 per cent in guilty pleas (Jeffrey 2014), making a real impact on the amount and type of criminal work that is coming to the Bar. Most of the criminal practitioners interviewed asserted that they had less work as a result of solicitors undertaking more advocacy hearings. In 2015, the Solicitors' Association of Higher Court Advocates launched 'The Court Advocacy Network', possibly in response to the Bar's online public access portal, an online platform through which solicitors can refer advocacy work to each other rather than instruct the Bar (Counsel 2015).

## XI. State Withdrawal: Reduction of Legal Aid – Civil Work

The introduction of legal aid franchising in the 1990s reduced and concentrated the number of civil legal aid providers, and by 1997, of the 12,000 legal aid firms, only 1,740 were franchised (Hanlon 2001; Hynes 2012). Further, the scope of civil legal aid was reduced, removing probate and property advice from its remit, and rates were reduced generally. Under the (some would say misnamed) Access to Justice Act 1999, personal injury cases (aside from medical negligence) were no longer eligible for legal aid and 'no win, no fee' conditional fee agreements (CFAs) were introduced. Whereas legal aid had been a loan, underwritten by the state and recoverable, the new system was market-driven and ultimately led to inflated costs and questionable behaviour by claims management companies (Hynes 2012). It has been subject to further reform under the Jackson proposals, enacted in the Legal Aid, Sentencing and Punishment of Offenders Act 2012 (LASPO) which took effect on 1 April 2013.

Further dramatic cuts to levels of civil legal aid payments were introduced by LASPO. Underpinned by neoliberal principles, the government's view was that it no longer had the responsibility to fund litigation through legal aid, arguing that this only led to speculative and meritless disputes (Fitzgibbon 2013). With some exceptions, public funds were removed from many areas of civil law, leaving an estimated 650,000 people without legal advice, as Citizens Advice Bureaux (CAB) and law centres also lost funding (Baksi 2014b). By the summer of 2019, the amount of legal advice centres in the country had halved since 2013 (Bowcott 2019c) and in the first five years the number of legal aid providers fell by a further 20 per cent (Asthana 2017). There was a 74 per cent drop in volume of civil legal aid cases initiated in the first eight months of the LASPO, far greater than predicted by the government, largely due to the smaller numbers of solicitors offering legally aided services and the public perception that now no civil cases were eligible for funding (Legal Action Group 2013). The Justice Select Committee inquired into the impact of the LASPO, and the Law Society and the Bar Council reported a year on, in April 2014, that this latest batch of cuts had had a highly detrimental impact on access to justice in terms of people's ability to find and access legal advice and representation (Law Society 2014; Bar Council 2014a). In July 2014, the CAB reported that they were unable to refer 92 per cent of people who came to them to the appropriate specialist legal advice they needed because of the cuts and that there had been a 62 per cent rise in those seeking help (CAB 2014). Government figures in 2016 showed that since the LASPO, there had been an overall reduction in civil legal aid workload to one-third of the pre-Act levels (MOJ 2016b). The Bach Commission (2017) estimated there to have been an 84 per cent drop in the number of civil actions initiated and the most recent statistics show that the figures continue to decline. Personal injury claims reduced a further 11 per cent in the year 2018/19 and in only 54 per cent of civil cases did both parties have lawyers (MOJ 2019a).

Further, it is thought that over half the costs saved from the civil legal aid budget have simply moved to other public bodies as a result of the cuts. A dramatic increase of litigants in person, especially in private family law cases, is placing a great strain on the family justice system, with hearings taking longer, increased delays and uncertainty around court listings. Mediation, rather than attracting more people in the first year after the cuts, dropped by almost 40 per cent, mainly as there were no lawyers directing parties to it. Levels continue to fall, the most recent figures available indicating a drop of 14 per cent in the year 2015–16 (MOJ 2016b). The Bar Pro Bono unit reported an increase in 47.2 per cent in applications for assistance in areas where funding had been cut.

The effect of these cuts on barristers has been dramatic, many reporting that the volume of work and level of fees have gone down. Some have changed or broadened their main areas of practice, and many work longer hours to compensate. Others have left the profession because of income insecurity, leaving the Bar Council (2018) to conclude that the long-term sustainability of the publicly funded civil and family Bar is under threat. Whilst the state has pledged £3 million to support litigants in person in response, it has done little to assuage practitioners' fears. Instead, it has suggested that money should be spent on solving issues earlier, not in court, and unmeritorious claims should be discouraged. It envisages other fora for early dispute resolution, such as legal hubs in GP surgeries, where no specialist advocates would be needed (MOJ 2019c).

## XII. *Transforming Legal Aid*

Criminal legal aid expenditure (not fee rates) rose between 2000 and 2005, prompting the next Lord Chancellor, Lord Falconer, to blame the lawyers, under a supplier-induced demand thesis, though evidence suggests the increase was attributable to changes in the system, the costs of which had not been properly accounted for (Cape and Moorhead 2005). Lord Carter of Coles (2006) was charged with reviewing the procurement of legal aid, and his report (the Carter Review) proposed that fixed and graduated fees should replace hourly rates. Despite strong reservations expressed by the Constitutional Affairs Select Committee and opposition from the profession to the scope of the reforms and their likely effect on the quality of work, they were unilaterally imposed on existing contract holders (Boon and Levin 2008).

In April 2013, six months ahead of schedule and a week after the implementation of the LASPO, the Coalition government launched its consultation on a further shake-up of legal aid, this time targeting criminal, prison and public law work.[2] Its aim was to cut the legal aid budget by a further £2.2 million. Critics were drawn predictably from the legal profession and the judiciary, but also from

[2] *Transforming Legal Aid: Delivering a More Credible and Efficient System* (CP 14/2013, 9 April 2013).

a wide variety of organisations, groups and individuals, even gathering support from large parts of the media as time went on (eg, Bentham 2013; Bowcott 2013). Little financial information was provided to justify the cuts and there was suspicion that the figures had been manipulated and that the statistics on barristers' fees were misleading. Many felt that the cuts had nothing to do with austerity, but were ideologically driven. The UK Statistics Authority subsequently publicly reprimanded Chris Grayling, the Minister of Justice, over the misleading statistics the MOJ had produced on criminal barristers' earnings (Baksi 2014a).

There were and continue to be concerns that as a result of these cuts, many are unable to access legal advice or representation and that numbers at the publicly funded Bar are diminishing, as it is so hard to earn a decent living (Peacock 2014; Schraer 2019). Lawyers gathered in protest outside Parliament on 22 May 2013 and outside the MOJ on 4 June 2013. For the first time in its history, many practitioners mobilised and effectively went on strike across England and Wales for a half-day on 7 January 2014. Despite the government dropping certain proposals, by the end of February 2014, it indicated that cuts to fees would go ahead. The CBA's response was to organise a whole day of strike action on 7 March 2014, which was supported by a wide selection of practitioners in other areas, whilst at the same time embarking on a month-long refusal to accept 'returns', both of which received an enormous amount of media coverage. Sections of the Bar were under attack and whilst not all felt that the Bar Council or other groups within the profession were sufficiently supportive, there was a relatively united front, backed by strong rhetoric to reinforce the profession's position. Unlike previous indifference or hostility towards the Bar, there was considerable support in the media, from the Church and various independent bodies and charities involved in the sector. No doubt prompted by the cumulative effect of the above, the MOJ negotiated a deal with the representatives of the Criminal Bar Association (CBA) and the Bar Council at the end of March 2014, whereby there would be a suspension of cuts to barristers' fees until after the 2015 general election, but the first half of the 15 per cent cuts to solicitors' fees was to go ahead (Baksi 2014c). On 8 July 2014, the Bar negotiated a temporary truce with the MOJ with regard to Very High Cost Cases (VHCC) (Bowcott 2014a). The second tranche of cuts to solicitors' fees was effected in July 2015, but was later suspended in April 2016 under Michael Gove, the new Justice Minister (Bowcott 2016a). Although public awareness and media coverage of the cuts to prison and public law cases were overshadowed by the robust campaign of the CBA, critics of these other cuts were no less vociferous (Wagner 2014). The High Court ruled that the proposed residence test for legal aid was discriminatory and unlawful (Bowcott 2014b), a decision later upheld by the Supreme Court.[3]

The dispute over levels of criminal legal aid continues, with the CBA periodically threatening further action (Bowcott 2015; Fouzder 2015). In April 2018, the

[3] *R v Lord Chancellor* (2016) UKSC 39.

Advocates' Graduated Fee Scheme (AGFS) was introduced, leaving the majority of criminal practitioners aggrieved that once again they were being grossly underpaid. A few days later, they took action, this time by refusing to take on new work. This was called off in June 2018, when members of the CBA narrowly voted to accept a £15 million deal offered by the state, pending a consultation on how that would work. By the end of November 2018, this figure had risen to £23 million, with a promise that there would be a one per cent increase on all fees (BBC 2018). In June 2019, the CBA voted overwhelmingly to take strike action in respect of prosecution fees paid by the CPS and, once again, over defence fees under the AGFS (Bowcott 2019a). A compromise was reached regarding CPS fees to barristers and, at the time of writing, the MOJ is undertaking a fundamental review of the criminal legal aid system, including all the defence fee schemes, and will report in the summer of 2020. It has further agreed to accelerate its reconsideration of payment for unused material, fees paid in cracked trials and uplifts in paper-heavy cases, and to come up with proposals by December 2019 (Slingo 2019).

The effect of these cuts on publicly funded practitioners cannot be overstated. Interviewees for this study explained how their professional lives have been affected, details of which are explored in the following chapters. Whist all barristers have had to reconceive their working practices due to increased competition and less work, it is especially pronounced in the case of those whose practice areas were and are dependent on public funding. The nature and strength of feeling on this topic is reminiscent of when solicitors lost their conveyancing monopoly and accompanying income security, when one described it as: 'Not so much reform as butchery' (cited in Sommerlad 1995: 181).

## XIII. The Neoliberal Bar: Independent Regulation and the Legal Services Act 2007

In 2001, an Office of Fair Trading report recommended that unjustified restriction on competition in the legal profession should be removed (Vickers 2001). The government responded with a report into competition and regulation in the legal services market. Its report[4] concluded that 'the current framework is outdated, inflexible, over-complex and insufficiently accountable or transparent' and an independent investigation was commissioned. David Clementi reported in 2004 (Clementi 2004) and the government broadly accepted his recommendations and published a White Paper in October 2005,[5] setting out three planks upon which reforms were to be built: a new, independent oversight regulator, the Legal Services Board (LSB); the single complaints-handling and consumer redress body,

[4] *Competition and Regulation in the Legal Services Market. A Report Following the Consultation 'In the Public Interest?'* (July 2003).

[5] *The Future of Legal Services: Putting Consumers First* (Cm 6679, 2005).

the Office for Legal Complaints and the facilitation of the innovative Alternative Business Structures (ABS), helping the legal sector to become more responsive to consumer needs by permitting non-lawyers and lawyers to form legal partnerships and companies as vehicles for the provision of reserved legal services. This was subsequently enacted in the Legal Services Act 2007 (LSA). Its claim was to enshrine the key elements of professionalism in a market model. The legal profession was to be both a business and a profession (Boon 2010), competitive, accountable and transparent. This transformed how barristers were expected to perceive their vocation and conduct their working lives.

The Bar Council had, in 2006, already separated the functions of regulation and representation by forming the BSB, but it was now under the overarching control and supervision of the new LSB. Since January 2014, the BSB has adopted a risk assessment approach to the supervision of the profession. Regulatory supervision obliges chambers, entities and individuals to manage risk so as to prevent non-compliance from materialising or prevent recurrence where it has occurred. Those deemed to be in the higher risk category attract closer supervision than others. The BSB has further relaxed the provisions of the Bar's Code of Conduct, permitting barristers to, inter alia, work in a dual capacity as self-employed and employed practitioners, investigate and collect evidence and witness statements, attend police stations, undertake correspondence and conduct litigation on behalf of a client (ending the solicitors' monopoly) and set up an ABS or entity.

This is a major departure from the traditional model of the provision of legal services, with the force of the market sweeping through both limbs of the profession and imposing great competitive pressure on them (Susskind 2013). On the other hand, it represented the interests of state and market forces controlling professional work, causing some to wonder if this will ultimately undermine the very essence of professionalism as traditionally conceptualised (Boon 2010; Sommerlad 2011). The reforms seek to eradicate distinctions between legal professionals in order to open up competition between lawyers, introduce new providers and capital to the legal services market, and promote the merging of different professionals within organisations (Boon 2010). New entities can now be made up of only lawyers (authorised bodies) or lawyers and others (ABS). The initial ABS licences were obtained in October 2012 and, for the first few years, all were granted by the SRA. Since the BSB's ability to grant them in April 2017, there are no precise figures on how many have been created. Survey research indicates a low level of intention to set them up, though some practitioners indicated interest in joining barrister-only managed/owned structures, particularly those doing criminal and family work, who are struggling to survive as a result of legal aid cuts (Bar Council 2014a; BSB 2017b). Chapters 3 and 7 explore reasons for this apparent reluctance on the part of practitioners to innovate in this way.

Finally, whereas at one time professional services were delivered on a local basis, developments in information and communications technology have significantly changed the nature of the corporate sector of the legal profession, with firms developing a global presence to cater for the increasingly sophisticated corporate clients. With greater competition and less secure employment structures, law firms are having to rethink how they work and the traditional system of referral to the Bar in many areas can no longer be relied upon. Susskind identifies three drivers of change affecting the legal profession, and though the bulk of his analysis relates to the solicitor branch, he predicts a knock-on effect at the Bar, resulting in a smaller profession, providing bespoke advocacy and advisory services for highly specialist and complex areas of work only. The first driver of change is the 'more for less challenge', whereby firms are requiring lawyers to increase their workload, yet have reduced their budgets in order to be profitable; the second driver is the ongoing liberalisation of the legal services market to provide more choice for the consumer and greater competition; and the last driver is the impact of information technology, which has and will continue to radically change how legal services are provided (Susskind 2000, 2010, 2013; Susskind and Susskind 2015). He envisages a very different landscape of legal services providers, which will include legal services traditionally provided by the Bar and solicitors being done by, inter alia, global accounting firms, legal 'know-how' providers, legal process outsourcers, high street retailers, legal leasing agencies, online legal services and legal management consultants. In some areas his predictions have proved true: the Co-op is now the largest legal provider of probate services (Rose 2018) and more family disputes are being resolved without lawyers or by mediation, overseen by non-lawyers (Maclean 2015; Maclean and Eekelaar 2016). Furthermore, in the name of cost-effectiveness and speediness, there has been an increasing shift from traditional court hearings to settling cases via mediation or round table meetings, collaborative lawyering, alternative dispute resolution, and dispute containment and avoidance. Together with the development of digital courts, online dispute resolution and virtual hearings, regular advocates are getting and will continue to get much less work (Moorhead 1998; Susskind 2013; Cross 2016; Rozenberg 2019).

The above account of the recent reforms seeks to set the stage for the rest of this book. Barristers are not just having to adapt to a very different commercial and competitive landscape; many are fighting for professional survival and have to persuade the state, the media and potential clients that their very existence and skills are valuable and worth preserving. Needless to say, these are very challenging times for many, and it is how different barristers across diverse practice areas have responded and adapted to these significant challenges that is explored in the chapters that follow.

# 3

# The Business of Chambers

> The chambers that are now starting to introduce CEOs and things like that tend to have more structure and tend to run better as businesses and I think the old style chambers are going to find themselves increasingly squeezed, if they haven't got anybody taking a strategic overview.
>
> A7, Bar marketing consultant

Most barristers operate within organisational collectives known as chambers. Of the 13,171 barristers in independent practice in 2018, only 595 were sole practitioners. The rest work within one of the 413 sets of chambers in England and Wales, most of which are in London.[1] This chapter explores how this idiosyncratic professional grouping – chambers – has changed in the last 30 years and why. The regulator's research concluded that, despite the liberalising rules under the LSA, the traditional chambers model strongly prevailed, whereby barristers remain self-employed and independent, but are grouped together as a collective, sharing the costs of office space and support services (BSB 2017b). There has been little innovation in the development of ABSs at the independent Bar for the delivery of legal services and some of the reasons for this will be explored later in this chapter. Nonetheless, the traditional chambers model has evolved significantly, evincing a more commercially oriented and customer-centred approach, a more management-driven structure and governance, a significant increase in the size of chamber membership, and a strong strategic awareness of branding, visibility and collective identity.

There has been scant research on these developments at the Bar. By contrast, the prominence of the new commercial and managerial logic, which has been evident in the restructuring of City and other law firms since the mid-1990s, has provoked a substantial academic debate on how this might have affected legal professionalism and whether the professional service ethos has been undermined, giving way to enterprise and market concerns, and if the two are incompatible (see, for example, Muzio 2004; Ackroyd and Muzio 2007; Faulconbridge and Muzio 2008; Boon 2010; Somerlad 2011; Evetts 2015). Muzio and Kirkpatrick (2011) noted how organisational and market logics could turn law firms into managerial professional businesses. The appearance of performance appraisals,

[1] Bar Standards Board, 'Key Statistics', 2019, https://www.barstandardsboard.org.uk/news-publications/research-and-statistics/statistics-about-the-bar/practising-barristers.html.

mentoring and management from above amounted to new disciplinary technologies, whereby professional identities are formed or shaped by and behaviour is monitored according to new management objectives. However, they also noted that professionals were not passive victims of these changes, but were dynamic and adaptive. Collegial professions were 'actively colonizing new organizational spaces, structures, practices and systems' and were 'deploying these to sustain traditional occupational objectives and rewards' (2011: 296). So, rather than these changes marking an end to professionalism, they can be viewed as a layering or evolution of it, a renegotiation whereby structures and processes may change, but traditional values and practices continue (Cooper et al 1996; Paterson 1996; Evetts 2015). This chapter analyses the new, modernised and more flexible chambers model, which has also been shaped by commercial and managerial concerns. It questions whether, in relation to the Bar, these changes have any impact on academic or practitioners' notions of legal professionalism. The developments in terms of how chambers are structured, staffed, governed and used are inextricably tied up with the Bar's reaction to (or, less commonly, anticipation of) wider changes within the profession. As Abbott noted (1988), professions adapt when external and/or internal changes occur, and the reforms discussed in the previous two chapters have prompted new organisational features in order to support its efforts to develop new expertise, compete for or maintain work and comply with new regulatory requirements.

Those interviewed held different views as to why chambers' structure and organisation had changed. One senior clerk felt it was because barristers themselves are now drawn from a different demographic, which includes women and people from all backgrounds, and this change 'brought with it a certain commercial acumen that wasn't there before' when there were 'quite a few people who had their own income and when they weren't in court they were off shooting with the Duke of X' (A5). One senior practitioner felt that the drastic cuts to legal aid and a government with a budgetary crisis had obliged the Bar to modernise its structures. This research found that the extent of chambers' development and modernisation varied hugely across the sets visited and was dependent on the types of work done, the numbers of barristers, their physical location, the resources available and, critically, the approach of key individuals within them. It would be simplistic to assert, as the BSB (2017b) research does, that the traditional chambers model prevails without a more thorough investigation as to what this model now comprises, how this has affected barristers' working lives and what it means in terms of conceptualising professionalism.

## I. The Traditional Chambers Model

Whilst the BSB's (2017b) report gave a succinct summary of this model, it is worth elaborating upon, not simply to give a sense of structure and governance, but to understand the sentiment and ethos that lay behind how barristers organised their professional workspaces and staffing. Until the end of the nineteenth century, it was common for barristers to practise alone, renting rooms in one of the Inns of Court (Abel 1986). From the end of the nineteenth century until the end of the twentieth century, the Bar ceased to receive direct instructions from clients and to negotiate directly with them (Abel-Smith and Stevens 1967). Most practitioners grouped together in small sets of chambers, sharing the cost of the overheads and the services of the clerk. As outlined in Chapter 2, in a bid to distinguish themselves from solicitors and all matters concerned with 'trade', barristers were expressly forbidden from advertising their services or tout for work. As a referral profession, briefs came in from solicitors via the clerk, who negotiated fees (barristers were not allowed to discuss payment either) and distributed work. The clerk received a percentage of each brief fee by way of remuneration (Flood 1983). The running of chambers was a largely informal affair, with no official oversight, leaving each head of chambers and clerk to determine how things were organised and how work was distributed. By the 1950s, this arrangement gave cause for concern. One newspaper asserted that 'the office inefficiency of many barristers' chambers is a disgrace to the profession … this is because they are run not by barristers but by their clerks, who are wholly untrained in modern business methods' (*The Times*, 19 December 1959, cited in Hazell 1978c: 117). By the mid-1960s, most sets were still fairly small, with 6–12 members, but nonetheless, few had accounting systems or annual audits and practitioners, the Senate nor the Bar Council were not particularly concerned about this lack of accountability and organisational inefficiency, perhaps taking the view that as self-employed practitioners, it was up to the barristers to decide how to run their chambers (Hazell 1978c).

The head of chambers was usually the most senior member, who was almost always a QC and remained at the helm until retirement or death (Hazell 1978c). How decisions were made depended largely on his (until about 30 years ago, it was almost always a man) personality or the tradition within that set. More often than not, important matters were discussed at a General Chambers Meeting, where a vote might be taken, though the head generally had the final say. Some sets were less democratic than others. One barrister (B36) interviewed noted that when he joined chambers in the 1970s, the head of chambers ran it 'like a private fiefdom, with a drunken clerk'. The distribution of work and fees were very much the domain of the clerk, upon whose goodwill a junior's practice was very much contingent (Flood 1983). As numbers gradually increased, ad hoc committees arose to deal with discrete issues and barristers volunteered to carry out many of the administrative tasks, such as negotiating rents or refurbishment of chambers with the Inn. These matters were done in their spare time and in a manner of their own choosing. Little was centralised and organisational practices varied across and within chambers.

Abel (1988) noted that in 1984, the average membership of chambers in London was 7–16 barristers, although in the Temple, where most of the common law sets were situated, 65 per cent had at least 20 people. By 1986, only two sets had more than 30 members and the largest had 45 (Abel 1986). As numbers grew, chambers gradually acquired some support staff in the form of junior clerks, a receptionist, a part-time fees clerk (dedicated to billing solicitors and chasing up payment), typing services and sometimes an administrator, who did chambers accounts and organised the upkeep of the physical spaces. However, there was still no official oversight of chambers' management or a uniform method of running a set.

All sets on circuit were general common law practices. Only a few sets were truly specialists, situated mainly in Lincoln's Inn or Gray's Inn (Morison and Leith 1992). Hazell noted that in 1978 the main specialist chambers comprised about six sets apiece, concentrating on tax, shipping, patent and planning law, and two on libel and admiralty work (Hazell 1978d). Chambers were identified by their geographical address (eg, 6 King's Bench Walk) and, if there was more than one set in the building, also by the name of the head of chambers. Obliged to practise from an address within one of the four Inns of Court and to be a member of chambers with a clerk, barristers in London were confined to a narrow, geographical area in mostly Grade II-listed buildings which are old-fashioned, inflexible and largely unsuited to being modern office spaces. Designed around a medieval, collegiate model, the Inns are enclosed complexes, catering to collective needs with a chapel, hall and library, and offering more private spaces in terraced houses around squares (Warren 1978). Overcrowding was (and remains) a perennial problem, with practitioners often sharing rooms and basic facilities. Critics pointed out that by deliberately obliging practitioners to practise in chambers within the Inns, the profession forcibly kept numbers of new entrants down, effecting one example of market closure (Abel 1988, 2004a). Since barristers were not allowed to attend solicitors' offices, client conferences were always held in these cramped, if historic, surroundings. It was not until 1987 that barristers in London were allowed to set up chambers outside the four Inns of Court (Zander 1988) and gradually some have begun to do so, especially since the rents inside the Inns were increased to market rates. A deeply individualistic profession, these groupings of self-employed practitioners were largely driven by practical considerations of cost sharing and no more. In the non-specialist sets, chambers as a group often had no particularly brand or identity and many were made up of practitioners with diverse practices, often in unrelated areas of law or, in the case of more junior members, with wide general common law practices. It was rare for practitioners to move and many remained in one set of chambers for their entire career.

Chambers was thus the professional home for barristers and their fellow members, and clerking teams were their regular, daily colleagues, sometimes for the entirety of their careers, all working in the same building(s) at the same collective address, even though they operated as individual, self-employed units (Morison and Leith 1992). Everyone knew one another well, shared rooms and contributed to varying degrees to the rather haphazard administration. It was in this small environment that new practitioners were trained not just in law and legal practice, but also in the ethical behaviour of the profession. The degree and methods of professional socialisation are discussed further in Chapter 8 on the Bar community, but the main point here is that the structure and hierarchy of chambers facilitated an environment that shaped and controlled its members. Common identity was (re)produced through shared educational background, vocational training and experiences and work culture, as was common within professions (Evetts 2015).

## II. The Growth of Chambers and the Rise of Specialist Teams

Since each set of chambers is free, subject to overarching BSB regulation, to arrange its affairs as it wishes, no two chambers' organisational structures or staffing are identical, but there are strong similarities in how many are organised. The most obvious, visible change since the 1990s is the increased size of chambers membership. The average set size had grown from 16 in 1986 to about 60 in 2011 (Pike and Robinson 2011). Many are now considerably larger. Of the 19 sets that formed part of this research, 11 had more than 60 members, two of which had over 190. To some extent, this increase was precipitated when the Inns started charging commercial rents, which small chambers could not afford. One chancery practitioner (B36) commented that 'rents were very, very low, but once they started doing up the premises and charging huge commercial rents, these places became completely, you know, the small chambers just became unviable'. The bigger the membership, the lower the shared costs of IT packages, law report subscriptions and staff wages. Some of the circuit chambers have become much larger 'mega sets', with offices in the provinces, sometimes also in London, and aiming to compete on a national level:

> Generally speaking, in the provinces, what you've seen happening has been the growth of large sets, which are increasingly multi-centre sets, where they have so many people that they can run viable specialist teams … which will have anything from, say 200 to 500 members and, because of the sheer size and scale, will be able to buy in services at affordable rates.
>
> B27, civil circuit practitioner

Most barristers on circuit used to be generalists. With the drop in work and increased competition from solicitors, many smaller circuit sets are no longer financially viable. By joining forces and merging with other sets, they have been able to create large specialist teams. Specialism is considered to be the only way to survive and, indeed, flourish across the whole of the Bar, not just on circuit. In order to secure enough work in any particular area, it is considered better if there is a significant group within chambers who share a specialism to attract the work, return it within chambers if necessary, build a reputation as a group and offer a wide range of experience and expertise to cover all levels of complexity:

> I wouldn't say we're big. 80-odd practitioners is not large given the range of specialisations we cover … To be really specialist you need critical mass in an area, so for

> example, if you're a set of 25 and you've got eight or nine family, you've got six or seven who do PI, Insurance and some who do a bit of crime and a bit of this and a bit of that, they're not really big enough to be a magnet for work, seven, eight or nine people.
>
> B13, commercial set

Some of the larger chambers run a number of different specialist teams, almost like mini-sets within a set: '120, I think. That's big, not abnormal, but it's big. It's very flourishing. People keep wanting to join … we're specialists within groups. Effectively, we run five or six separate outfits within chambers' (B2, multi-practice set). Many of the general common law sets have grown in this way, and whereas in the past solicitors routinely instructed chambers that offered services across a wide range of practice areas, marketing a generalist set is now seen as problematic, as professional and lay clients prefer to go to narrowly specialised experts. As a result, many chambers have had to recruit to increase the number in each of their specialist teams and create viable sub-groups that can be marketed on their own, under the wider brand of being a multi-practice set. However, there are disadvantages to being in chambers with a large membership:

> I think some practitioners in those sets feel that they are either being ignored, their practice isn't being developed, they don't get an opportunity to have a reasonable voice … those are some of the feelings that I felt when I left chambers and we were not that mega large at the time.
>
> B18, criminal barrister, 21 years' call

One of the Chambers Directors agreed that it was hard to clerk all the barristers properly when the numbers got too high:

> Just like ordering a Chinese takeaway, because it's just a matter of numbers and how anyone in the world can actually manage that many people … There are different hurdles in regards to managing an individual practice and it's my role to ensure that I can spend enough time with each individual to make sure that each of those hurdles in their career is gained.
>
> A8, Chambers Director, multi-practice set

Many interviewees noted that there is considerably less loyalty to chambers now: 'It's been like a revolving door' (B20) or 'I'm afraid, it's less of a club now and it's more of a business and people are leaving and coming all the time' (B19). Between the time of the initial fieldwork in 2013/14 and the follow-up interviews in 2018/19, just under a third of this modest sample of participating barristers had moved chambers (three had moved twice) and two clerks had also moved (both of them twice). One administrator who has worked in a set for over 40 years noted that: 'A lot of them, very young, a lot of them who don't really know the history of chambers, the loyalty is perhaps not quite as cohesive as it once was' (A1). Some practitioners now take a much more pragmatic and less sentimental view of chambers, often guided by financial concerns. The notion of a chambers family is less appealing than professional advancement, especially to newer entrants.

Moreover, the higher number of barristers in a chambers calls for a proportionate increase in clerks and support staff, and not all sets can afford this and are operationally under strain, with too many members and not enough staff. This was especially apparent in the smaller circuit and less specialised London sets visited. There is therefore a tension between the need for some chambers to expand, in order to keep costs down and to build and consolidate specialist teams of a sufficient number and weight, and the undesirability of being in a set so large that practitioners fail to get sufficient individual clerking attention and clients feel they are not getting a personalised service. Further, the trend to specialise, sometimes very early on in a career, can be limiting. Some practitioners could spend their entire junior careers being led by a QC and will have never cross-examined a witness themselves (Singh 2013). Some interviewees confirmed this:

> We have a lot of youngsters who become almost sort of personally attached to the silks, as silks like particular juniors and they don't get enough into court in my view and they tend to get very specialist practices and they earn fortunes … it's not actually necessarily the best way to build a long-term practice, because that area of work might go. I mean often it works but … I favour something of a more general approach.
>
> B36 Chancery practitioner, 38 years' call

Practitioners of one specialism are often unaware of case law in another that is relevant across disciplines (Singh 2013). However, since solicitors have themselves become more specialised and have undertaken much more advocacy in the lower courts and at interlocutory stages, the Bar has had to become even more niche and expert in order to distinguish its services. There are two aspects to consider here: first, how an area of law might become a recognised specialist area; and, second, how an individual, previously known as a generalist, becomes a known expert in one area. The latter is considered more fully in Chapter 5, which explores how barristers market themselves in a bid to get work. Recognition as a specialist area requires mobilisation on the part of those in the practice area:

> We have some people who specialise in costs law and they are extremely successful but they actually went, I believe, to the Directories, and they said 'Costs law is a new area, you need to have a section rating costs lawyers' and they went and made a pitch to the publishers and they persuaded them to kind of invent costs law and then of course they themselves (laughing) appeared, because they are very good at costs law.
>
> B28, specialist civil silk, 25 years' call

As the specialism becomes more established and increasing numbers practise within it, practitioners create a specialist Bar Association to represent their interests, provide educational training, perhaps a journal and conferences. Most specialist practice teams within a set of chambers will therefore also belong to a specialist Bar-wide association, which will give their practice area more gravitas and support. Thus, these practice teams are recognised not just within chambers, but also as part of a wider group across the profession. This process of identifying and creating an area of work and then seeking formal acknowledgement of its existence and the right to do it from a professional association is a critical part of professional development, where a jurisdictional claim is made and established (Abbott 1988; Fournier 2000).

## III. Location: Front Stage, Backstage and Chambers as a Virtual Space

Significant changes have occurred in terms of the physical space within chambers and how it is used. With an increase in membership, more room is needed, yet even chambers with large turnovers cannot always expand, as space in the Inns is scarce. A set seeking to grow is unlikely to find new premises adjacent to it and many prefer not to have annexes too far away:

> We're at capacity … we have got very, very limited possibility of people now shifting round and moving and sharing rooms … I'm always looking for more space but it's very difficult … We don't want to leave the Inner Temple, we really don't want to have to move. There isn't anyone nearby that is likely to move.
>
> A2, Administrative Manager, civil set

This reluctance by some to move outside their Inn is in some ways a practical concern. Three of the four Inns are within very easy reach of the Royal Courts of Justice, with Gray's Inn being slightly further away. All have dining facilities in Hall, libraries and some parking facilities. But the attachment goes deeper – the Inns are the customary home of chambers and barristers and some still think the picturesque, historical settings are attractive to lay clients and in keeping with the Bar's traditional identity and image.

In many chambers, whether within or outside the Inns, the interiors and layout have changed, with more emphasis being placed on the appearance of reception, waiting and conference areas in a bid to make them more professional-looking and user-friendly to clients: 'Bearing in mind that you've got incredible competition from these sets who are, you know, have all the latest facilities, flexible meeting spaces' (A7, Bar marketing consultant). The focus is on client service and satisfaction rather than barrister use, in keeping with the more commercial and competitive spirit that has emerged at the Bar in the last couple of decades. Many chambers have been refurbished extensively, with large, plush reception areas, rooms with partitions that can fold away, creating larger spaces for seminars and with video-conferencing facilities. There is a more corporate feel in these 'front' spaces. Behind the scenes, however, it is not uncommon for barristers to be in much smaller rooms, mostly shared, with piles of boxes containing case files stacked in their rooms and the corridors:

> We are now having to sell ourselves to the public and to solicitors in a way that we didn't have to before. And we're having to use marketing tricks and tools of mainstream

> commercial life which professionals didn't really have to do many years ago … But chambers will not be a series of rather nice panelled Georgian offices with pedestal desks and bookcases, lined with rather impressive books. It will be, front of house will be sleek, smart and swanky, and out the back you will have rabbit hutches for the lawyers … you wouldn't show the clients out back, you'd show them the smart, swanky stuff out front.
>
> B1, common law set

Although some barristers interviewed revealed an attachment to the physical notion of chambers, others felt that the historic premises must give way to a more flexible and economic model. IT has liberated barristers from working in chambers, with instructions being sent via email and conferences held over the telephone or video-link platforms:

> I believe the future is in just providing a service. I mean I can go to a solicitor's office and have a conference. What people want from me are the pleadings or the advice or me to turn up in court, don't they? So they don't need this anymore (indicating the room in chambers).
>
> B6, circuit practitioner

Whereas previously practitioners were expected to come into chambers every day and indeed had to in order to collect briefs which were often contained in large files, now more work from home, unless in court or conference, and it is common for them not to have an allocated desk in chambers:

> I do much more at home than I used to … Nobody has their own room in chambers anymore. It's all hot-desking. We've got about twice as many barristers as we've got space to seat them.
>
> B5, circuit set

One circuit chambers visited during this research had no individual barrister rooms at all, just one large library room, where they all worked and a few smaller conference or telephone rooms, with a flexible space they shared with the other businesses in the building for more formal conferences. In an effort to reduce overheads, as barristers' incomes fell, this was a more economic and practical model. Other sets have changed their layout to cater for large numbers. One large London set has configured the shared use of desks/rooms according to practice area: 'On the third and fourth floor we have a touch-down area, which would be like hot-desking, and on our third floor, it's mainly family and immigration practitioners' (B45, mixed disciplinary set). Some chambers allow practitioners to choose whether they want their own desk, to share an allocated one or just to hot-desk and pay accordingly. Further, since barristers are now permitted to attend solicitors' offices for conferences, chambers have ceased to be the only place they can meet. With the development of IT, face-to-face meetings happen less frequently: 'I mean half the time they don't even come to chambers. It's email, all email, telephone and quite often you have conferences elsewhere' (B38, civil set).

Most chambers have remained within the Inns, but during the last 25 years, more sets have moved out and some are purchasing their premises, giving whichever members want or can the chance to invest in them:

> For me, it's a real bonus in terms of the building … you can design and build a proper barristers' set of chambers, which has been done, so you can expand if you want to, with a hot desk-room, or not, whereas in the Temple, it's all Grade II listed. The rents in the Temple are the same as the rents outside … People looked around and thought 'well, our clients would much prefer air conditioning and nice lifts and lovely windows, rather than these creaky old places with dusty staircases'. So people began to move out and you borrowed the money.
>
> B44, Head of Chambers, multi-disciplinary set

> It's open to everyone to buy into the building and most people use it as a pension fund.
>
> B43, mixed practice set

A significant change of use has thus occurred regarding the physical premises of chambers. The focus (and expense) is now on the showroom common parts, catering to visiting clients, with financial and spatial constraints and IT developments making barrister use of secondary importance. Nonetheless, many continue to work in chambers regularly. Some sets still have daily tea for all to attend or host a Friday night drink after work. In larger sets, where many 'hot-desk', practitioners admitted to not knowing all of the members, though the touch-down areas were large and sociable and they knew everyone in their team(s). One commercial barrister noted that in his set, everyone had their own room and it was a 'bit like monks in cells'. He did not know everybody's name, but he knew most by sight. In larger sets, barristers have set up mentoring schemes, giving new members a link with and a chance to meet more senior members. Despite these developments, most interviewed insisted that there was a collegial atmosphere in chambers and that the open door practice, whereby barristers go into each other's rooms to discuss a case or a point of law and bounce ideas off each other, remained very much alive. The true nature and extent of collegiality at the Bar is examined more fully in Chapter 8.

## IV. The New Commercialism: Business and Management

Many of the barristers interviewed came from sets that now employ staff over and above the traditional employees. This is not simply in response to the increased membership, but also to adapt to the dual development of the managerial requirements and commercialism that has pervaded the administration of chambers in the last 25 years or so. Morison and Leith (1992) noted the recent appearance of practice managers in their 1992 study, but research on marketing at the Bar in 1998 found that it was still unusual to find specially appointed business managers in the sets they visited (Harris and Piercy 1998). A new transparency and accountability, largely driven by regulation and commercial awareness, has transformed how chambers are run and who is involved in running them. Although the roles and job titles vary across sets, it is now common to find Administration Managers, Chief Operating Officers, Practice Development Managers, Business Directors, Marketing Managers, Chambers Directors and Chief Executives, or any combination thereof, in chambers. Some are concerned with administration and regulatory compliance, others with business strategy and practice development. In sets where such personnel do not exist, largely due to the added expense, the clerks have undergone some form of management training and are encouraged to adopt a more commercial approach to the running of chambers.

Chambers managers or administrators on the whole have no legal training, but have come from the business management sector. One interviewee spoke of his chambers' experience in the mid-1990s, when an administrative manager was brought in. Although now the norm, at the time her actions were innovative, creating a whole new structure around which chambers was organised and run:

> She set up a whole series of committees … she had interest groups so that each practice area … would have its interest group … and they would have meetings and discuss what initiatives they wanted to pursue … then she set up Call groups … if you had issues about inadequate work for juniors, as opposed to silks, or senior juniors or something, we do have groups which meet and address those issues. Then there's the Financial and General Purpose Committee … we have a Business Development Committee, we have a Marketing Committee, we have a Budget Committee.
>
> B36, Chancery set

A whole series of divisions of labour within chambers have been renegotiated in the last 25 years, creating a quite different professional dynamic. Decision-making is often made by committee or, in very important matters, chambers vote. A head of chambers will rarely impose her or his will, occasionally having to step in if an impasse emerges. In only one of the sets visited did the head of chambers make all the decisions, in consultation with the senior silks. Often there are two joint heads, especially in very large sets. In most cases, these figureheads are now elected for a fixed term and chambers have a written constitution. All interviewed viewed this more democratic structure of governance as an improvement. One recalled his arrival at the Bar in the early 1990s: 'The whole hierarchical nature of the set, the sort of stuff that went along with being a barrister, which I associate with some kind of fossilised British class system, was something that I found very hard to take as a young man' (B25, criminal practitioner). Many chambers now ensure that the junior end is represented on their management committees. One even had a specific junior practitioner committee who met regularly with the clerk to share ideas and concerns.

The new managers employed by the barristers have duties that are more developed than those of early administrators, who might have done some accounting, VAT returns, banking, salaries and rental matters. Now a manager can be in charge of everything, aside from barristers' practice development, including tasks such as: organising marketing events, collating and updating Bar directory entries, practising certificates and professional insurance (Bar Mutual) applications, building maintenance, recruitment and training of staff, absence control, staff appraisals and salary reviews, initial collation and sifting of mini-pupillage and full pupillage applications, compliance issues and any other operational procedures in chambers. Some are also involved in wider strategy: 'She has an input into our overall strategy, including our business strategy and she is very much responsible for keeping us abreast of things, what we should be doing or might want to do in terms of quality assurance' (B48, Joint Head of Chambers, specialist civil set). The Legal Practice Management Association (LPMA) was set up in 1996 and now has a membership of over 130 people:

> Some people are members of both the Institute of Barristers' Clerks and the Legal Practice Management Association, so we do have some clerks who are part of the LPMA and there tend to be also chambers directors. CEOs also tend to be members of the LPMA.
>
> A2, Administrative Manager, civil set

The organisation runs workshops on '[t]he Jackson reforms or whatever. They will hold sessions on the various aspects of that' (A2) and holds events to update its members on relevant developments within the legal sector: 'If anything controversial is going on that we need to know about, like … the pupillage gateway changed across to a different provider' (A2). Chambers managers have liberated the clerks, the heads of chambers and other barrister volunteers from a number of administrative tasks, which they previously undertook in a rather piecemeal fashion when they had the time:

> One barrister was looking after the leases on the building, and would liaise with the Inner Temple about the problems with refurbishments and things like that. Another barrister would look after leases on photocopiers. Someone else would be on an IT committee and a lot of the HR issues used to go to the head of chambers and so all that was taken away and put into my remit.
>
> A2, Administrative Manager, civil set

These changes have happened gradually, in conjunction with a growing commercial awareness at the Bar, and it has taken some time for them to be streamlined and rationalised. There were a number of tales of disastrous early attempts to incorporate such managers into chambers, sometimes due to the hostility of the clerks' room: 'We did try. Had somebody for a couple of years. She was a complete disaster. She couldn't manage the clerks' (B32, circuit set). It has taken time and experimentation for managers and barristers to find a way of working with and around the idiosyncratic ways of the profession. One chambers' manager (A2, civil set) was very proud to assert that all chambers information is now centralised, accessible on one computer system, coherent and uniformly branded: 'There was a woeful lack of central electronic filing … all staff were filing things individually on their C drives. No one made any use of the server … so there was no sharing of information or very little sharing of information.'

A key task for the administrators is ensuring chambers' compliance with regulatory requirements. The latest BSB approach to regulation of chambers management is one of risk-based supervision, placing the onus on chambers to comply, with only those identified as being 'risky' in some way being put under close inspection by the regulator. As it happens, many of the administrative protocols were already in place prior to the BSB taking over independent regulation, in the form of the optional but widely adhered to Bar Mark: 'They had Bar Mark here anyway, which is was the – it's slightly different, but it's like a starting block for making sure that your company is compliant' (A8, Chambers Director). Another administrator (A1) expanded on this: 'We have a Chambers manual and appendices … It's our bible of what we do, everything – chambers' management, recruitment policy. A huge, house book, which we, when we applied for quality mark, had to get everything in order. That appeared in 2003.' Chambers are now, for example, obliged to have policies on discrimination and fair selection processes in recruitment, maternity policies and complaint procedures which are brought to the attention of a client at the outset of the relationship. The increase in regulation has led to an increase in the work needed to be done to comply with this. In chambers that do not have the staffing capacity to do so, this aspect of administration is sometimes sub-contracted out. One chambers director took the view that total compliance was unrealistic: 'I can tell you wholeheartedly that they can regulate and regulate and regulate, as they do. The reality is 90 per cent of chambers are just not up to being able to comply. They can't. It's impossible, they just haven't got the manpower' (A8, mixed disciplinary set). Some chambers have declined to recruit such staff, either because they felt their clerks were able to expand their roles to include any new tasks or because they could not afford the additional personnel. A couple of clerks noted that their workloads had increased significantly to absorb all the additional management and marketing duties: 'There's tons to read … there's a much bigger admin job for me … you just squeeze it all in. You know, we don't have lunch hours' (A3, senior clerk, common law set).

With some variation, the organisational aspects of chambers are more centralised and are considered by most of those interviewed to be more efficient. Many barristers no longer have to carry out many of the discrete tasks they used to, but new responsibilities have emerged, a change manifested in the numerous committees that have sprung up. Aside from practice group/team committees, there are recruitment, financial, management, strategy and marketing, to name but a few, which are all manned by barristers in conjunction with management and business staff. The practitioners fund all additional costs of such staff from their contributions to chambers. Critically, chambers have no outside investors or shareholders. On the one hand, this can result in under-investment, since barristers themselves have to meet the cost of any innovation. There was a noticeable difference in the levels and type of staff employed in the large or specialist sets and the smaller ones. As the BSB's (2017b) research found, chambers' budgets for marketing were generally low, though in a number of specialist civil or commercial sets visited, considerable sums are set aside for marketing staff, promotion and branding. Chambers dues are calculated in different ways according to the set, but in essence all pay a percentage of their income towards the running expenses (rent, staff, marketing etc). A very successful commercial set will have a lower percentage: 'It ranges from about eight, nine per cent to about 28 per cent if you're a crime set. The average at the Bar would be between 15 and 18 per cent' (B13). However, not having to account to investors means that change is often driven by budgetary concerns and then shaped by the barristers and their management employees and their shared objectives, rather than outside interests.

## V. The New 'Super Clerk'

> The clerking role at all levels has changed beyond recognition ... the clerking role back when I first started was basically to sit at the desk and wait for the phone to ring and then distribute work out to the membership.
>
> A8, Chambers Director, mixed disciplinary set

Although traditional clerking remains, a new breed of clerk has emerged at the top of the clerking hierarchy. Operating under a variety of names – Chief Executive Officers, Commercial Managers, Chambers or Business Directors – and often with university degrees and wide business experience, these clerks have duties that go beyond the traditional ones of a senior clerk. One barrister described their Business Director thus:

> He's like a super clerk. He is a super, super senior clerk. Business development directors who are below him, they are the senior clerks ... He oversees practice development, overseeing the clerking as a whole from a very senior level and inputting into business development.
>
> B48, Joint Head of Chambers, specialist civil set

These 'super clerks' have taken a step back from day-to-day clerking and are involved in overall chambers strategy, which might include practice development for individuals or practice groups. They attend meetings with existing instructing solicitors or potential new ones and are involved in general chambers development, which might include the setting up of an ABS or forging new alliances with lawyers abroad. Therefore, the most senior clerks' role has been transformed from an untrained, idiosyncratic controller of work distribution to a modern, efficient and commercial overseer and strategist: 'The whole ethos of clerking has changed. Mainly brought on by the advent of technology. Also there was, or there is a view now, that the old style of clerking has its place, but it's not an overriding thing in a set of chambers' (A5, Senior Clerk, common law circuit set). The clerks below these super senior clerks are also much more commercially driven and all will now undergo some kind of formal training, whether it be in relation to the IT clerking systems or management courses. Gone are the days of quirky, individual practices in the clerks' room, where the head clerk ran a private dominion:

> When I was a junior clerk, I was required by my senior clerk to sit on a wall for 45 minutes with an aerial in my hand whilst he watched TV and watched a football game – a TV aerial, so that he could get reception. I had to sit there for 45 minutes so he could watch the game and then I went into the window to do my DX and came back for the second half. That is an absolutely true story. That would never, ever, ever, ever happen in today's world.
>
> A8, Chambers Director, clerking for 25 years

The Institute of Barristers' Clerks (IBC) offers, inter alia, two-year B Tech clerking courses, which junior clerks attend for one day every fortnight, as well as evening classes and diplomas in business administration. It also runs shorter, seminar evening sessions on matters such as Chancery Division listing. One set of chambers organised in-house training for clerks on public speaking, networking and business management, and offered them bonuses if chambers' turnover exceeded a certain amount, as an incentive to work together and harder. Many chambers have divided up the clerks into teams, sometimes by practice area or according to the rank of the practitioners they clerk. The clerking team, or members of it, will meet with the corresponding team of barristers regularly to discuss matters such as strategy for getting work, developing new areas of work, existing levels of work or distribution of unallocated briefs. One barrister felt this arrangement delineated the clerks' responsibilities more clearly, made them more accountable to practitioners and perform less haphazardly.

## VI. Chambers as a Business

There has been a concerted push across the Bar to transform and modernise chambers' administration and governance in order to:

> Make us much more corporate as an organisation and therefore much more attractive to bigger firms … we are a business, we monitor as if we were a business, we report as if we were a business, we're a business … we provide extra value to certain clients … we provide them with 24 hour contact … it's not 'I'll go home at five o'clock and then you can't ring me at the weekend'. It's like we have to be more professional about it.
>
> A8, Chambers Director, multi-practice set

Even the language used has changed. Referring to a set of chambers as a business is in itself a startling development for those raised on the traditional model. Clerks frequently referred to barristers in chambers as 'the membership', as if they were elements of a corporate body, and the websites of a number of sets no longer use the old terminology of 'clerks' or 'pupils', preferring 'practice managers' and 'trainees' instead. It is generally accepted that sets of chambers need an overall management and business plan in order to target, get and maintain work, and to provide a modern, efficient and customer-centred professional service. A need for a strategic overview is deemed crucial: 'What happened was there was more of a look at how can we, we, as a collective, bring work in. Not so much as Charlie the clerk will go to the Witness Box and come back with a coat, pockets full of briefs, but how can we do this now, how can we take it forward?' (A5, senior clerk). Yet some chambers have not brought in commercial expertise, preferring to run things as before, either due to a lack of understanding of what they might achieve or because they feel threatened by such changes:

> There isn't any centralised strategic thinking and that I think is a source of some potential discomfort amongst members of these chambers. We did actually have a sort of one-off strategy meeting recently … and it was perceived to be actually rather ill-tempered … there were some rather big questions raised by people about how do we respond, for example, to the new business environment, and whether or not we should be going to work with or employing solicitors and becoming Tesco's plc business structure and that sort of thing, but this was taken by some people as criticism of the way in which chambers was currently managed.
>
> B15, specialist silk, civil set

Evident from the interviews was the fact that not all barristers welcome the new commercial approach and this was not necessarily dependent on seniority and the ability to remember 'how things were'. Indeed, there were some very forward-looking participants who were senior members or heads of chambers. Interviewees generally accepted the new management and clerking initiatives as positive developments, but there were those who resolutely resisted notions of dramatic change, such as new business structures. Moreover, not all senior clerks agreed with the new management and business 'turn', preferring to acquire a more commercial outlook themselves. For them, these new 'outside' experts lack the essential knowledge of the Bar and barristers, and thus fail to integrate new methods of working successfully:

> I'm an old fashioned clerk, always will be … I'm not a lover of practice managers … [they] mainly sit and cause trouble to be honest … I was brought in because they had a practice manager and he failed, because, this sounds sort of protectionist, but it's not – it's 40 years' worth of knowledge. It's knowing how barristers react, how they feel. You know, they tell you things that you wouldn't dream of really. I've been told so many things being a clerk. You're a father confessor, you're a psychologist, you're a psychiatrist, you're a theatrical agent. You've got to be all these things to be able to do the job and they tend to bring people in from the commercial world, who are no doubt extremely good at what they do, you can't deny that fact, but there's a gap in knowledge, which is very, very important – the barristers and the way barristers' think, the way they behave, their attitudes, their concerns, their worries … it has to be run like a business, but running alongside that is the whole ethos that has always got to be there. The integrity. The honesty. All these different things.
>
> A5, senior clerk, circuit set

The above extract reveals a complex view of the new developments. On the one hand, a clerk might feel threatened by the new management regime or be caught up in a nostalgic ideal about the clerking role. On the other hand, there is a palpable sense of pride about a job well done – a job that is nuanced, delicate, complicated and not simply concerned with market logics. Above all, there is a sense of deep affection for the clerking role and the barristers 'within the fold'. A few of the clerks and practitioners interviewed were barely able to conceal their glee when recounting how their chambers employed a manager and it was a complete disaster, so they had to get rid of them and revert to the traditional staffing structure.

However, on the whole, old methods of clerking have been updated and displaced by market and management logics. Clerks are no longer paid a percentage of all fees, but a flat salary with a far more modest incentive bonus of anything between 0.5 and 1.5 per cent. They are expected to have more skills and business acumen and have to be much more proactive in getting work. A few chambers have recruited clerks specifically to run and coordinate direct access work. One barrister recounted how his set also has a personal support lawyer to keep members updated on new developments in the law and carry out research for cases where necessary. Most interviewees had never heard of this kind of arrangement. The prevailing view from the interviews was that chambers are run much more efficiently, more professionally and more commercially than before, and that barristers and their support professionals are much more conscious of the need to provide a good service to their clients:

> Over the course of my career it's become very, very much more professional. What I mean is that I feel that we are more accountable, I feel that we're less of a boy's club, less introspective, better regulated, better run, better understanding of the service that we provide, better client relations.
>
> B15, specialist civil silk, 28 years' call

This contrasts sharply with Harris and Piercy's findings (1998) that, despite their developed communication skills, barristers showed little if any interest in customer relations and that there was a distinct division between the barristers, who did the 'thinking' in chambers, and the clerks, who simply enacted what had been decided. Relations between barrister and clerk and client are now much more equal, respectful and collaborative and, as Faulconbridge and Muzio (2008) found in relation to law firms, barristers have put in place new organisational and management structures to support rather than displace professional values. Their self-employed status protects them from managerial subjugation. However, there is wide differentiation across the Bar in terms of how organisational and commercial matters have developed, largely because of the relative independence of the practitioners and of chambers as collective units, and due to very varied levels of confidence, interest, resources and know-how.

## VII. Chambers' Branding

In step with the developments to make chambers more corporate, the branding of sets has become commonplace. One chambers director noted: 'We went for complete brand awareness. Last year we were at every event there was to be at. We had our brand everywhere' (A8, multi-practice set). Chambers now hire website designers and professional photographers to create an online presence that reflects their identity:

> I think it's all about a recognition by chambers that in addition to the old structure of all of us being a collection of individuals, that in the modern world we need to have some sort of brand identity as a group as well.
>
> B20, specialist civil barrister, 38 years' call

A marketing consultant (A7) noted that 'you're trying to design a website that reflects the ethos of its practitioners'. For the more general common law sets, it is harder to brand successfully, as they must first identify which area of work they do as a collective and want to be known for: 'It won't work for [x chambers] because they are a generalist set. They can't do PI or employment, because they've had to be fighting against people who are established at doing just PI or just employment.' As indicated earlier in this chapter, in the past it was common and considered beneficial to offer services across a wide range of practice areas within one set of chambers. Now sets of chambers will only attract work if they are considered to be *the* experts in any particular area or, more commonly, sub-area within a specialism: 'I don't think our chambers at the moment are particularly known in any one area as being excellent, so consequently it's really very much a common law set that is trying to react to massive change' (B4, common law set). Even so, some common law sets have successfully rebranded as 'multi-' or 'mixed disciplinary' sets, cross-selling barristers from different teams to provide a complete service for clients or putting forward members of the family, immigration and housing teams, for example, to provide different units of specialist advice in one case. In these cases, chambers have actively recruited barristers who specialise in particular areas to bolster existing practice groups, sometimes recruiting whole teams, expert in a new area, to complement another group already within the set. Getting into one of the established Bar Directories is now an all-important marketing target and the entries for chambers serve as a good example of the promotion of chambers as a collective, rather than a random group of self-employed practitioners sharing office space and staff:

> It's become a rather two-tier Bar now. The sets that are doing well are the specialists and the commercial sets, who genuinely specialise and have brand reputations in their area of practice, and that is usually signified by them being able to get into the legal directories, which are Chambers and Legal 500. Those two. That is the Holy Grail of marketing actually.
>
> B1, common law set

Some chambers have abandoned the traditional address title for a name of a famous judge or barrister who was once in the set: Hailsham, Atkin, Wilberforce, Henderson and so on. Others have converted it into a more modern, catchy abbreviation: 1 Crown Office Row is now 1 COR. All have logos that adorn their webpages, notepaper, emails and Twitter accounts, and consistent branding across chambers is considered essential. One administrator (A2, civil set) commented that: 'A lot of money had been spent on branding, which was excellent, but there was no one at staff management level making sure things went out with a corporate identity.' Since her arrival, she has ensured uniformity:

> The right fonts and the same fonts we use on letters, the same kind of styles and templates for a Word document, a PowerPoint presentation, things like that. And it might sound trivial, but in actual fact it does go a long way in making things look much more professional.

## VIII. ABS and Going 'Global'

As indicated in Chapter 2, under the LSA, the rules concerning the structuring and financing of legal service providers were liberalised. In relation to the Bar, a number of momentous changes were introduced, including permitting barristers to set up an ABS, liberating them from the traditional chambers structure, or allowing them to create new or ancillary 'add on' units, such as LLPs or companies. Barristers can now be part of interdisciplinary practices or litigation and advocacy entities. They can work in dual capacity as self-employed and employed practitioners (not on the same case) or share premises with other non-barristers. The SRA started licensing ABS entities in October 2011, but the BSB only became authorised to do so in March 2017. Thus, the few early barrister-led ABSs were set up and regulated by the SRA rather than the BSB. At the time of the original fieldwork, there had been little innovation in this regard: 'I think it's fair to say that since the Act was passed, quite a lot of time has been spent trying to work through what that means' (B1, common law set). Recent research indicates that interest remains low (BSB 2017b).

In interviews, many barristers displayed a remarkable lack of knowledge or interest in developing any new structures in order to deliver their services more effectively, competitively or commercially:

> Q: Do you have any ABS or ProcureCos or …
>
> A: (interrupting) No.
>
> Q: Do you have any need for anything like that?
>
> A: No, I don't foresee it happening.
>
> Q: Is it something your chambers have even talked about?
>
> A: No, no.
>
> B20, specialist civil set

> What would they be doing?
>
> B14, commercial set

> In terms of ABS and things … I don't think we'd ever thought of it. I think there was some idea of setting up a ProcureCo … I have to admit [to] … not being particularly entrepreneurial or interested in these kinds of things.
>
> B19, common law set

A handful of interviewees said that their chambers were actively looking into setting up some form of entity or ABS, even if they had not yet quite worked out what to do with it, but this and other structural innovation, whilst the subject of some discussion, had rarely been acted upon, both at the time of the original fieldwork and the follow-up interviews five years later: 'I know that it's been under discussion for ages. I'm sure we're not alone in contemplating going into, if not partnerships, alliances, maybe ad hoc ones with solicitor's firms on a particular contract or job' (B2, mixed practice set). Even such contemplation was contingent on at least one member of chambers having some sort of commercial outlook and understanding:

> Most members of chambers are, I think, absolutely ignorant about ABS or what they do or what they could do. [Name of barrister], who is dealing with it, is very, very up on it and is setting it all up, which I'm very grateful him doing it, he's put a lot of work into it, and I think when it is set up, we're then all going to see how we can use it and whether it's going to benefit chambers and how we deal with it.
>
> B44, head of chambers, mixed disciplinary set

At the Bar conference in 2015, one practitioner speaker noted that flexibility was key to a successful career. The modern barrister had to be an advocate, a businessperson and an entrepreneur. Practitioners needed to diversify and re-invent themselves to survive (Hill 2015). Yet not all are entrepreneurial or business-minded, and nothing in their training has prepared them for these challenges and transformations. A strong sense of uncertainty about what setting up an ABS would achieve was evident in many interviews and was coupled with a suspicion that anything they did set up might fail, jeopardising the reputation of chambers:

> It's something I wanted to set up in advance, because I said 'This could be interesting, it could be potentially very useful'. Let's set it up and the idea of the ABS here, we haven't called it [name of set], we've called it by a completely different name, because if it succeeds it doesn't matter what it's called, and if it doesn't succeed then it won't have [name of set] written all over it and we can just drop it.
>
> B44, Head of Chambers, multi-practice set

One barrister interviewed had set up an entity, an LLP, which is regulated by the SRA as it pre-dates the BSB's power to do so. It employs barristers (who remain regulated by the BSB), solicitors and paralegals. The model used had no top-heavy partnership, with expensive associates below. The barrister described it as 'a thin top level, with a strong lean resource below' (B50), made up mainly of paralegals or junior barristers working on secondment. The work was very specialised and fees were fixed. Their actual operations were more akin to those of solicitors, having given up all court advocacy. However, using their title and experience as barristers in their view gives them more credibility and cachet than if they were simply solicitors. This particular entity had to pay regulatory fees to both the SRA (for the LLP) and the BSB (for the individual barristers), and insurance was expensive and difficult to find as companies were not sure what kind of cover to give this new set-up. He also noted that running a business such as this involved a lot of extra work and he and his partner were obliged by the SRA to undertake a management course. Only about three or four other participants envisaged creating something different from the existing arrangements. One commercial barrister projected:

> The new rules come in under which the company could create a SupplyCo. In other words, the company could supply the legal service and it would then allocate work to a barrister who would still be … for example, if IBM goes to [name of chambers] or Barclays Bank more likely, goes to [name of chambers] and says 'We've got this work, we want you to do it. This is a case worth £5m in fees, it's a billion dollar claim. 5 million in fees, litigation will take 18 months to 2 years, can you do it for 5 million?' 'Of course', the clerks rub their hands and say 'Absolutely delighted'. Our SupplyCo under this model would have employed paralegals, an accountant, some solicitors and then the SupplyCo, [name] Chambers Ltd would instruct the barristers.
>
> B13, head of commercial chambers

The few that are engaging, albeit slowly, with these new opportunities see new ways of working and of restructuring their chambers as essential to their survival. One specialist civil and commercial silk (B48) commented: 'It's about to change dramatically and if you don't think about it and look at the options, you're going to die, so you have to and you can't just live in the past.' However, most see absolutely no need to change the existing chambers structure, which they consider to be sufficiently flexible and much cheaper. More prosaically, there are chambers that have taken advantage of a limited company structure through which to channel chambers' finances, giving them various tax advantages. A number of (mainly) commercial chambers have opened annexes or acquired office space, or have created alliances with lawyers abroad in places like the US, the Gulf or Russia, largely to draw in work for the barristers in London or to provide a working base in a location where they already have some work. Although nothing like the presence of large global law firms, this is nonetheless a significant development in the Bar's international presence, represented by the Bar Council's International Committee, with a small yet significant group of barristers engaging in business opportunities and attending conferences abroad (Pinto 2015). The initial fieldwork took place before the 2016 referendum, but of those interviewed in 2018/19, none was able to comment on whether leaving the EU would affect any international alliances or their work more generally. At the time of writing, the political upheaval and uncertainty surrounding Brexit makes it difficult to anticipate its effect, if any, on the profession.

## IX. Online/Virtual Chambers

'Clerksroom' is the largest public access portal apart from that of the Bar Council and was launched in 2001 with two barristers and one clerk. It now has 80 barristers on its books and 20 clerks, taking 10 per cent of each fee or at least £600 per month. Barristers are only accepted if they already earn more than £100,000 annually. More recently, it launched Billy Bot, the robot junior clerk, and has innovated shared office space in London for those needing a room to rent on an hourly basis for conferences and meetings (Granville Stafford 2015; Bindman 2018). There are a number of smaller portals (eg, Barristers Online, MyBarrister, Barristers Direct and Absolute Barrister), and practitioners who operate via these or similar ones are often also members of traditional sets of chambers. There are no figures on the number of practitioners doing this and only two of those interviewed had signed on with these portals, but had done almost no work from them. The amount of barristers listed on some of the websites seems modest. More research is needed to establish how many barristers are using these platforms, for how much work, what they think of them, how customers are experiencing this way of finding legal representation, how they rate the service and the fees charged.

## X. A Traditional Chambers Model or Something New?

These findings point to an evolution of the chambers model, which in turn marks an evolution in barristers' professionalism. The concept of enterprise has become a dominant feature, which is driven by managerial and market logics. This shift is reflected in the new chambers re-organisation and staffing, with a focus on customer care/service, efficiency, compliance and commerce (Evetts 2015). The profession appears to be looking outwards, customer-facing, for the first time. The reconception of what kind of clerking and management staff are needed has been further shaped to support larger numbers of practitioners, divided up into specialist teams.

Nonetheless, elements of the essence of traditional life in chambers remain: the collegial room sharing; the barrister-led decision-making about chambers' strategy, albeit now in collaboration with business and management experts; the essentially unchanged financial structure, whereby a percentage of each member's income pays for chambers administration; the presence of clerks and clerking duties, which, although modernised, remains the same in the sense that work always passes through them and they agree the fees. Typical features of ideal-type professionalism also prevail, evidenced by barristers retaining or developing new areas of specialisation, honing their expertise even more narrowly so as to give them exclusive jurisdiction or at least an edge in these micro-markets. Knowledge, skill, discretionary judgement and status remain features of professional life at the Bar. Although hyper-specialisation to some degree creates splinter groups, established professions have always had highly differentiated sub-communities, but remain held together by common training and a broader shared jurisdiction (Freidson 2001). Most of the interviewees felt that the new chambers model had not undermined core professional values, but that instead the new organisational structure and commercial focus have been absorbed into professional life without compromising it, supporting Faulconbridge and Muzio's research into law firms that found 'organizational tactics and mechanisms are ultimately defined and influenced by professional interests' (2008: 20). The degree to which these developments may have altered traditional Bar culture is explored in Chapter 7, but many were keen to stress that they felt that practitioners still retained independence from managerial interference:

> All the professions are now being dragged into the business world we live in. Cut throat … a lot of people came to the Bar because they didn't, they wanted a financially remunerative job which is interesting, without being really in kind of management, not having line managers, not getting into endless corporate meetings and to some extent the Bar hasn't.
>
> B19, civil/commercial practice, 15 years' call

Unless and until barristers develop more radical ABSs or entities and fundamentally change the way they do business and acquire investors, or more practitioners adopt hybrid status (self-employed and part-time in-house), it is likely that the revised, modernised, commercialised, but fundamentally recognisable chambers model will remain. From the reactions noted above, it seems likely that most barristers are reluctant to let go of it and would prefer to continue to work within this structure, and will resist more dramatic change for as long as possible, many perceiving that to work within an ABS would essentially make them like solicitors, which many were insistent they would never want to be. One of the first BSB-licensed entities was created by a criminal law set, which intended to use it as a corporate vehicle to bid for legal aid contracts. When the two-tier contract proposal was abandoned, the head of chambers noted that they no longer had any use for it and that, in his view, the traditional structures and ways of working in contentious matters would remain as they were (Rose 2016).

Yet, if one were to step back and compare the empirical data on the running of a set of chambers today with how things were done in, say, the early 1990s, the changes are significant. The increasingly monitored and regulated administration of sets, together with rules and guidance on how to attract, interview and recruit new members (which is examined in detail in the following chapter), have gradually eroded the freedom barristers once had to decide how to run their collectives, showing all the hallmarks of commercial organisations and in contrast to the traditional, autonomous professional (Sommerlad 1995; Evetts 2015). The new commercial outlook has obliged them to think and behave differently, ever mindful of the insecure nature of their practices and of the competition they face from other members of the Bar and solicitors. These changes are reflected in the discursive practices that have arisen. Practitioners, clerks and chambers staff spoke in interviews of being more professional, more efficient and uniform in their organisational arrangements, adopting managerial objectives. A number of interviewees described chambers as a business, having a business plan and a business manager or director. Many of the chambers web homepages lay great emphasis on being client-friendly. 'Efficiency', 'uniformity', 'business-oriented' and 'client-friendly' are notions that were entirely absent, or at least unarticulated, 30 years ago at the Bar. This linguistic turn, evident in many of the answers given during interviews, reflects a significant shift not just in outlook but also in what is happening on the ground. For some commercial and specialist practitioners, failure to innovate, whether by setting up alliances or annexes abroad or by exploring how new structures might benefit their chambers, is a 'head in the sand' approach that spells professional death. They see no future at the modern Bar for a historic, undeveloped model that has outlived its purpose and for those who are frightened to change or unable to adapt.

# 4

# Getting in, Fitting in: The Enterprising Aspiring Barrister

> I applied to slightly less competitive sets and had two coaching sessions with somebody who specialises in self-presentation. I did further mini-pupillages and more pro bono to boost my CV.
>
> B51, civil practitioner, one year's call

In an increasingly competitive environment, an applicant seeking to enter the profession must mobilise new skills and entrepreneurial flair to get a pupillage. This chapter investigates what students do to enhance their prospects of success and what transpires during selection processes and interviews. What are recruitment panels looking for and does the new regulatory framework really ensure acceptance based on merit? How is merit interpreted? Statistical data of the numbers qualifying and getting pupillage reveal just how hard it is to secure a place on this apprenticeship year (Zimdars 2010; BSB 2017a). Historically, incoming barristers paid 100 guineas to their pupil masters for the privilege, though pupillage, whilst traditional, was only made compulsory in 1959 (Hazell 1978e). This payment was abolished in 1975 and for the next 28 years, an unpaid pupillage was not especially difficult to secure, even if the process was often dependent on family connections or luck (Hazell 1978e; Boon 2014). Barristers continued with the long-standing tradition of training newcomers, but were under no obligation to recruit them at the end of it. Non-payment of pupils put a disproportionate strain on those with less means, so from 2003 all pupillages had to be funded, initially at the sum of £10,000 per year and from September 2011 to the tune of £1,000 per month, the first six months by way of award and the second six the same or via guaranteed receipts. Top commercial or specialist sets pay up to six times this amount (Aldridge 2015). From September 2019, minimum pupillage payments must reach levels recommended by the Living Wage Foundation and have increased to over £18,000 in London and a little less than £16,000 elsewhere (Walters 2018).

In the first decade of mandatory payment, the number of pupillage places offered dropped by 51 per cent (BSB 2015b). The reduction of work in many areas of practice, together with the obligation to pay pupils, has, in some chambers, meant that fewer or no pupillages are being offered. In any given year, it was estimated that about 3,000 students were competing for as few as 400-odd places (Wood 2010; Chambers Student 2019). Recent figures from different sources support this stark reality: only 41 per cent of students enrolled on the Bar Professional Training Course (BPTC) between 2012/13 and 2017/18 have started pupillage (BSB 2019c). In 2017/18, there were 1,351 graduates called to the Bar. At the same time, only 473 people started pupillage, places for which were also sought by students from previous years. In 2018, 2,089 aspiring applicants collectively submitted 14,516 applications to the profession's official portal, the Pupillage Gateway. About 100 sets of chambers recruit via this portal. Only 224 pupillage places were offered (Connelly 2018). Reviews of the entry processes, together with recent research, lament the lack of diversity in the profession, exacerbated by the drop in numbers of pupillages and increased competition to get them, disadvantaging BAME students especially and those from lower socio-economic or non-traditional backgrounds (Bar Council 2007; Wood 2010; Ilex Professional Standards et al 2013; Freer 2016, 2018; BSB 2017a). Further, the increased costs of the qualifying courses disproportionately affect these groups. A conservative estimate of a law student's debt is between £50,000 and £60,000. One Bar Council chair noted that if a student took the longest route to qualify in London, it would cost about £127,000 (Bowcott 2016b).

Despite this, there has been little qualitative research on how students view the application and selection processes or the criteria that chambers rely on when recruiting (BSB 2017a; Freer 2018). What are law students doing to prepare for a career at the Bar, knowing that there is a good chance they will not even get a pupillage, let alone a tenancy? How and in what way are they building their CVs to compete with one another? On what basis does chambers decided who to invite for interview? How do barristers assess applicants? Have the new regulations designed to impose meritocratic selection practices been effective? Drawing on barristers' and pupils' experiences, the focus of this chapter is on two aspects of getting into the profession: what attributes and skills a new entrant needs and how pupils are selected.

A glance at virtually any of the online profiles of young practitioners at the Bar reveals a significant shift, embodied in the strikingly different contents of their CVs, compared to older barristers. Based on interviews with pupils and young practitioners, this chapter interrogates why this is the case and what has brought it about. In keeping with one of the main themes of this study, the findings show that even a student/aspiring barrister must now be strategic, enterprising and able to market her/himself, long before s/he has even qualified. Having a good degree and passing the Graduate Diploma in Law (GDL), if necessary, as well as the BPTC are not sufficient, and new entrants must mobilise all forms of capital to secure additional experience and qualifications. Thus, a barrister's professionalism is being refashioned by an increased competitive and commercial turn, even in the pre-qualification period. Turning to selection processes, the regulatory framework imposes training and guidance on how selection and interviews should take place. How effective these are in ensuring objective, merit-based decisions is considered in the light of some of the findings. Despite new regulation and overt efforts by many to make selection processes fairer, this research shows that entry criteria continue to include subjective elements and display unconscious bias in favour of those who 'fit in'. The wider implications of both these sets of findings are considered at their respective sections in the chapter.

## I. Pupillage Places

Given the numbers of those qualifying and pupillage places available, chambers often need make no effort to attract applicants and can enforce high standards, making entry ultra-competitive (Rogers 2011). There is no doubt that the number of pupillage places has dropped since funding became obligatory, but this is by no means even across the profession. Some chambers, who undertake criminal or family work, no longer offer pupillages at all, due to lack of work at the junior end: 'We haven't had a criminal pupil here for three years. We always used to have one and various of our junior members were pupils … but its either three or four years since we had a pupil here' (B18, criminal circuit barrister). Even chambers that actively discourage applications are inundated: 'We do say on the website, "Don't apply". We still get over 100 applications every year. We do take mini-pupils … for experience, although I'm not sure there is any point' (B32, family and criminal practitioner, circuit set). Equally, some of the junior barristers interviewed indicated that they did not apply to chambers that did criminal work for financial reasons, a trend that has been noted across the sector, where the disproportionate rewards of commercial legal practice, together with the costs of legal education, are discouraging students from doing so (Webb 2015). One commented that this decision was made early on, during a mini-pupillage:

> I saw a week's rape trial and that was great, but I knew from the outset that I wouldn't want to do crime just because I knew that I would not earn any money and I'd never be able to move out and whilst I'm not in this for the mega bucks, you need to survive.
>
> B17, civil barrister, three years' call

Parts of the commercial Bar, by contrast, seem to be expanding and actively seeking to recruit: 'We took on seven pupils this year, which is unheard of … and that's because there is more and more work' (B13, head of chambers, commercial set). This by no means makes entry to commercial chambers easier. If anything, the competition to get a pupillage in sets that are obviously flourishing, where work is plentiful and prospects are good, is even steeper. However, it is worth noting that this 'internal differentiation' of uneven pupillage places (and work) is a consequence of wider 'system disturbances' (Abbott 1988: 117). The reduction in funding of the police and prosecution service and of legal aid in many areas of work, together with solicitors undertaking more advocacy work, has resulted in fewer cases being initiated and less work coming to the Bar, and so fewer pupillages are offered as a consequence. On the other hand, where practitioners have developed highly niche expertise in order to compete successfully for work, more pupils are taken on: 'The specialist Bar will just get stronger and stronger because we have two characteristics which should be absolutely unbeatable in any harsh market, which is very high quality with very low cost compared to solicitors' (B13, head of chambers, commercial set). Competition for pupillage across the Bar has become 'piranha like', as the same interviewee phrased it. One civil set had 180 applicants for two spaces, but many sets had more: 'You have a stack of about 800 applications a year … we select six' (B43, mixed disciplinary set), '400 odd applicants … to our final five' (B13, commercial set) or 'In come 400 letters asking for pupillage and there are probably two or three places' (B44, mixed disciplinary set).

How do students compete for these few spaces? There is some evidence to suggest that commercial and specialist sets like to recruit students immediately after their studies are complete, whilst other mixed practice sets expect them to have acquired other skills and experience before applying. Most students do not get a pupillage the first time they apply (Bar Council 2014b; BSB 2019c) and the majority that do eventually secure one tend to get it after they are qualified, many taking a further year or two to acquire additional skills and experience. All of the younger practitioners and both of the pupils interviewed felt that they had to build up their CVs, particularly where they have failed to get a pupillage first time round, to improve their prospects. As one head of chambers indicated: 'We're not looking for a normal CV, we want something special about the CV' (B44, mixed disciplinary set).

## II. The 'Special' CV

The findings from the interviews suggest that building a 'special CV' and enhancing employability is done in three general ways, none of which was the norm 25 years ago: by undertaking multiple, unpaid mini-pupillages in different sets of chambers; by acquiring a postgraduate degree or, less commonly, a PhD; and, finally, by acquiring other work experience, paid or unpaid, that is relevant or linked to some area of legal practice. One interviewee felt that people were starting pupillage later as a result: 'I don't think many early 20 year olds make it to pupillage and tenancy. Certainly in this set … there were six of us, just off of memory, I was 31, so two were 33/34, two were 30/31, one was 26 and one was 24/25' (B47, common law practice, two years' call).

The mechanisms of advancement, which are outlined below, reveal that students are very aware of how opportunity structures operate within this sector and strategise accordingly: 'Because it's so competitive now, in terms of getting pupillage, you really do have to, I certainly felt personally I had to go and demonstrate something else' (B46, family practitioner, six years' call). Like many entering other turbulent labour markets in an employment culture of insecurity, the focus is on 'identity work', (honing presentation skills and conforming to a particular organisational culture), improving one's competencies and actively cultivating cultural and social capital to make oneself more employable (Smith 2010). Employability is an individual's responsibility, where the risks and opportunities appear to be of one's own choosing and making, yet this notion ignores the fact that the resources needed to acquire employability are less available to many, excluding those who lack the means, the connections and the cultural know-how from competing on a level playing field (Smith 2010; Sommerlad 2011).

## III. Mini-pupillages

Formal vacation schemes in solicitors' firms play an increasingly important role as a gateway to that branch of the profession (Shiner and Newburn 1995; Shiner 2000; Francis and Sommerlad 2009; Sommerlad 2011). The same holds true of mini-pupillages at the Bar, which usually last about a week and are undertaken by students whilst at university, during the GDL and BPTC years and often after qualifying (Freer 2016). Of the junior practitioners and pupils interviewed, all except two (who had come into the profession from solicitor jobs) had done at least two mini-pupillages, but most had done many more, some as many as 11. All undertake this unpaid work experience to build up their CVs and are advised to do it by their tutors on the BPTC. The experiences they acquire also allow them to get a feel for chambers and what the profession is like, and to help them decide which practice areas they might be interested in:

> I'd done quite a few mini-pupillages … not as many as some people do … I think I'd done maybe something like six or seven overall … I didn't learn anything from a legal point of view, but it was a very good starting point … I think mini-pupillages are probably the only way that you can get a feel for the atmosphere in a set of chambers. I don't think that that comes across from the website, the interviews.
>
> B17, civil practitioner, three years' call

One interviewee was positively deterred from doing criminal law during a mini-pupillage: 'I saw crime … the case itself I found quite traumatic. A historic paedophilia case and made me think perhaps crime isn't something I can necessarily embrace' (B21, specialist civil practitioner, three years' call). Another junior had a similar experience with a sexual offences case: 'It was just awful, really grimy and I thought "OK, this is really not for me"'. He also ruled out family law work during another mini-pupillage: 'I had seen some family work and quite liked it, but knew that it was not likely to pay very well and worried that it would be grinding. That it would grind you down, doing it on a daily basis' (B23, specialist civil practitioner, seven years' call). Mini-pupillages therefore provide students with important glimpses and experience of the profession. Students get the chance to see what a barrister's work entails, to assimilate some of the professions' norms and practices, to sample different practice areas, to get a flavour of chambers life and a barrister's working day, and, crucially, to improve their CVs and bolster their pupillage applications.

How do students get these mini-pupillages? Unlike full pupillages, they are not regulated by the BSB, save for a few, which are 'assessed' (competitive to get, monitored and rated by chambers, with a view to obtaining a full one). Chambers advertise mini-pupillages on their websites and have an online application process, and many now only accept official mini-pupils via this route. Yet students continue to secure them via more unofficial and informal connections. One interviewee secured two mini-pupillages through chance meetings at law fairs:

> I did one at X chambers … and that was just because I met a nice woman when I went back to University for the Law Fair … and then the other one was at Y chambers … and again that was because I met someone at a careers fair.
>
> B17, civil practitioner, three years' call

Another interviewee explained that some of her mini-pupillages were 'unofficial', obtained through contacts of her mother, who was a solicitor, when she was still at school. Two more also obtained them via family contacts. This more invisible route to obtaining work experience still occurs and so acquiring a 'special CV' is achieved far more easily by those with more social and economic capital, possibly at the expense of less well-connected students (Bathmaker et al 2013). Relevant work experience is now a prerequisite to get on one of the BPTC courses (Ilex Professional Standards et al 2013) and many chambers' websites indicate that mini-pupillages on a CV are a requirement when applying for pupillage. Although chambers as an organisation can be discouraged (or, should the BSB see fit, prohibited) from taking mini-pupils via non-selective routes, no regulation can prohibit a self-employed practitioner from informally allowing a student to shadow her or him and thus selection for mini-pupillage retains an arbitrary element, favouring those with social connections and the ability to undertake unpaid work experience (Freer 2016, 2018). The Sutton Trust (2018) reported that 79 per cent of law internships were unpaid (54 per cent offer absolutely nothing, a further 17 per cent expenses only and eight per cent less than the national minimum wage). Of all sectors, the legal profession had the highest amount of internships yet the lowest levels of advertisements, high levels of personal connection and social segregation.

## IV. Further Educational Qualifications

> All ours, say they're all Oxbridge, they're not, about 50/50 Russell Group and Oxbridge but then almost all of them will either then be Cambridge LLM, Oxford BCL or about third have done the Harvard Masters. It's very odd, about a third have done Harvard and then this year, about 40 per cent have got PhDs.
>
> B13, head of commercial chambers

What is immediately apparent from this extract is that non-Oxbridge/Russell Group applicants are unlikely to even be considered for pupillage in this commercial set of chambers. It has become much more common for prospective pupils to have graduate degrees, something that was relatively rare in the past: 'What I would say is a big change even in my time, is a lot of people now seem to have multiple degrees, postgrads and things' (B19, mixed civil practitioner, 15 years' call). One pupil (B40) interviewed had done a non-law degree, a two-year graduate law degree and then a Masters in law at the University of Oxford ('It was a long and expensive route'). Another interviewee had done two Masters degrees before applying for pupillage: 'I think the choice to do two was just something I was really interested in. But then I knew it would probably be a good idea to apply for pupillage having done a Masters' (B45, family practitioner, seven years' call). This trend was almost universal amongst the young practitioners interviewed: 'I did an undergraduate law degree … I did it as a dual French and English law degree and then I did a Masters in France, specialising in EU law' (B47, common law practice, two years' call). Another had done a Masters because he felt that his first degree was not from a sufficiently elite university, so the decision was entirely strategic:

> Some people had suggested it to me, my undergraduate degree is from Sheffield, and there was a suggestion that it was possible sets were a bit snooty about that and that I could polish my academic credentials, so I did a Masters at UCL.
>
> B23, specialist civil practitioner, seven years' call

This perceived or real need to continue their education to postgraduate level (either before or after the BPTC) is a route only open to those with sufficient funds or those who are prepared to take on further debt. This raises a further, less discussed, economic and social barrier to entry into the profession, largely affecting students from disadvantaged backgrounds, who are considered to be more risk and debt-averse (Ilex Professional Standards et al 2013). For students who do not get scholarships, acquiring a graduate qualification is often not financially viable.

## V. Other Work Experience

Even top academic achievement is often not enough. Many sets look for added value, in the form of pro bono work, placements in solicitors' offices, working at the International Criminal Court or similar activities. All the junior practitioners interviewed had acquired such work experience: 'I did a Judicial Assistantship at the Court of Appeal for four months' (B19) or 'I went to the International Criminal Court and I think that helped' (B45). Another worked as a paralegal in a firm of solicitors, while another worked at a children's charity. Those involved in the selection processes confirmed that this is what they were looking for, one revealing that what they expect of applicants is extraordinarily demanding:

> If they can demonstrate that they are committed to pro bono, before pupillage … demonstrate that you've done that or doing some work at the Citizens Advice Bureau or

> running some advice surgeries or setting up your own … it's the ones that set them up that get the pupillages … that always impresses.
>
> B46, family practitioner, pupillage committee member

When referring to one particular set, well known for doing human rights work, a law student commented, only half-jokingly: 'You need to run an NGO in Gaza to get in.'

A number of interviewees came to the Bar slightly later, having gained experience in related work areas and impressing chambers with their knowledge and contacts. One had been a policeman and then an outdoor clerk for a solicitors firm. A couple more had worked as paralegals in solicitors' firms and one had worked as a commercial solicitor. One of the pupils interviewed indicated that because she did not attend a 'top' university, entering the barrister profession via her work history was the only way in:

> I worked as paralegal in a solicitors doing PI and then in an insurance company doing the same. I think it helped me get pupillage … I was quite conscious that I didn't go to a top university and I didn't get a first and so I kind of had to do that … I didn't go to very good university … and they pushed you down the solicitor route so the only things we ever really got talks about were the LPC and vacation schemes.
>
> B22, pupil barrister, specialist civil set

This pupil's university careers advisor seemed to think that since her or his institution falls outside the top section of the league tables, they should not encourage their students to apply for a career at the Bar. It seems clear from these answers that a student can no longer simply rely on a good degree and then pass the BPTC to get a pupillage. Whereas 25 years ago, further educational qualifications were rare, mini-pupillages were almost unheard of and other work experience was not required, aspiring entrants are now expected to have all three. Students are aware of this and have to strategise, building on their qualifications by undertaking extensive work experience or acquiring postgraduate qualifications (or both) just to get an interview. Many of the senior practitioners remarked that they would not get into the profession now because most, if not all, simply had a degree, a conversion course where needed, the Bar Finals exam and nothing more. Whether these additional qualifications or attributes now needed to get into the profession actually produce a 'better' barrister is a moot point. Perhaps these additional qualities simply give selection panels more criteria to work with when deciding whom to recruit in this hyper-competitive environment.

## VI. The Implications of these New Trends

Aspiring barristers now need to be enterprising. Acquiring more educational qualifications, undertaking numerous mini-pupillages and engaging in diverse extra-curricular activities and extensive work experience have become the norm, which students themselves regard as fundamental to produce added value. They recognise the need to build up their CVs, they formulate how to do so and they take the initiative to take the necessary action. These forms of self-improvement help them acquire the capital they need to get into the profession over and above the traditional qualifications and it is their responsibility to acquire it. This is their ticket to employability, reflecting neoliberal discourses and practices (Grey 1994; McNay 2009; Smith 2010; Gane 2012). Therefore, the problem of intense competition in getting a pupillage is not a problem for the BPTC providers, the profession, its regulator or even the state, but remains something to be managed by the entrepreneurial student, caught up in an 'assemblage of a learning apparatus' to achieve employability (Simons and Masschelein 2008: 391), amounting to Foucauldian technologies of self-improvement and self-assessment (Sommerlad 2011). Foucault conceived that power is dispersed so broadly and insidiously that it does not have to be overtly imposed from outside. A sense of what behaviour or actions are required is internalised and normalised to the degree that an individual will self-govern to conform, often having no overt awareness that these demands are often unfair, discriminatory and provoked by wider power structures and economic concerns. Thus, in one generation it has become normal for law students to pay market rates to outside providers in order to qualify, to work for no pay on multiple occasions and to acquire postgraduate qualifications to boost their CVs, all at their own expense. At the same time, more students are qualifying, yet the profession has drastically cut the number of pupillage spaces offered. All this has occurred when the Bar professes to be more diverse and open to all.

Having the necessary entrepreneurial spirit to become employable raises clear issues of equality. A student has to mobilise social connections and use cultural and economic capital to enhance opportunities to get unpaid work experience, secure mini-pupillages or study for an additional degree. She or he must have a 'feel for the game' (Bourdieu 1990: 66). One study interviewed 81 undergraduate students over a period of two years, focusing on how they sought to acquire different forms of capital to respond to this challenge. It found that working-class students focused more on getting good academic results, lacking the capacity to 'play the game': they did not have family or social contacts to secure the same kind of work experience as their middle-class counterparts, who often displayed an internalised understanding of the game and 'pulled strings' without actively recognising that these were the mechanisms that allowed them to 'get in' (Bathmaker et al 2013). So the playing field, rather than being levelled by an increase in access to higher education, remains uneven after graduation and is shaped by socio-economic and cultural factors. Similar findings have emerged from research into law firm vacation schemes (Sommerlad 2011), recruitment in elite City law firms (Ashley 2010; Cook et al 2012), in accounting firms (Jacobs 2003) and work placements in other industries (eg, the creative industries sector; see Allen et al 2013).

## VII. Pupillage Selection Processes

Once all the applications are in, how do the barristers on the pupillage selection committees actually decide which students to interview? All the participants in my sample had a selection process that involved humans, though one barrister recently explained on Radio 4 that initial selection in his chambers was conducted via an online 'interview', whereby automated questions were typed across the applicant's computer screen, the responses were recorded on camera and artificial intelligence systems categorised the footage to assess who should be called for interview (BBC 2019). Barristers taking part in the selection of pupils now have to undertake training in equality and diversity (see, for example, the BSB's Equality and Diversity Rules, Fair Recruitment Guide, Subconscious Bias and Pupil Equality Monitoring Toolkit) and it is unclear how this is reconciled with the automated approach. In any event, chambers retain the discretion to set their own entry criteria. The transparency and consistency in communicating these to applicants varies hugely across the Bar, with some chambers giving considerable specific information, from which a student can make an informed decision as to whether or not it is worthwhile applying, whilst others give very little. If chambers have elected to use the standardised Pupillage Gateway scheme, then applicants fill out the same application form for participating sets, but until recently were limited to 12 applications in any given year. This was raised to 20 in January 2019 and chambers are now all obliged to advertise their pupillages on the Gateway. The information given by chambers at this stage is crucial in helping a student decide which chambers to apply to. Students complain that many sets are simply too opaque or silent about their selection criteria (see Cordrey 2016). Many chambers have opted out of this scheme and run their own application and interview processes. Current figures suggest that only about 100 sets use the Gateway scheme exclusively, about half of all pupillages are managed by it and the rest deal directly with the applicants. In general terms, the selection processes are broadly the same: applications, the sifting process and then first, and often second, interviews, which include problem solving and advocacy tests:

> 180 applicants for two spaces … that goes down to 30, so we'd have 30 on first interview. Then it's sifted further and we would have 12 for the second interview … the second interview is just an interview, but they would be given a case or a scenario to talk about, to prepare in advance.
>
> A2, administration manager, civil set

The whole process is extremely long and onerous due to the sheer volume of applicants and the intense competition:

> 400-odd applicants say, interview maybe 150–200. 70 say, 60, 70, 80 come for a week … So then now out of that 60 or 70, by which time we've got a file on them, because we've got interview notes, we've got the week notes, in which they do a bit of assessed work for us, and we choose, let's say, 15 or 16 for a final weekend of interviews and then the

> final weekend, we pay all the expenses so they come to London, we pay to put them all up and so on and then we will be down to our final five and by that time, you just have to look at the CVs of these youngsters.
>
> B13, head of chambers, commercial set

## VIII. The Sifting Stage

As indicated in the above extract, the first stage is sifting through the paper applications and deciding who will be invited for an interview. A time-consuming and unenviable task, this is sometimes done by a very junior member of chambers or by administrative staff (Freer 2016) and, it seems, now even by a computer. By contrast, some sets oblige every member of chambers to participate in the sifting process (in pairs) applying a pre-calculated marking scheme that is designed to be as fair and non-discriminatory as possible and to fit chambers' entry criteria, whatever they may be. The following extracts come from a group interview with three members of one such chambers:

> We do the marking and selecting for interview over a period of about a month … we have a compulsory system in chambers, which means that everybody has to do it, the marking.
>
> You do it in a team … you have a pile of applications and you each have the same, and then you have your criteria … and you have to mark them in each category … and then you compare it with your partner, so you do your individual assessment and you discuss it … and the pairs select six.
>
> Then there's this meeting, so all the pairs come together and if there's any disagreement about who has been put forward for interview then it's discussed.
>
> B43, B45, B46, family law practitioners, multi-disciplinary set

Yet even this meticulous system necessarily has a subjective element, since each set of chambers has its own entry criteria and the BSB, although providing guidance, permits chambers considerable discretion. A member of the same set continued:

> We comply with equality and diversity policies and also BSB requirements, and their requirements aren't really detailed – it's just things like anonymising applications. it's general, they leave it to your discretion. We have a marking criteria – education and a sort of fit with chambers' ethos, probably to demonstrate people's commitment to our ethos.
>
> B45, family law practitioner, seven years' call

This particular set of chambers had very clearly spelt out its 'ethos' on its webpages and the membership in the set was diverse, but the fact remains that being the right 'fit' will always contain an unknowable and arbitrary element. Many chambers actively market themselves to try and attract the 'right kind' of applicants':

> We do uni stuff – Oxford University Law Fair, we do the main law fair at Lincoln's Inn, we do law student drinks in chambers which we've started in the last year … That's

> the City University and so they would be invited into chambers for champagne and sushi – we've done three of those this year … we approach people and we've got drinks in chambers and that seems to go quite a long way in attracting the kind of people we should encourage to apply.
>
> A2, administration manager, civil set

What image is this chambers trying to project? Who, one wonders, are these ideal applicants and, perhaps more tellingly, what kind of student is likely to be at home in this kind of reception? As Freer's research (2016, 2018) shows, many non-traditional entrants are discouraged from coming to the Bar, as they are intimidated by the profession's social practices and historical settings.

The following extract was echoed in many answers, where barristers assert that there is a greater degree of transparency in the process, whilst at the same time showing that selection sometimes retains a subjective aspect:

> It's very transparent, I mean, we have – in come 400 letters asking for pupillage and there are probably two or three places … We have a committee who does that, who spend two full weekends, sifting through all these letters and coming out with maybe 40 … they do it by the rules … I think they are more open about the process. I think people choose for what they think is going to be good for chambers. They choose the best … we don't choose because we think we ought to have someone who's 'green' in chambers, we choose what we think is the best.
>
> B44, head of mixed practice set

How is 'what is going to be good for chambers' or 'the best' defined? How is merit assessed? To what degree do people recruit in the image of themselves based on unconscious bias? These selection criteria remain nebulous, despite increased accountability and openness. A more obvious bias in the initial sifting process is a reluctance on the part of recruitment committees, especially in commercial and chancery sets, to consider applicants who did not go to Oxbridge or a Russell Group university, only 'occasionally' drawing from a wider pool:

> We certainly do Oxbridge every year, because it's a regrettable fact that we're still heavily Oxbridge-oriented … we have open days now, where we send invites out all over the country to all the Russell Group universities and others … and we pay for anybody and they come from all over the country … so they have a day in chambers … we do 100 at a time now, so we're getting 200–300 people coming here … it's a charm offensive … we're very anxious that we're not just getting Oxbridge, because occasionally you pick up an absolute gem from somewhere else, absolute superstar.
>
> B13, head of chambers, commercial set

The last sentence is particularly revealing. Despite assertions that chambers seek to recruit from a wider pool, this interviewee indicates that it remains exceptional to recruit someone who does not hold an Oxbridge degree. Figures of the 2011/12 pupil intake show that 28.4 per cent of pupils had Oxbridge degrees and a further 35.8 per cent were from Russell Group universities (Bar Council 2014b), a vast improvement in terms of educational diversity from the previous year, where Oxbridge students accounted for 35 per cent and Russell Group universities some

64 per cent (Bar Council 2012). One interviewee was told that where she went and what grade she got for her undergraduate degree were 'converted' into points during her application's assessment:

> It's terrible when you spend all that time doing application forms and then you don't even get an interview … It's because maybe you didn't score very highly in where you attended university. In fact that was the feedback that I got from a few sets the first time that I applied. It was 'Oh you just didn't score highly enough … if you get a first you get 10 points, if you get a 2.1 you might get 8 points, but it depends how high your 2.1 was. If you went to Oxford and you got a 2.1 you're going to get a higher grade than if you went to Leeds and got a 2.1' … so I needed somewhere that was going to look beyond that … so there were only a few places where I could've realistically applied to.
>
> B22, pupil, specialist civil set

How common is this method of assessing applicants? The relatively small sample of this study makes it hard to know, yet this particular chambers clearly used where the applicant went to university and what degree she got as either a first filter in the selection process or at least as one measure in determining how many 'points' the applicant received in that filtering process. Parts of the profession display a strong preference for and belief in the reliability of academic results and credentials, especially commercial and chancery sets (Ilex Professional Standards et al 2013; BSB 2019b). Research into how elite law firms select formal vacation scheme students has found that this focus on elite education privileges middle-class students who attend Oxbridge and Russell Group universities, having often attended fee-paying schools before that, thus disadvantaging students from lower socio-economic backgrounds (Sommerlad 2011). Moreover, many large firms offer training contracts to students in the second year of their undergraduate studies in an attempt to recruit the best students before they are offered jobs elsewhere. At this stage, they have no degree results, so A levels are the only indicator of academic capability and which university they are attending (Boon 2014). Certain sets of chambers are strongly influenced by a student's educational background. One participant commented:

> It's all very well to say 'yes, we should be equal opportunities' … it's meaningless because if you don't have the work that traditionally people from state-educated, non-lawyer families did when they got to the Bar, you won't get those people going to the Bar … Legal aid, publicly funded work. Unless you've been to Oxford or Cambridge, you're not going to get into one of these big sets offering their own pupillages at £60,000 a year are you? … The big mistake they made was to cut unfunded pupillages … it was a chance for someone to have a go, and lots of times that person was taken on.
>
> B41, mixed common law set, 31 years' call

Therefore, this particular barrister feels that one of the unintended consequences of funding pupillages is that rather than making the Bar more accessible, it has reduced the opportunity for many to get in. Some chambers cannot afford to offer as many pupillages as they used to and are more cautious about whom they do offer them to, often using academic credentials as the driving indicator of suitability.

Since many non-traditional applicants do not meet the traditional requirements of 'merit' on paper, they are less likely to be offered pupillages (Freer 2018).

Apart from discriminating against certain entrants, this focus on academic excellence raises vexed questions that continue to challenge the Bar's professional bodies and academics. Aside from issues of fair access and diversity, is this focus too narrow? Are other skills and attributes being sidelined as a result? If advocacy is part of the core of the profession's skill base, does it follow that those with top academic achievements make the best advocates? Not all are of this view: 'I'm not convinced that the people who excel as academic lawyers or academics in general, necessarily make the best barristers. They may be clever but … (laughing)' (B24, head of mixed circuit set). The answer depends somewhat on what kind of practice a student seeks to acquire. Commercial and chancery barristers regard academic excellence and an intellectual approach as vital to that kind of practice and, rightly or wrongly, other areas of law are perceived by some as needing less rigour in this respect. These practice areas can be largely document-based and some practitioners in this area commented that their working lives had more in common with solicitors working in commercial law firms than barristers at the publicly funded Bar. Advocacy skills in these areas are more often deployed, for example, in skeleton arguments or during round table meetings than in court, but even then some feel that a purely academic approach has its disadvantages, evidenced by the poor quality of some courtroom advocacy and drafting decisions of junior barristers:

> They don't seem to have any idea of how it works in court, except theoretically … What they don't learn is not being overdramatic and as if you are addressing a jury … Keeping it on a sort of conversational tone … they are too formal, they exaggerate … they could have been at it for five or six years and they still haven't got a clue about how to gauge your court and gauge the situation and they produce absurd skeleton arguments … nearly always you notice just regurgitating the notes in the White Book … they're just playing safe … It makes things too long, like the book type skeleton arguments and I think it is increasing the expense of litigation.
>
> B14, commercial practitioner, 39 years' call

Very recent quantitative research into how chambers advertise and select pupils supports these findings that during the sifting stage, academic credentials were across all chambers the most important criteria applied in selecting who was chosen for interview, and especially so in what that study termed Business and Property chambers (BSB 2019b).

## IX. The Interview Stage

After the initial sifting comes the interview stage. The numbers involved and the style of interview vary, but the ideal-type process would consist of interviews that contain exercises or questions that all candidates address, so that they can display legal reasoning, argument, critical thinking and advocacy skills or potential. This is the approach recommended by the regulator, reasoning that judgements will be based on objective merit. Certainly applicants are expected to be thoroughly prepared. One young practitioner commented how she felt she had made a lot of mistakes during her first interviews, so before the next round of applications, she thoroughly studied where she had gone wrong. One recently recruited tenant (B51) gave some indication of what was involved:

> I would read a lot about each chambers to which I applied, particularly focusing on recent high-profile cases in which its members had been involved. I would typically do research on these and base applications on those cases, knowing that I would have things to say on them in an interview should they arise, which they often did. That was how I attempted to personalise each application to the specific set of chambers.

The BSB recommends that chambers implement objective methods of assessment during interview and some chambers follow this approach:

> Twenty minutes is about a problem that is common to all of them and it's quite illuminating actually how they approach that. I think this is important, to have that kind of objective standard … then it's kind of structured 'Where do you see yourself going at the Bar? What are your interests? How would you be self-promoting, what marketing would you do?' Bit about their interests … They're different depending on the CV, to an extent.
>
> B19, mixed practice set

But despite good intentions, regulation and training, questions are inevitably always going to contain a more personal element about the actual person being interviewed and there was evidence that in some cases, the regulators' recommendations are completely ignored: 'Some, they would give you a problem in advance, some they would give you a problem on the day. Here it was just an interview, finding out about you and that was the case with probably about half of the chambers' (B40, pupil, family law set). Even sets that have 'objective' processes still include opaque criteria when making their final decisions:

> They get the 40 … interview them all and then they make their choice … they set them tasks, they interview them, they are looking for people who are bright, have got something extra, a bit of value added on top of the normal stuff, who are personable … I'm not going to have positive discrimination.
>
> B44, head of chambers, mixed set

This last extract merits closer analysis. Whilst it is clear that efforts are being made to make selection and interviews more transparent, objective and meritocratic, there are still certain invisible processes at play. How does one assess if an applicant has 'something extra' or 'a bit of added value'? What makes someone 'personable' or 'bright'? In a profession where self-presentation is all-important and used daily, whether during advocacy in court, during negotiations or in conference, a high premium is placed on a person's demeanour, erudition, eloquence and social confidence. Aside from educational and technical ability, cultural proficiency is essential. Given that potential ability as a barrister is hard to assess during an interview, mastery of cultural norms and values, evidenced by self-presentation during that exchange, translates into cultural 'fit', promoting attraction to recruiters, facilitating 'smooth communication' and conveying competence and credibility (Gorman 2015: 126). As discussed earlier, acquiring such mastery is often dependent on the social and cultural capital an applicant has, which in turn is often shaped by her or his socio-economic background, and, as indicated in this chapter's opening quote, one applicant had two coaching sessions to hone these skills.

## X. Discussion

It is hard to evaluate the extent of any conscious and unconscious bias that comes into play in these selection processes and whether recruiters are unwittingly seeking to reproduce themselves, choosing applicants who share their educational and socio-economic background because these factors make them a better fit or 'good for chambers' (Grey 1994; Nicolson 2005; Gorman 2015). Recent statistics reveal that BAME applicants are half as likely to get a pupillage than their white counterparts with similar educational attainment (BSB 2017a). Certain practice areas seems to call for different attributes and, for some chambers, top academic ability and achievement are paramount. Given the numbers of applications, some filtering criteria are necessary. Moreover, the funding of pupils can be a risky business, as not all pupils are later deemed good enough to be offered tenancies, so barristers exercise more caution in selection. Abel (2004a) would argue that the construction of 'merit', based on academic credentials, is simply a means by which barristers protect their interests and restrict entry, and that there is nothing to stop chambers acquiring more physical space and let the market decide how many lawyers are needed. Barristers routinely respond to this charge, and many did so during the interviews by emphasising that high-quality academic skills and intellectual rigour are (and have always been) essential to providing a high-quality service. Furthermore, in the current climate of competition, there is even more pressure on chambers, like law firms, to recruit the 'best' people, traditionally judged, in the main, on academic credentials (Garth 2013). Not all are convinced. This 'fetishisation' of merit has been described a seemingly legitimate step in appearing to make entry criteria equal, but as Sommerlad says, citing Aristotle, although 'everyone agrees that justice in distributions ought to be according to merit in some sense, they do not call merit the same thing' (Sommerlad 2015: 123).

So, where does this leave the aspiring entrant? A whole range of additional and different skills are required to get into the profession now. Whereas before students had to pass the Bar Finals examinations, undergo a cursory interview that was more of an informal chat and were more or less guaranteed a pupillage in a set of chambers, even if not in one from their top choices, much more is now required of them. The aspiring barrister must be enterprising. The recruitment process has normalised this. She or he has to be proactive and must have mobilised multiple resources and connections to dip in and out of different chambers on unpaid work placements to narrow down what she or he wants to do and why. Oxbridge and Russell Group degree holders retain an advantage. Many hold post-graduate degrees and have worked or volunteered in other, related fields. In the context of this extreme competition, those who apply for pupillage are necessarily risk-takers. They need to be robust, persuasive, self-promoting and self-assured in the unfamiliar chambers environment during interviews and must face the harsh reality that the odds of being accepted into the profession are stacked against them. A barrister's professionalism, even in this pre-apprenticeship phase, has been refashioned by a competitive and commercial turn. It forms part of a larger shift in the profession, whereby all barristers are now expected to be self-motivated and entrepreneurial in getting work, an analysis of which forms the basis of the following two chapters.

# 5

# Getting Work

## *The New Marketeers*

> I think you have to be a lot more efficient, you've got to be a lot more proactive and you've to be a lot more responsible for your own practice than you used to be … I think in the old days people were just taking it for granted that there would be a brief on the desk every morning and they would go off to court and that was it. Now, to get any decent brief you've got to be proactive, you've got to go out there, you've got to find solicitors.
>
> B44, head of mixed disciplinary set

Two key developments, facilitated by regulatory changes and the growth of IT, have reshaped how a barrister goes about building a practice. First, the ban on barristers advertising was lifted in 1990 and has gradually resulted in the profession marketing its services. This chapter explores the different marketing methods used by practitioners and their attitudes to self-promotion. Second, the introduction of licensed access in 1990 from certain professionals and then more general direct access from 2004 permits barristers to be instructed directly by the client, without the services of a solicitor (Boon and Levin 2008). This new way of getting work, by targeting the lay client directly, is explored in the next chapter.

A common view, as expressed by a Bar marketing consultant, is that 'law itself isn't enough to build a practice as a barrister anymore' (A7). During the 100 years or so when the Bar was an entirely referral-based profession, a practitioner (and often the clerk) adopted a somewhat passive role in securing work. Advertising for work was strictly prohibited, likened to being involved in trade and wholly unbefitting for a gentleman's profession (Burrage 2006). As the primary consumers of the Bar's services, solicitors knew their market and advertising was deemed unnecessary (Abel 1988). During the post-war boom years and up until the early 1990s, when work was plentiful, this approach was sustainable. Since then, numbers coming into the profession have increased, yet the amount of work has diminished, obliging barristers to take a more active, commercial approach to generate work and to acquire new skills in self-promotion and marketing.

As Chapter 2 has set out, the reduction of work available to barristers over the last two decades is significant. Fewer civil actions are being initiated, due to the removal of legal aid in many cases, but the significant increase in court issue fees has also contributed (Rose 2014). A claimant must now pay £10,000 to initiate a claim worth over £200,000 in the High Court and, until July 2017 (when the Supreme Court ruled it unlawful), Employment Tribunals started charging fees in 2013 that ranged from £390 to £1,200 to bring an action, causing a 79 per cent drop in cases (BBC 2017). Work, previously carried out by barristers, is now being done by solicitors. One family solicitor (S2) said that he carried out much of the interlocutory work in his cases and generally instructed counsel later, unless the case was complex, involved a lot of money and/or required a 'hyper-specialist'. Civil practitioners felt that the Jackson Reforms in 2013, which made CFA uplift and after the event insurance premium payments irrecoverable between parties, resulted in a reduction of lower value CFA cases being initiated.

Competition comes not just from outside the profession. Chambers and barristers are increasingly competitive with one another when bidding for block work from local authorities. There are also more practitioners in specialist areas, all trying to get the same work. In some areas the volume of work is decreasing. The amount of criminal prosecutions has almost halved since the government cuts to the police and CPS's budgets, which has had an inevitable knock-on effect on the Bar (Fenhalls 2019). Criminal law solicitors are under considerable financial pressure to keep advocacy work in-house, even if they may not have sufficient training, experience or time (Fitzgibbon 2015; Hunter et al 2018). Many of the junior criminal practitioners interviewed noted that when they started out, it was very hard to get any work at all or any work beyond the most basic bail applications or remand lists for the CPS:

> The *Quincy* years, as I describe them, happen when you are perhaps three years' call. You've initially bits and bats of work from your pupil master's solicitors, say token favour. Then, if you're a reasonably good looking woman you sometimes then get more work off sad, middle-aged little bastards who think you might sleep with them. When it becomes absolutely apparent that you've not going to do that, then everything tails off and I call them the *Quincy* years, because you could perhaps have a bail application in the morning, but there wasn't really that much work after that and you would always be home in time to watch re-runs of *Quincy* at about 12.30.
>
> B30, circuit criminal practitioner, 18 years' call

In the past, a handful of surplus briefs might have been returned to other sets of chambers on a daily basis if there was no one to cover them. This almost never happens now as clerks are reluctant to send work elsewhere. One barrister commented that even within sets, people are not always willing to share contacts: 'People in this set have their solicitors and they very jealously guard them' (B19, common law set). In this new climate, barristers no longer have the luxury of waiting for work to come to them. Not all have fully embraced this: 'They believe that the old rules still apply: they sit in the back room and the clerk will arrive at five o'clock and say "There you are Sir, there's your case for tomorrow". It's not like that anymore' (A5, senior clerk, 40 years' clerking). With online courts already being piloted in certain cases, where civil claims are dealt with in a more inquisitorial style and without the use of lawyers, a further chunk of junior work stands to be lost as the initiative unrolls to include more kinds of cases. Predictions are that by 2022, most civil disputes will be dealt with through an online court, though the current reform programme is behind schedule (Briggs 2015, 2016; MOJ 2016a; Rozenberg 2017, 2019).

## I. Barristers and Solicitors

Until relatively recently, the relationship between barrister and solicitor, mediated by the clerk, was the only channel through which to cultivate new and maintain old sources of work (Harris and O'Malley 2000). A common (mis)representation, often used to explain the difference between the two branches, likens a solicitor to a GP and a barrister to a consultant specialist in advocacy and complex advisory work. This analogy, whether accurate or not, no longer applies, as the differences in function have been all but eradicated: many solicitors have become more specialised and do more advocacy, whilst barristers can now receive instruction without them and conduct litigation. In any event, it belies the 'complex social interaction surrounding the getting and keeping of work' and the delicate balance needed to keep both parties happy (Morison and Leith 1992: 27). Historically, barristers viewed themselves as more expert and specialist, and some were seen as patronising to and dismissive of solicitors, regarding them as mere conduits between them and the lay client (Morison and Leith 1992; Harris and Piercy 1998; Harris and O'Malley 2000). One interviewee confessed as much:

> When I think of the way that I treated solicitors when they first instructed me as a junior barrister, aged 24, and how I sort of looked down my nose at them … I liked them but I felt this sense of … superiority.
>
> B15, specialist civil silk, 28 years' call

Yet solicitors were the repeat client, if not the actual client in any particular case, upon whose repeat instructions a practitioner was entirely dependent. Whilst pleasing the lay client was essential, this could be achieved by getting a good result rather than by indulging in extensive customer service skills, which was left to the solicitors (Morison and Leith 1992). This did not detract from the barrister's professional duties to the lay client, shared only by her or his duty to the Court, but in terms of cultivating relationships, it was the professional solicitor client who was critical in the development of a barrister's practice (Harris and O'Malley 2000).

Given that barristers were not encouraged to socialise with solicitors in case this was construed as touting for work, developing an ongoing professional relationship was often a slow process and in the early years a young barrister was especially dependent on the clerk to direct work her or his way and introduce different solicitors. The general view was that solicitors had their preferred chambers and practitioners and that there was no need to advertise. It was felt that if a practitioner were not good, she or he would get little work (Zander 1968).

However, the process is more complex. For example, barristers often complain that solicitors suddenly and inexplicably stop instructing them; work is often unevenly/unfairly distributed within chambers, with, for example, women being pushed to do certain kinds of work (family); the clerks used to be largely unaccountable for their choices of brief allocation (Kennedy 1978); a chance 'return' could set a career on a new path and solicitors would sometimes select a less able barrister, perhaps with a good client manner or fighting spirit. As practitioners became more experienced, the clerk would start repelling work deemed too junior and would try to divert more complex and better-paid briefs their way, so the process of getting the right kind of work would begin anew (Morison and Leith 1992).

## II. The Self-Promoting Barrister

Solicitors are still the main source of work for the Bar (BSB 2017b), but practitioners are much more proactive and aggressive in their efforts to get work from any source and have had to develop different skills to complement this new approach. One such skill – marketing – has proved challenging for some and antithetical to their traditional ways of thinking and working. In the early years of advertising, O'Malley and Harris (1999: 874) found the legal profession particularly resistant to it: 'Marketing represents an abomination to legal professionals' and that 'attitudes are likely to preclude greater marketing applications in the future'. Practitioners have almost no training (or none at all) in business or marketing matters and some of the older generation are culturally averse to any forms of self-promotion: 'I don't like it … it's just not in my blood to blow my own trumpet. You were brought up not doing it, weren't you? An absolute anathema' (B14, 38 years' call). Osiel (1989/90) and Burrage (1997, 2006) both note how in the nineteenth century, when solicitors and the new accountants were taking advantage of the commercial, trade and industrial growth that swept across Britain, the Bar actively shunned new opportunities or areas of work to preserve its status as specialist advocates, market concerns being of secondary importance. Muzio and Flood (2012) also note that entrepreneurs abounded in the solicitor profession during the same period, with lawyers actively participating in industrial enterprise, supporting and investing in their clients' new businesses and creating legal infrastructures to accommodate their clients' interests. On the whole, the Bar did not engage in such activities to the same extent.

Contrary to O'Malley and Harris' predictions (1999), there has nonetheless been a dramatic shift in the attitude of many practitioners to advertising and promoting their services and in how they seek and maintain work levels, with a variety of marketing models being utilised. Now that they face steep competition for work from solicitors and within their own ranks, barristers have adapted, have devised new ways of getting work and have found new markets to penetrate to compensate for work lost (Abbott 1988). As noted in Chapter 3, chambers, as collectives, are much more market-oriented, with relationship marketing models in place, where the interaction between the supplier and the customer is central and their relationship is more equal and collaborative (Gummesson 1997; Woo and Leelapanyalert 2014). Aside from management-led marketing, which forms an integral part of a chambers' business plan in many sets, individual practitioners are now expected to proactively market their services and be self-motivated in getting work. The rhetoric at the Bar Conference in 2015 revealed that being flexible, diverse and able to re-invent oneself are considered essential attributes, and that barristers can no longer be just advocates, but must also be businesspeople and entrepreneurs (Hill 2015). This attitude was reflected in some interviews: 'I think if you're not prepared to self-market as a barrister then you're not going to succeed … now it's absolutely essential. It really, really is. There are people who are a bit more old school about it' (A4, deputy senior clerk, circuit set).

Some barristers' continuing dislike of self-promotion may have less to do with the snobbish avoidance of involving themselves in trade and more to do with low levels of confidence in this area. Many have never had to actively market their services and despite the new commercialism and expectations that barristers will market themselves, BPTC students are given no training in such matters and many do not realise the need for it until they are in practice:

> I think in a very naive manner I just assumed, especially somewhere like (name of) chambers, I just thought 'Ah, big chambers, they must just have work constantly pouring in' … but obviously as soon as you actually get thrown into this you realise that's not good enough nowadays, because there are some great chambers out there and some great individual barristers and if you want this work you have to really fight for it now.
>
> B21, civil barrister, three years' call

This research found a wide range of reactions to marketing and self-promotion, together with a noticeable differentiation across the Bar in terms of the degree to which barristers have adapted and adopted new ways of getting work. Marketing initiatives can be broadly categorised as follows: online self-branding and high internet visibility, including the use of social media; marketing themselves in groups/teams; individual marketing; diversifying their practices and flexible working; actively cultivating solicitor relationships and undertaking direct access work. All, except the very new, participate in seminars to solicitors. All have web profiles and most have business cards. Thereafter, the degree to which individuals participate in marketing endeavours varies enormously across practice areas, years of call and chambers.

## III. Online Branding, High Visibility and Social Media

All chambers have a website and each barrister has a web profile. Sets have employed designers, hired professional photographers and put together branded websites, which are corporate and internally consistent in terms of look and message. If a practitioner has been involved in any notable case or has received accolades from one of the directories, this is instantly transformed into a bite-size branded puff:

> I think people set store in the fact that they have been ranked or mentioned in the directories and certainly all our barristers use it ... they use the icons in their CVs and in their emails. They use the quotes in their CVs and on their web profile, so it's very much something that is wanted and valued.
>
> A2, administrative manager, civil set

Barristers are thus much more visible than before (Thompson 1995). Whereas the profession's governance and activities were once opaque and individual practitioners were rarely known to people outside the legal world, now they strive for prominence and the net is flooded with competing listings and promotional material of those fighting to find a place in the market. This new visibility permits both professional and lay clients to scrutinise a barrister's professional practice history:

> Clients are increasingly sophisticated. You can find out anything you want about anybody by just going on a website now, so there's a very, very high degree of transparency. You have all these booklets, Chambers and the Lawyer who provide these ratings, so you can work out who's who, you can get recommendations and if you want you just, you know, a point of contact is always on the website, you can ring up a clerk and find out if it works for you.
>
> B13, head of commercial chambers

Whilst there is undoubtedly more transparency about a practitioner's experience and expertise, there are ongoing demands for more upfront information on fees (BSB 2017b; YouGov/London Economics 2018). More barristers' work is now charged on a fixed-fee basis, but practitioners prefer hourly fees, which can truly reflect and reward the actual time spent on a case. Nonetheless, much has been done by practitioners to make themselves more visible. Chambers obtain web analytics and tailor their sites accordingly. One design agency took the view that barristers' websites are too complicated: 'They say "we've looked at a lot of barristers' websites and ... the big thing is they just have far too many words"' (B27, head of marketing committee, circuit chambers). Another senior practitioner noted:

> We've done a lot of research on who clicks on what, and you know what you want to develop. I mean the figures are absolutely stark. People are really disinterested in background information, they want to see the CVs of the barristers and that's probably 90 per cent of the clicks.
>
> B13, head of commercial chambers

One set of chambers sent out a questionnaire to all their instructing solicitors and concluded that it is the lay clients, rather than solicitors, who looked at the barristers' CVs. As one personal injury barrister (B6, 22 years' call) commented, having a web profile can have its practical uses: 'They've been on the website and stuff, if only to find out what you look like so they can find you at Court', but conceded that 'at higher levels there's much more scrutiny and decision'. The professional and lay clients have more information and thus more control when choosing which barrister to instruct. Styles vary from set to set, but often the CVs are extensive, listing prizes, awards, articles, books, part-time judicial positions and any reported or high-profile cases in which a practitioner has been involved. One family law solicitor reported that she always looks at these profiles, often to clarify the background and experience of the barrister. The amount of years' call is not always representative as, for example, some solicitors with many years' practice later cross-qualify and then come to the Bar.

Raising one's professional profile can also be achieved by using different social media platforms. Many of the barristers interviewed are on LinkedIn, but few seem to actively use it, other than to have an account and collect contacts. New practitioners seem much more comfortable with these networking sites, yet innovation in this regard is not always encouraged: 'I was absolutely gobsmacked that chambers didn't have a LinkedIn page so I created one while I was a pupil and I got hauled in front of [name of barrister] who was "Why on earth have you done this?"' (B12, common law set, four years' call). There are more ambitious LinkedIn users, who participate in international exchange chats, in which they share legal analysis or news with other lawyers or academics. Some barristers are active users of Twitter and they consider it to be an effective marketing tool and will often use it to promote a blog they might have written, comment on a case in which they have been involved or link followers in to any number of articles on legal developments and news. Twitter is regarded as an efficient, fast and easy way to keep abreast of legal updates, to network or to rebut inaccurate media reports. However, a number of interviewees displayed a real lack of knowledge about Twitter or whether or not chambers even had an account: 'I don't know. I don't think so. Do you think Twitter is a good thing for chambers?' (B36, 38 years' call). A few were openly hostile to the idea of it and the prospect of embracing any social media as a marketing tool seems unlikely: 'I'm willfully anti these kinds of things. I can't see myself doing Twitter and blogs' (B19, civil practitioner, 15 years' call). Some spoke about it in a way that revealed that they did not understand it – 'I'm not interested in what Phillip Schofield's doing this morning and stuff like that' (B7) – an impression that was confirmed by a Bar marketing consultant (A7):

> Barristers don't understand how it works … and generally I think it's because they are scared because it's new. It's a new world. I find a lot of fear in barristers about marketing generally, about anything about putting themselves out there. I think barristers are perhaps resistant to learning new skills outside the law.

Administration of a chambers' Twitter account is sometimes done by the clerks and administrative staff, who post information fed to them by practitioners. Alternatively, specific barristers are chosen to be in charge: 'He does Twitter for the simple reason that he doesn't drink. There is no danger at all of inappropriate late night tweeting' (B32). Despite a large number of criminal barristers using Twitter to follow developments in the highly contested legal aid consultation, few seem interested in using it regularly as a marketing tool.

For those who have engaged in social media, it is an easy way to write about law, whilst also raising their profile: 'Google juice. Get my name out there. People mostly very positively link my work in other places and they get interesting comments … it gives me more clout, people take more notice of me' (B9). For sole practitioners especially, creating an online profile is essential. Without a clerk to mediate, this kind of barrister has to attract all her or his work unassisted, relying on word-of-mouth recommendations, but also taking full advantage of different kinds of social media. The more online platforms a barrister appears on, the better, not just in terms of wider exposure, but as a form of re-assurance to a browsing potential customer:

> When I've got time, I blog … LinkedIn yes, I make quite a bit of use of that … it doesn't bring any business directly, but it does help me keep in touch with people. It's a good way to remind someone that you exist … I encounter someone and I connect with them via LinkedIn and that adds an extra reinforcement to the 'I gave you my card' or they gave me their card … I get lots of emails from LinkedIn because people want to connect to me … It's another way for people to have heard about me and generally if people have heard from several different ways, they're more comfortable with it. The blogs, I've had a couple of bits of business out of them.
>
> B9, specialist civil sole practitioner, eight years' call

Those who blog feel that their time is better spent writing this kind of output. It's faster than writing journal articles, not as 'lightweight' as tweets and 'you're better off if you've written something that's online because then people can find it and it's a wider audience and it stays there forever' (B11). Newer members of the profession are generally more adventurous and blog tactically in the hope of developing new work:

> I wouldn't blog about personal injury for example, because although I do a certain amount of it, I don't really want to. I want to do more commercial and property stuff, so I try and blog about anything that's of interest in those areas in the hope that they would lead to work.
>
> B11, civil/commercial practitioner, 18 months' call

Another young practitioner explained how she was trying to narrow down her expertise and blog on that alone so as to be taken seriously as a specialist in that field. Most of the older practitioners did not engage with social media, saying that they were not interested in it, it did not bring in new work or they did not have time.

The process of acquiring and, to varying degrees, developing an online presence marks a significant new development at the Bar. A generation ago, aside from the occasional criminal practitioner who might have conducted a high-profile case, most barristers were unseen and, to the public, largely unknown figures, mere names on chambers lists in the perfunctory directories and in the doorways of their buildings. A relaxation of the rules banning advertising coincided with the internet boom and barristers are now highly visible professionals, whom members of the public, professional clients or other barristers can look up, see photographs of and whose academic and work history is available at a click of a button. Many have individual entries and appraisals in the Bar directories. Shaped and guided by professional web designers, photographers and marketing consultants, barristers have engaged in sophisticated forms of professional identity and self-presentation work.

## IV. Marketing in Groups/Teams

Grouping together into practice teams is a development that first emerged in the mid- to late 1990s. It marked a shift from the totally individual approach to getting work to a collective and collaborative effort, whereby barristers market themselves as individual practitioners *within* specialist groups, offering expert advice at all levels of seniority and/or in different sub-specialist areas. As one senior clerk (A3) explained:

> I think years ago people were just individuals within chambers. They had their own practice … we've got a lot more teams now, so people are saying 'You've got to get involved, you've got to do a talk, you've got to produce a paper on it, to keep our profile'.

Aside from the pupil barristers or those in sole practice, all those interviewed were members of one or more practice teams or groups within their set. Each group has to market itself. In some chambers, a team has to bid for money from the general marketing budget and justify its use. These specialist teams prepare events, such as seminars, lectures or conferences on specific areas of law, targeted at specific solicitors who already (or might in the future) instruct them. Accredited for CPD, the seminars were a very successful way of attracting solicitors to get their points, listen and have a drink. Until the SRA changed the requirement for solicitors to actively clock up a certain amount of CPD hours, seminars were a very popular tool for marketing. Law firms invited specific barristers, perhaps fresh out of an interesting case, to go in-house and present to the solicitors there. Seminars vary in style and form, but can comprise a small group of practitioners, from mixed levels of call, presenting on different aspects of one topic or on different topics: 'Three of us and then, for the first time ever, we've got an external speaker, a medic, talking about peripheral nerve injuries' (B6, personal injury practitioner). Given that solicitors now rarely sit behind barristers at court hearings, many junior barristers remarked that if they did not have seminars, they might not actually meet any solicitors. Whether these seminars achieve their intended purpose of bringing in new work or cementing relationships is hard to gauge. In the field of family law, there were different opinions:

> If somebody speaks well and they're knowledgeable on their subject, obviously it's a good starting point … but none of that really helps as to how good somebody is in court or how prepped they are on the day.
>
> S1, family law solicitor, 20 years' qualified

> We have a constant, constant continuing education programme, so in any one month, we will have three or four junior members of the Bar coming to talk … it will definitely influence us.
>
> S2, family law solicitor, 24 years' qualified

> I've done market research for a couple of different chambers and when I say 'How do you instruct new barristers?' … and it's always, well predominantly, 'I have to see them on their feet', and it's often when they're on the other side in court.
>
> A7, Bar marketing consultant

> Do you know what the solicitors tell me? They tell me that the marketing that works for them is the one-to-one relationships.
>
> B39, family barrister, 24 years' call

Some barristers take part in seminars rather begrudgingly, unconvinced that it does their practices any good at all, and resent the amount of time it takes to prepare these presentations: 'I don't think I've ever had a piece of work come, a new piece of work, come as a result of a talk that I've given to a firm of solicitors. I really don't think so and it's perfectly possible that solicitors have actually stopped instructing me' (B15, specialist civil silk). Others find the social interaction in a marketing context awkward: 'I attend a lot of marketing events when clients come here or we go to them. If I'm completely honest, I hate it. I hate it. I hate the idea of selling myself. I hate the small talk' (B17, civil practitioner, three years' call). Two complained that these events have too many speakers and last too long, leaving no time at the end for networking. In any event, since November 2016, solicitors are no longer required to attend an obligatory amount of CPD-accredited events and are now permitted to address their continuing competence in a less prescribed and more flexible manner. As a result: 'Putting on seminars is no longer as effective as marketing – it is now necessary to pitch topics incredibly carefully so there is a genuine demand for them, or to move to more social type events' (B12, civil practitioner, 10 years' call).

There are other ways in which barristers come together to target new custom. For certain kinds of work, chambers now bid as a group for bulk instructions from, say, local authorities, often making their offer deliberately low to undercut other sets. One chambers director described how a small group of barristers decided to build a whole new practice area. They identified which conferences and seminars were being held on the topic, specific barristers attended them to learn and cultivate contacts, whilst the clerks started talking to solicitors in that field. A barrister from a different chambers noted that it is the most enterprising that innovate:

> [P]rincipally as a result of the individual activities of about four or five able and ambitious people … You have to have people, individuals who bring the work in, that remains the case. You can develop, and in these chambers we have developed, some [type of] work … about five or six people do a lot of that work and that has involved active marketing.
>
> B49, specialist civil/commercial silk, 29 years' call

Alternatively, some teams persuade their set to recruit a whole new team, which they 'bolt on' to complement and extend the work of an existing practice group.

It is common for practice teams to produce regular newsletters or 'alerters', which they send out to solicitors in hard or e-copy or display in the waiting areas of chambers. These cover new developments in their area of specialism. Some of the personal injury barristers interviewed explained: 'You're normally asked to digest a case and put some comment' (B6) or 'It's a review of recent cases over the last month and also legislation and also just general developments in PI' (B1). Whilst some claim that these cement relationships – 'We do get, quite regularly, quite good feedback … most people who receive them are people who instruct chambers anyway' (B1) – others concede that given the fact that so many chambers produce them, it is likely that many go unread, but remain important: 'It's not really the fact that they read them, it's the fact that you are sending them out, because you're reminding them that "we are here and we know what we're talking about"' (B15).

Many chambers strategists, whether from a marketing, management, business or clerking point of view, now seek to be more sophisticated in relation to how they entertain. Whereas most chambers host annual parties or arrange social outings to which they invite solicitors, the aim now is to be much more specific in terms of whom they target. One chambers director banned large parties and focused on specific marketing events for specific practice teams, inviting not just key solicitors, but other sources of work, such as general counsel, from large organisations. Chambers might now distribute a guest list with the invitation to encourage people to come. In some sets, even the more junior clerks received marketing training so that they would be more confident and skilful at talking to solicitors at such events.

These team efforts to maintain old and attract new custom mark an evolved collaborative spirit at the Bar, where practitioners work together for the good of a collective (practice group or chambers), as well as for their own advancement. The individual, self-employed practitioner has additional duties and obligations to others under these communal branded practice groups and in some ways they must operate as if they are in a commercial organisation, rather than simply as an autonomous professional (Evetts 2015).

## V. Individual Initiatives: Specialism, New Practice Areas and Diversification

Despite the fact that some chambers now employ marketing specialists (full/part-time or for consultations/workshops), practitioners are nonetheless expected to actively promote themselves. Barristers can no longer rely on many types of work that used to be considered staples and many of those interviewed have already branched out into new areas or seek to do so, or have become known for a specific specialism. Whereas 25 years ago a barrister might have said that she or he was a family law practitioner, this would now be considered far too generalist:

> What you tend to notice is that different family barristers have different recognised areas of expertise. For example, [name], in [chambers] – he has developed an absolute expertise in, for example, international relocation of children. He's a person to use there. [Name], up at [chambers], again I would go to him, for example, if there were Schedule 1 applications – Financial provision for a child born out of marriage … I think most senior lawyers in London kind of know the strengths and weaknesses of members of the Bar in terms of what they're very good at.
>
> S2, family law solicitor, 24 years' qualified

One interviewee did family law work, specialising in a particular non-accidental injury to children in care proceedings. If one already had a general area of specialism, zoning in on one niche part might be feasible. However, for more general common law practitioners, re-inventing themselves as hyper-specialist experts can be hard. Where a whole practice area is under strain, many seek to branch out at the same time into an already competitive field. One criminal practitioner had no desire to change his practice – 'I'm quite an ideologically committed criminal barrister' (B25) – but most of the others interviewed felt that they had no choice but to diversify as '[e]veryone is competing for the increasingly small puddle of work that is available in crime' (B8) and seek, with varying degrees of success, to branch out into new areas. For them, private prosecution, extradition, regulatory or any privately paid work are good sources of income. One junior undertook a mix of education appeals, police regulatory, health and safety, nurse and midwifery, and General Medical Council work, and hoped to develop all of these so that he could phase out his less well-paid criminal practice. A couple of medical negligence juniors noted that they now faced increased competition from criminal law barristers, who had started appearing in the Nursing and Midwifery Council or the General Medical Council Tribunals, fora that were traditionally the preserve of specialist civil practitioners. One family and criminal law barrister found educational appeals to be a new source of work:

> It's quite seasonal, that's the problem. As soon as the secondary school places come out you get a flood of parents enquiring … In this case there are 24 other parents in the same situation, so I've had three of them in together, written an advice … we advertised in the *Primary Times* school magazine saying we're cheaper than solicitors (laughs).
>
> B32, family and criminal circuit barrister, 13 years' call

However, as one criminal silk noted, there was less regulatory work available for more senior practitioners and '[t]he good stuff is jealously guarded by those who specialise in it' (B2).

Re-inventing oneself as a new specialist requires an entrepreneurial spirit, marketing skills and confidence, which they may not have:

> Some think it's, and this always amazes me, think it's beneath a barrister to try and go and get their own work … and you just think we're not in the eighteenth century

> anymore and others are scared. Others are scared of trying to move into new areas. They've got no confidence in themselves that they'll be able to do it.
>
> B33, criminal circuit barrister, six years' call

A few practitioners readily admit that self-promotion does not come easily to them: 'I'm just not really interested, no. I can't really explain, I'm a bit like [name of barrister] – he's considerably awkward' (B19, civil barrister, 15 years' call). Barristers have worked within a strictly controlled, sheltered framework for so long that many do not have the necessary skills, experience or commercial imagination to take advantage of the sudden freedom to innovate. One criminal silk noted:

> The real thing actually is that most criminal practitioners have certainly not had another job outside being a criminal barrister, but the vast majority have only ever been in one set. They don't even know what another set looks like. They don't have another way of understanding how things might operate. One of the talks I give quite regularly is 'How do you develop an international practice?' and you'd be amazed. The criminal Bar don't think they've got any international part in their work at all. I would say 90 per cent of criminal cases, probably a bit less than that, 70 per cent, have got an international element. You take a drug importation, money laundering …
>
> B37, criminal silk, 30 years' call

Another common way to acquire different expertise is for newer members of chambers to spend periods of up to a year on secondment in law firms. The perks are considerable. Hired on a fixed and regular salary to work in-house, they return to chambers at the end of the period with solid ties with the firm in question. Solicitors prefer using barristers to locum solicitors from agencies, who they think produce low-quality work. Barristers are also seconded out to the CPS or other in-house positions, giving them a chance to develop new skills in new areas of law:

> I did a secondment to the Nurse and Midwifery Council … for four months … in house, and presented their cases and that gave you the avenue to then move into other areas and then I started defending there.
>
> B33, criminal circuit practitioner, six years' call

Members of chambers see this as potentially beneficial to everyone in the set, as more work is likely to follow from these sites once the secondment is over, perhaps spilling over to other practitioners. Some barristers have acquired hybrid status, whereby they work a contracted period of hours for a firm on a fixed retainer, whilst continuing with their own practices in chambers the rest of the time. The number of barristers working in this dual capacity in 2018 was 413.[1] The prospect of guaranteed work/income provides security when in certain practice areas there is none. A couple of those interviewed intended to do this and one had actually done it at the time of the fieldwork, working in-house for a commercial firm

[1] Bar Standards Board, 'Key Statistics', 2019, https://www.barstandardsboard.org.uk/news-publications/research-and-statistics/statistics-about-the-bar/practising-barristers.html.

two or three times a week for a fixed fee as a consultant. Another had been offered a similar arrangement for personal injury work:

> I'm like a consultant, so he will, instead of my hourly rate – now at the moment the clerks aim for £250. If I say I'll do it for £175, he'll bill his clients about £230 or something and instead of giving it to the clerks, he'll keep it and I'll get £175. I'll have to give a bit of it to my clerks, probably because it might be imprudent not to.
>
> B5, civil circuit practitioner, 28 years' call

Although he will get less per hour and will give his clerk some of his fee, this practitioner envisages getting a guaranteed amount of work each month. The solicitor meanwhile can charge the client less and make a profit.

These recent trends to specialise as much as possible, adopt flexible and hybrid working patterns, brand as a group and utilise different marketing techniques whilst at the same time being more accountable and transparent, mark a shift to a form of commercialised professionalism. Barristers' services are now a commodity to be sold in the market. The Bar now promotes a culture of enterprise which has a distinctly different logic compared to traditional professionalism and, as discussed below, personalises and individualises work relations, requiring a practitioner to develop sophisticated communication and social skills (Hanlon 1998; Evetts 2015).

## VI. Relationship Building

Of all the individual marketing endeavours, cultivating relationships with solicitors was considered to be by far the most important and effective: 'It's entirely connections. I mean it's like, sort of, the world of Georgian politics. It's all to do with alliances and who you know. It's not a surprise' (B2). After the advertising ban was lifted, barristers slowly started to realise that they no longer needed to be so reliant on the clerks:

> My main marketing strategy is to be nice to my solicitors and ring them up a lot … I used to leave it to the clerks, rather sort of respectfully. I didn't really think about particularly developing a relationship with solicitors and now I do have relationships with solicitors and clerks really don't come into it so much.
>
> B5, civil circuit barrister, 28 years' call

However, it requires more than just building up a rapport, but crucially involves selling oneself as *the* specialist to go to:

> You know it's basically all about cementing your solicitor relationships and you do that by getting on with them personally and trying to convince them that you are expert in your field, and that's the most difficult thing.
>
> B1, civil barrister, 24 years' call

Practitioners seem to be much more solicitous and considerate to what used to be regarded as the 'lower' branch and relations are much more respectful and mutual: 'It's less snotty, it's much more respectful, barristers are making themselves much, much, much more available in terms of mobiles … it's more collaborative, much more explanation … so it's changed a lot' (S2, family law solicitor, 24 years' qualified). Solicitors shop around for the Bar's services much more overtly than before. A potential new solicitor might ask for a free trial or a 'beauty pageant', as one practitioner (B10) called it, whereby they phone up, express an interest and request a free introductory chat, come into chambers and assess the barrister for half an hour. Barristers are more accommodating in this regard than they might have once been. Whereas socialising with solicitors was strongly discouraged until the early 1990s, now it forms a central part of marketing. There are:

> Lots of schmoozing events, drinks parties and things like that. I take old chum solicitors out to lunch and just remind them I'm there and still firing and they find out what I'm up to these days and that sort of thing … I've had to cultivate the younger ones a bit and certainly keep the older ones warm, so you do have to put yourself about quite a bit more than you used to … I don't like it. I don't mind having lunch with the ones I know, who I've become friendly with.
>
> B14, commercial barrister, 41 years' call

Practitioners have to instigate this contact: 'You have to be proactive, you have to go and chat. You have to go and spend a lot of time talking to solicitors who have that sort of work' (B44, criminal silk) and some are extremely strategic and tactical in approach:

> If I had to target, it's the 'freshies', the ones that are just out of training contracts. What I offer them is 'you can call me any time in respect of any case. If you don't feel confident going to your supervisor, come to me'.
>
> B46, family practitioner, six years' call

On the circuits, barristers tend to have a closer relationships with local solicitors and many now go to the local Law Society events with them, rather than the Bar Mess dinners that, in some areas, have become rare occasions and serve no marketing function. They often attend seminars or go to the races or other sporting events together. One circuit clerk noted that it was hard to network with solicitors, as they are spread out over a greater geographical area than in London and going to see them required a lot more effort and time. All agreed that networking successfully required strong social skills: 'You need to be a social person. You need to be a social animal. You need to be making connections' (A7, Bar marketing consultant) and 'the most particular skill I think, is the ability to go out and speak to solicitors … and present yourself very smoothly' (B44, criminal silk, 36 years' call). The Bar Council now offers optional general marketing training, as well as more specific workshops such as the 'Soft Skills Development Course'.

Whether they are aware of it or not, barristers are deploying key aspects of the relationship marketing and market-oriented models to attract work, evidenced by the much more client-centred approach, more equal power balance in their relationships with solicitors and their willingness to be flexible, cooperative, collaborative and available. Some are innovative and ambitious, diversifying and renewing their practices to compensate for work lost elsewhere. There is much evidence in support of Abbott's (1988) professional development thesis at work here, with barristers compensating for the loss of their advocacy monopoly and the loss of work more generally to solicitors by creating new work areas or straying into areas of practice normally undertaken by other types of chambers. The levels of success achieved within and across chambers depend on a number of factors: how vigorously or successfully efforts to get work are explored and executed; how competitive a new area is; what confidence and skills a particular barrister feels she or he can utilise to re-invent herself or himself; and the attitude of individual barristers, the most influential members of chambers and their business/management staff, who as a group can effect change.

## VII. Attitudes to Marketing

Some chambers and individuals are clearly ahead of the curve when it comes to proactively marketing their services. A few barristers even receive coaching on how to achieve their personal goals in practice development. However, a significant number of those interviewed struggle to know what to do, how to adapt and grapple with the new possibilities: 'If you look at [name] or [name] Chambers, they are modern, forward-thinking, progressive and they are already blogging and tweeting. However, most chambers are not' (B1, mixed set). This study found very contrasting approaches to getting work and marketing, ranging from members of chambers 'writing articles, getting on the radio, getting on TV. We had media training a few years ago' (B48, civil/commercial set) to interviewees, who were not even sure if their set had a marketing committee. One barrister found himself in charge of chambers marketing by default because no one else wanted to do it. Finding volunteers for these tasks is not always easy. After all, none of these administrative posts offers remuneration, so chambers very much rely on the goodwill and interest of practitioners to take on these extra responsibilities. All the clerks and staff were positive about marketing and insistent that practitioners should make active efforts to self-promote, but some of the barristers interviewed were ambivalent and regarded marketing as something outside the normal scope of work and time-consuming. This echoes earlier findings that legal professionals are resistant to it (Harris and Piercy 1998; Vickerstaff 2000). But attitudes are more complex and contradictory than this, exhibiting a mix of dismissiveness of and defensiveness about marketing and a lack of confidence about how to do it, whilst at the same time conceding it was necessary and effective:

> That's a change over my time, it's all marketing now. It's really quite boring … I have to say there are people who are very good at marketing and they've got good practices. I think it is important and I'm terrible at it, I've never done it. I've always thought you can just rely upon doing work quite well.
>
> B19, civil practitioner, 15 years' call

A handful of practitioners insisted that they carried out no marketing at all, but when questioned more specifically revealed that they participated in the development of their web profiles, prepared directory entries, obtained new work as a result of a team effort, spoke in public and gave seminars. One specialist civil QC claimed to have a purely instrumental view of it: 'I've given talks. It's the most convenient way to do 10 hours of CPD, so I speak at conferences – once or twice a year. I get some odd little, quite good little cases out of that' (B49). There are many sceptics:

> I'm open to it as a concept but I sometimes wonder, do we get value for money and how do you demonstrate that this works or is it just slightly emperor's new clothes? You know, everyone seems to say you have to do this, but are you wasting money?
>
> B24, head of common law circuit set

There are those who are utterly convinced that marketing does not bring in work and are uncomfortable with the thought that it might:

> When I worked on the solicitor side of things, I wasn't at all influenced by blurb … I don't think there is anything wrong with self-advertising, but I don't think it works. I'm in a number of books, directories, I'm in two or three of those but I've not had any work from it, the top 500 and whatever else. I'd know straight away if someone new instructed me from that. I'd be very suspect of a person who briefed me because I gave him a good time at a rugby match. That wouldn't be a very nice way. I don't know. I don't do it.
>
> B4, barrister, 24 years' call, former solicitor's clerk

For many of the more senior practitioners, the only way to market themselves is by performing well in court in front of other lawyers, often on the other side. Technical excellence is what matters in terms of getting work, a view that is supported by research in Scotland and New Zealand (Palihawadana and Barnes 2004; Thomas et al 2001):

> I'm quite old-fashioned. I take the view that if you're any good, the solicitors will ask for you and you don't really need to do a lot of this stuff, but you prove your – you market yourself in court as it were.
>
> B7, criminal barrister, 29 years' call

One specialist QC felt that any other marketing at silk level was likely to fail:

> I'm extremely old-fashioned. I think marketing is grossly overrated at silk level, because the only way to keep, to build and keep a practice as a silk is to get repeat work and to get work from people you've been against. You do it by impressing people.
>
> B49, specialist civil silk, 29 years' call

These assertions that this stance is old-fashioned is indicative of just how central marketing has become at the Bar, as a concept if not a full-blown reality. Some feel outnumbered, out of date or have to justify why they do not do it. Others feel that perhaps they should be doing it, even if they do not really believe it works, because that is what they are being told by the marketing, management and business staff in chambers, the Bar Council and the specialist Bar Associations and at the annual Bar Conference. Nonetheless, for many, a recommendation remains the only important way of getting new work and it might not necessarily come from the solicitor client:

> I don't think there is evidence to say that you get new work. I think you get new work through all manner of different means and the most likely way is by some kind of recommendation … I get work from people who are serving prison sentences at Bullingdon because they speak to their cellmate.
>
> B18, criminal practitioner, 21 years' call

Senior practitioners, from this sample, on the whole displayed more reluctance to self-promote and one view was that 'the bottom end of chambers is in some ways the most dynamic bit of it in terms of chambers strategy and that sort of thing. We all tend to be quite turned on about marketing' (B12, civil barrister, four years' call). This may be because many older practitioners have established practices and enough work. However, despite protestations that they did not like it, that it took up too much time ('You should be doing a half day a week marketing. That's the aim' (B1)) or were hopeless at it, many of the more senior barristers nonetheless (begrudgingly) engaged in marketing. Some actively embraced it, whilst conceding what hard work it was:

> I would say I work very, very hard at marketing … I go to conferences, I speak on panels, I make sure I'm going out to breakfast or lunch with solicitors … I'm very proactive but I'm very unusual … I wrote the book because I thought there was a hole in the market and I thought it was quite an interesting subject … But to be honest with you, it's all a serious, serious slog and it's very, very time-consuming … the book's been an amazing marketing tool. I have actually got one case I know directly from the book, because I saw the email that preceded me getting the instruction.
>
> B37, criminal silk, 30 years' call

Only one barrister spoke of marketing to other members of the Bar, 'which I've always said is as important as marketing to solicitors, you need your peers to know that you are in the game and that you are good. That's critical. People forget that' (B48, commercial silk, 28 years' call).

It is impossible to generalise why some are better or more interested in marketing than others, but factors that tend to influence this are: whether or not they have enough work, though few are complacent; how senior they are; what their views about marketing are; how confident, sociable and entrepreneurial they are; whether or not they belong to a specialist set or specialist team within it, which might be easier to promote; how innovative those within their team are and whether or not chambers as a whole provide marketing resources, support, guidance and innovation.

What can one conclude from these developments? Many of the older practitioners who have sufficient work resist most of the more enterprising ventures in self-promotion and claim that things are very much as they used to be, with work coming in on the basis of technical performance and attendant reputation. But for new, younger members of the profession, things are very different than they were for incoming barristers 30 years ago. They are expected to market themselves if they want to succeed, to devote much time and effort into raising their profiles, by undertaking some or all of the marketing initiatives examined in this chapter. Therefore, it is difficult to conclude that things are as they used to be and that these developments have not reshaped what is required, in terms of not just skills, but also attitude. There is much evidence to reveal a significant shift in, first, how barristers get work and, second, how they view their role in that process. The traditional passive approach has been displaced by a more commercially imaginative and aggressively enterprising spirit. Some practitioners are proactively expanding their practice areas, creating new specialisms and encroaching on each other's traditional jurisdictions, in order to acquire a reputation in new areas. Many engage in a number of promotional and marketing activities to further their reputations and brand. Whether seeking to survive in a publicly funded practice or taking advantage of the liberalising rules in how to attract work, this new self-motivating and self-promoting barrister is required to be flexible and resourceful, savvy and highly visible as she or he seeks to compete in the rapidly evolving markets for legal services.

# 6

# Direct Access

> We've all got to try and get work wherever we can and if I don't sign up for direct access somebody else will and if nobody signs up the solicitors will keep all the work for themselves.
>
> B2, criminal silk, 26 years' call

> I hardly ever do direct access work and am instinctively wary of it.
>
> B36, chancery practitioner, 42 years' call

In 1990, Direct Professional Access (later known as Licensed Access) was introduced, permitting professionals, such as accountants, to instruct barristers directly, without going via a solicitor. In 2004, a truly public access scheme was launched and has slowly expanded to cover almost all kinds of work, as permitted by the rules[1] (Boon and Levin 2008; Flood and Whyte 2008). Since January 2014, barristers, if they complete the training, are now also allowed to conduct litigation, removing the last significant difference between them and solicitors. They can now issue proceedings or commence defences to proceedings, as well as carry out all the attendant ancillary functions. Despite these developments, the profession's own promotional rhetoric and the Direct Access Portal set up by the Bar Council in 2016, solicitor referrals remain the main source of work for the Bar. In a 2013 survey of about 2,700 barristers, 77 per cent of them did no direct access work. Of those who did, nine per cent said that it accounted for less than five per cent of their gross fees. Most direct access cases related to family and civil law work and were done by younger practitioners (Bar Council 2014b). In 2013, the restriction on juniors under three years' call accepting direct instructions was lifted to give them another way to develop their practices following the large reduction of work brought about by the LASPO. By 2015, Bar Council statistics showed an increased interest in direct access work, with 6,425 barristers registered as being trained, although there are no figures as to how many actually do it or how much of it they do (Granville Stafford 2015). Many barristers indicate that they would like to do it (Flood and Whyte 2008; BSB 2017b), yet it seems from the scant data available that not many of them do very much. Nearly half of those interviewed for this study

[1] *BSB Handbook 2019* rC119–31.

had done no such cases ('none at all, thank goodness', B20, specialist civil). Some had not properly thought about it ('It's probably something I ought to look at', B36, chancery). Most of the other participants had done a modest amount, perhaps a handful of cases a year. One mixed practice administrator revealed it amounted to 2.5 per cent of the chamber's annual turnover. Four or five interviewees had built up more significant direct access-based practices – one said it accounted for about 30 per cent of his work, another 10 per cent. Only the sole practitioner participant and the barrister who had set up an LLP relied almost exclusively on public access instructions. Their practices were very specialist and both had given up courtroom advocacy. Only a couple of those interviewed had signed up on one of the online portals (eg, Clerksroom Direct, Riverview Law and MyBarrister) offering clients direct access to barristers.

Why has direct access work remained marginal for most practitioners, particularly when so many struggle to maintain sufficient levels of work? This chapter investigates attitudes towards direct public access work, despite the somewhat low levels of engagement with it. Flood and Whyte's (2008) interviewed and surveyed barristers who explicitly undertook direct access work, so were predisposed to it. Their research pre-dates the implementation of the LSA, permitting the emergence of ABSs, and was before barristers were allowed to conduct litigation, so the topic is worth revisiting. Whilst the BSB's (2017b) study on the provision of legal services at the Bar includes aspects of direct access, there have been no in-depth qualitative studies on barristers' experiences of it. It has been reported that barristers see it as a potential area of considerable growth (Granville Stafford 2015) and, given how much work has been lost as a result of cuts to legal aid, it seems logical that more will seek some form of direct instruction. If this proves to be the case it is possible that it will significantly reshape the organisational structure of chambers and working practices at the Bar for the reasons explored below.

The fieldwork for this study uncovered different attitudes to direct access work. On the one hand, views were fairly negative. Certain kinds of cases were deemed unsuitable, even if permitted by the regulations; direct, unmediated contact with clients was often perceived as problematic; clerks and practitioners worried that solicitors – their main source of work – would feel threatened by the Bar attracting direct access work. The perception was that they would stop instructing barristers if they appeared to be 'stealing' work from them. Finally, for many, direct access meant they would become like solicitors, which they did not want. On the other hand, many felt that they should do more direct access, that it is very cost-effective for the client and has enabled some practitioners to increase their workload when instructions from solicitors have dried up. One specialist civil silk noted that he no longer did any as his qualification had lapsed, but he felt he should renew it as the experience was '[q]uite positive when I did it. One can usually provide assistance immediately and for not very much or even nothing, to a client who deserves it' (B49). Three commented that when they were approached to do unsuitable cases, the result was a role reversal, whereby they redirected lay clients to solicitors, supplying their traditional clients with work, something Abel (2004a) foresaw and

Flood and Whyte (2008) noted. An ongoing challenge for the Bar is finding effective ways of letting the public know that it can instruct a barrister directly without going via a solicitor. A handful of participants felt that few members of the public knew that this was possible.

## I. Fees

One of the main advantages of direct access, from a client's point of view, is that it is much cheaper to instruct a barrister than a solicitor: 'That is what our USP is for direct access, definitely … they could borrow 3, 4 or £5,000 and then they can have their case conducted, whereas if they're using a solicitor it's going to cost them £25,000. The saving is huge' (B39, private family finance practitioner, 24 years' call). This is the case across practice areas:

> We ought to do direct access, you just ought to do it. I mean, there is no reason not to do it … Relative to the bill that would be put in by Freshfields for preliminary appraisal, you know, £40,000, the Bar is much cheaper. The Bar is good value.
>
> B49, specialist civil silk, 29 years' call

> We're much, much cheaper. I've done cases where … all the legal things I drafted – witness statements, all the pleadings I did. I did the advices, everything … We had a trial and as I recall, I think my fees were in total about £15,000–£20,000. His [the solicitor's] were in excess of £60,000.
>
> B26, civil barrister, 25 years' call

Solicitors' organisational structures, profit targets and overheads are such that their fees are significantly higher and in all areas of work, the savings by going directly to the Bar can be enormous. Some clients are becoming aware of this and have started instructing the Bar directly:

> Everyone was worried in the beginning of the 1990s that the likes of Herbert Smith would come in, set up advocacy units and take away our business. In fact, the reverse happened. Their clients were fed up with the fact that they were trying to have hoisted upon them in house advocates who knew nothing, had no experience and were just there to generate fees for the firm … the Bar is still half the price or less of comparable solicitors, who have such high overheads. So your marketing position is, what I used to call 'Brain on a Stick' economics.
>
> B13, commercial silk

Accepting such instructions has sometimes obliged barristers to charge a fixed fee by working out in advance how much time the work will take without a solicitor having assessed the case first. Many clients ask for this. The client is obliged to pay upfront, a huge perk for many, who are used to waiting months or years for payment, but it is often hard to predict the fee accurately and barristers generally prefer to charge hourly rates. Direct contact with the client and lack of commercial experience makes some feel awkward about charging and reluctant to bill for the full amount of work done: 'I'm very bad, I don't know how you are supposed to deal with it. I suppose one view is you ruthlessly charge for every minute you spend on it, but I don't' (B5, civil circuit practitioner, 28 years' call). Others think that some clients regard direct access as some kind of pro bono service or think it will be a cheap deal: 'People think that direct access is virtually free, that's one of the big problems with it. 'Do I have to pay for it?' (B19, civil work) or 'A lot of the direct access clients we get don't want to pay very much' (B43, family law). One barrister felt that she was more likely than a solicitor to tell the lay clients what she thought the outcome of their case would be, which would not just keep costs down, as decisions could be made earlier about settlement, but would also be re-assuring for the client:

> I've had two direct access clients … and both of them said to me that what they don't get from the solicitor is the answer. So they've used a solicitor and they've found that what they get is a lot of preparatory stuff – how much money have you got, give me all the bank statements and lets have a look at it and what they can't get for them, is 'This is what is likely to happen' and so I've sat with the same client who has already spent £8,000 on a solicitor and I've said 'This is a schedule and this is what I think is going to happen' and they came to me specifically for that reason.
>
> B39, family finance practitioner, 24 years' call

## II. Suitability

Not all cases are deemed suitable for direct access, even if they satisfy the regulatory criteria. As Flood and Whyte (2008: 143) found, cases that only need barristers to give 'red light/green light opinions' are popular with clients as they are done quickly and more cheaply than a solicitor. A planning appeal for a surveyor, tax or intellectual property advice and some aspects of private family law advice are examples of cases where direct access was deemed by participants to be wholly suitable: 'Finance is probably the best area for it … I think probably with finance it's easier, because you can give them a list and say "These are the documents we need, bring them all in and I will sort out the rest of it for you"' (B41, family finance). One family lawyer felt that direct access was suitable for grandparents or other relatives wishing to intervene in care proceedings, and found that solicitors or local authorities often recommended it to such people. The nature of the case and the type of client often determines whether or not the arrangement will work. Although barristers can help a client draft a letter, direct access does not permit them to conduct litigation, unless they are specifically qualified to do so. The client will have to instigate or respond to proceedings and deal with the correspondence (with guidance perhaps), as well as do much of the preparation and document collation, tasks usually done by a solicitor. Practitioners found that many clients find it stressful and confusing, and demand a lot of support, requiring them to engage in a much closer relationship with the client than they are used to.

This, in turn, obliges them to spend much more time on a case, time which they are reluctant to charge for.

However, for the sole practitioner participant, direct access was his main method of getting work and for him it was the repeat custom that mattered:

> I want someone who will ring me up every month or every six months, but who will keep on sending me their work. And I have a number of clients now, for whom I am the 'go to' person … almost identical to being a solicitor.
>
> B9, sole specialist civil practitioner, eight years' call

However, as a sole practitioner, without the support of chambers, he actively turned away court advocacy work, so in a sense his role is more akin to the old solicitor model: 'I rebuff anyone who asks me to help them with litigation. A lot of barristers do direct access advocacy … I don't feel, me on my own, that I can cope with the stresses, strains' (B9). Ironically, the barristers who have administrative support from chambers felt that they did not have the ability to take on direct access clients in cases that went beyond advocacy or advice. They could not envisage and did not want to draw up witness statements or undertake document preparation of any substance:

> One of the problems for public access is … you wouldn't have the resources to be able to do it as an individual member of a set of chambers … For my practice I can't see the advantages of it particularly, because I work for claimants who suffer personal injuries either in the clinical negligence field or otherwise and I wouldn't want necessarily to represent them without the filter of a solicitor, because I haven't got the support staff, I don't want to start taking witness statements. I don't want to, you know, I just really don't want to go there.
>
> B15, specialist silk, 28 years' call

Even now that the liberalising rules under the LSA permit barristers to restructure or form alliances that will facilitate paralegal or other support to do such tasks, almost all those interviewed were not interested in going down that road. There was also a sense that existing structures in some areas of work did not lend themselves to direct access instruction. Much defence personal injury work, for example, comes via the Medical Defence Union, which has its own in house solicitors. Other organisations, such as the police force, also use in-house lawyers, and they themselves often instruct solicitors first. A client is unlikely to bypass these in-house legal facilities and go straight to a barrister for advice. In criminal defence work, especially in cases of serious crimes, the framework discourages direct access work, though criminal appeals or privately paid driving offences, for example, could be suitable:

> They're normally in prison for a start and it's simply doesn't work. They will be seen by solicitors, when they are first arrested. They will see them in the police station, normally will keep the same solicitors, so there will not come a time when they'll think 'Oh, I know, I'll go to a barrister direct'.
>
> B3, criminal circuit barrister, 33 years' call

Before the cuts to legal aid, most solicitors routinely instructed counsel, even if they wished to do their own advocacy work, so as to be available for clients. Spending all day in court kept them away from their offices too long and was not good for business:

> You've got to bear in mind that at any point during the day we might end up having a couple of hours completely unsolicited with one of our clients. You know, it's not in the diary. If you were in the middle of a trial you couldn't do that.
>
> S1, family law solicitor, 22 years' qualified

The daily schedules of many barristers who do a lot of court work do not always allow them to be available for direct access customers. Clients often want immediate advice and support, and dealing with them without an intermediary solicitor is something new for barristers:

> I have done two [direct access] family cases. They were both horrific … constantly on the phone and demanding answers … residence, both of them and people would phone up at 10 am, when you'd just gone to court and then would be harassing the clerks throughout the day, 'Well she hasn't got back to me'. 'No, she's in a trial' (laughing).
>
> B32, family and criminal law circuit barrister, 13 years' call

Direct access seems to work well, according to the barristers interviewed, where the structural framework does not direct a potential client to an in-house legal facility first, where the client is not in prison, where a self-contained piece of advice is sought, where extensive administration or evidence gathering is not required and where the client accepts that the barrister might not be available for a whole working day, when in court. Any or all of the above are examples of what can work well within the existing chambers model. However, once the work includes what would traditionally have been seen as solicitors' work, many of those interviewed regarded it as 'too much trouble' (B31), problematic or undesirable. Only a few were happy to make adjustments in terms of securing administrative, legal or other expert support and described how their chambers have created alliances with paralegals or small solicitor firms, to whom they delegate some of the document or evidence-gathering work. One commercial practitioner described how a large corporation and a foreign government had both gone to his chambers as their first port of call. The barristers then decided what support was required from solicitors and other experts, and, within the agreed budget, divided up the work – a complete reversal of the traditional referral arrangement. From the client's point of view, this is much cheaper than having a law firm distributing the work. However, this kind of arrangement was not common amongst those interviewed and one wonders how many barristers are interested in and have the skills and support to coordinate and handle all aspects of very large, complex cases. In the case of the sole practitioner whose practice is almost completely based on direct client referral, the barrister ceased to do advocacy work completely and took on a role more akin to that of a solicitor, precisely because he did not have sufficient support to do both. Additionally, the only participant who operated the LLP had also given up court advocacy work so as to be available to clients full-time.

This raises one of the critical points about this kind of instruction. If barristers engage in significant amounts of direct access work that goes beyond straightforward advisory and advocacy elements, do they in fact end up operating as solicitors in all but name? Flood and Whyte noted that barristers did not want to become the 'functional equivalents to solicitors' (2008: 143) and, as explored below, this study found the same for almost all of those interviewed. More broadly, is it possible to do large amounts of direct access work and provide expert advocacy services at the same time? Many practitioners predicted that if direct instruction begins to dominate, many practitioners will effectively operate as solicitors and only a few will remain specialist advocates, operating within a recognisable chambers model. Most explicitly stated that they had become barristers precisely so that they could avoid the work traditionally done by solicitors.

## III. Client Contact: 'I Don't Want to be a Solicitor'

When asked about direct access, interviewees referred to solicitors as buffers, shields, cushions, barriers, safeguards or defences from the lay clients: 'you don't have the protection, if you like, of a solicitor' (B8) or 'I quite like having that nice insulating blanket of a solicitor between me and the client' (B12). For many civil practitioners, their job is intellectual legal problem solving, working alone and involves some advocacy. For those who do certain areas of civil work, even advocacy will not always feature highly, so their interpersonal communication skills may not be either particularly good or necessary: 'We're not used to explaining things to clients or dealing with clients without the solicitor mediating and so it does require different skills' (B1, civil practitioner, 21 years' call). Even some of the more junior barristers do not like the idea of close client contact: 'I do not enjoy direct access work for individual members of the public and much prefer having a solicitor to gatekeep for me in such cases' (B12, civil practitioner, four years' call). One barrister, whose practice comprised over 30 per cent direct access work, commented: 'It has been a lesson in how valuable it is to have a solicitor between you and the client in the old-fashioned system' (B5, civil practitioner, 26 years' call). This reaction was voiced across the whole range of age/experience. One relatively newly qualified practitioner chose to go to the Bar on the assumption that client contact would be limited:

> I don't mind it in principle. I have to say, obviously I went into this profession – I don't have any desire to be in a client-faced thing, so I wouldn't say that I don't like contact with clients, but I would rather have less of it, I think, than more.
>
> B17, civil practitioner, three years' call

Few barristers interviewed intended to qualify to conduct litigation, stating that they would have become solicitors had they wanted to do that kind of work. One commented that 'even this direct access-lite is enough client contact' (B32, 13 years' call). One argument for retaining some distance from the lay client is that the barrister maintains independence of thought and judgement and can give better, dispassionate advice without feeling the need to please the client or tell her or him what they want to hear. In fact, solicitors often rely on barristers to deliver more difficult messages to clients. Further, if the case does not go the way a solicitor had hoped or predicted, she or he can blame the barrister, whilst preserving good client trust and satisfaction with their services (Morison and Leith 1992). Others like having solicitors as sounding boards, with whom they can discuss aspects of the case. Solicitors also 'buffer' the Bar from the more difficult clients or vexatious litigants. Having professional direct access clients or in-house HR send work are considered ideal direct access cases: 'Not necessarily professional clients, but sort of, switched on, educated clients' (B26, civil barrister). Although only a few are quoted below, many of those interviewed perceived that a significant amount of direct access clients were in some way irrational:

> You do get quite a few nutters, which I think having solicitors in between filters out. One suddenly understands why it's such a nice idea having solicitors in between (laughing).
>
> B5, civil circuit barrister, 28 years' call

> A lot of it's absolutely time-wasting, you know. People with a plastic bag full of papers and they basically want you to take over as solicitor for six months. I mean I had one horror story with a man. I thought I was just doing this one application … then it just got, you know, besieging me with stuff even though I'd been retained to do one thing.
>
> B19, civil barrister, 15 years' call

> I'm certainly keen to try and avoid taking on sort of litigants in person, who are loonies basically, of whom there are plenty about.
>
> B11, civil barrister, 18 months' call

The direct access rules permit barristers to turn work away: 'I've had maybe 30 a year. 15 are clearly lunatics, so I say "I'm sorry, I can't help you" … Once you've got rid of the lunatics, it's absolutely fine' (B49, specialist silk, 29 years' call) or 'We do get quite a lot of direct access, potential instructions that come in that is turned away' (B17, civil barrister, three years' call). However, turning work down is practically a new skill: 'You also need to develop the ability, which of course you never had to do before, of saying no to people, and say "No, I'm not going to do this, I don't want this case, go away"' (B24, head of circuit chambers). Whether or not direct access attracts a certain kind of litigant, who perhaps has had trouble getting solicitors to act for them is hard to know, but the high number of similar responses, even within this small sample, seems to suggest a common perception that direct access clients are especially difficult. However, not all agreed and it could be that barristers simply are not very good at or do not like the complexity and messiness of client contact: 'They're not all nutters, that's not correct … my experience of direct access so far has been, surprisingly, that in fact that they've been rational, intelligent. They actually know their case quite well' (B15, personal injury silk, 28 years' call). One made the point that between barrister and solicitor in a conventional instruction arrangement, there is a great deal of trust. Both are likely to keep attendance notes of telephone or face-to-face discussions, they know how the system works, speak the same language and misunderstandings are less likely to arise than when dealing with a lay client. There was, no doubt, also less emotional investment in a case. One interviewee appreciated just how much extra care and work was involved in a direct access case and why perhaps solicitors charged more:

> You've got to keep files and make attendance notes for every discussion ... ethically it is very awkward and I see how hard solicitors, that's where some of their bills come from ... you've got to have it all in apple pie order.
>
> B14, commercial barrister, 41 years' call

One practitioner felt that the high level of complaints from direct access clients had made him reluctant to do much work of that nature:

> You have to be more careful. I'm also on the Professional Conduct committee of the Bar Standards Board. I sit on that committee and we investigate, for want of a better word, or at least we receive complaints of misconduct, which we analyse and either dismiss or recommend should go before a disciplinary tribunal ... and there are certain areas of work that tend to generate complaints of professional misconduct and direct access is one of them ... My experience of sitting on that committee means that I'm very wary about dealing with public access cases, direct access cases.
>
> B1, civil barrister, 25 years' call

## IV. Offending Solicitors: Biting the Hand that Feeds You?

One repeatedly expressed fear during the fieldwork is that by doing direct access work, a barrister will upset her or his existing instructing solicitors by appearing to take work away from them. As Flood and Whyte (2008) found, there was a notion that it would lead to a reduction of work from solicitors. One clerk commented:

> It is a double-edged thing as I said earlier, because some solicitors that I've been out to see and spoken to ... They're not keen on the fact that barristers will have direct access to clients and they're not very happy about it and so that may have an impact on our referral work.
>
> A4, deputy head clerk, circuit set

Even so, in the current shortage of work, practitioners are prepared to take the risk:

> We spent a lot of time debating what we were going to do about direct access and whether we were going to rub it in solicitors' faces or not. There is a separate section on the website for direct access and it is pretty clearly there, it's not hidden away.
>
> B32, family and criminal law circuit barrister, 13 years' call

Views across practice areas and even within practice areas are mixed. A couple of family law practitioners felt that in private family work, which lost most of its legal aid support under the LASPO, there was great scope for developing direct access work. Many people, who now find themselves unable to get legal aid for any divorce matter, might have enough money to pay something for legal representation. They hope to charge a lower fee than normal, but one that will undercut solicitors and attract the clients directly. By contrast, one family law solicitor was not convinced that direct access would ever develop significantly and did not perceive it as a threat to her work levels at all:

> I don't think in reality any barrister who is busy, which they are if they're good, is going to have the time to deal with the day to day minutiae of it … I think that the people that we're instructing are so busy doing their normal, everyday work, I truly don't see that they would find time to deal with. And also, well I don't know how many barristers are going to take it up, but most people go to the Bar 'cos actually they don't like the client access (laughing).
>
> S1, family law solicitor, 22 years' qualified

Further, in her experience, clients going through a divorce were reluctant or unable to do even basic document preparation or form filling: 'People are phased by it and what we take for granted as being something we can do very easily, Joe Blogs actually finds it quite tough' (S1). In any event, quite often, when any kind of case is turned away from chambers as being unsuitable for direct access, the client is nearly always redirected to one of their instructing solicitors. This solicitor conceded that the Bar has become a source of some of her firm's work. In turn, solicitors send clients who do not have much money directly to the Bar because they know it will be cheaper:

> In some ways it's been quite good, because if a case comes to us that isn't for a barrister, direct access, needs a solicitor in this case, we can then send it to them. And likewise, when they get a client, who hasn't got that much money, they can't be bothered with it, they say 'Listen why don't you go and see a barrister direct, I know a chambers I can introduce you to', and they come.
>
> A3, head clerk, common law chambers

## V. Public Awareness

Making the public aware that direct access to a barrister is possible is a challenging task. Many people know little about the Bar and less of its structural machinery. In an effort to improve public knowledge, the Bar Council has an official direct access website. Many chambers also have their own individual websites, linked to their main ones, but designed in the hope that they show up early on Google searches. Some have dedicated direct access clerks, who process online enquiries and decide how to distribute the work. But practitioners find that even their instructing solicitors are not always aware of different practice areas within the same chambers or that they do direct access work:

> I frequently meet solicitors in other areas of work, so immigration for example, and they say 'I didn't know you did family work, your chambers … I didn't know you had a direct access team, because I sometimes I am able to refer and I just want to refer clients because we don't do family at our firm and we have something straightforward that wouldn't require a solicitor' … so that's when you know marketing isn't working. Just to have it as a link on the website is not enough.
>
> B45, family practitioner, seven years' call

The BSB (2017b) survey research stressed the need for barristers to clarify to the public exactly what services they provide and to package them more commercially, giving upfront information on fees. So, whilst barristers feel they are being more transparent, visible and competitive (which they are in comparison to a generation ago), there is still a need for some to hone their business and marketing strategies.

Some practice groups invite in-house Human Resources officers or consultants to their seminars, hoping for direct instruction. This can work well in some areas. One employment practitioner, for example, noted: 'I've been really, really impressed, you know. When you have a good HR person, they're more help to you than any solicitor is, because they know that much more' (B17, civil practitioner, three years' call). Two of the circuit sets in this study advertise their services in the local paper and one offered free surgeries: 'That brought work but out of probably six, seven, eight appointments you might get one fee-paying case. It is good publicity' (A1, administrator, mixed set practice). One circuit clerk planned to target large local companies and invite their relevant officers to a series of Health and Safety seminars, which the chambers was setting up with the local chamber of commerce and would feature several of its members. Certain practitioners and many commercial chambers target overseas work for direct access. Some of the promotional work is done via the Bar Council's International Committee:

> The International Committee's remit is to promote the Bar overseas … Whenever I meet someone at a conference, whether here or elsewhere, but a foreign lawyer for example, and I say 'Did you know that you can instruct the Bar directly?' 'No? really?' I say 'Did you know that you can cut out the middleman, so it's cheaper and quicker for the client? And did you know that we're not a competitor to you, so we won't steal your client?' 'Really?' And so that message is a really important message for the Bar.
>
> B37, criminal silk, 30 years' call

Barristers can offer cheaper prices, expertise and pose no threat, as a solicitors' firm might, of luring clients away. They mostly wish to be instructed for discrete pieces of work rather than on a client retainer. However, international clients can find certain things about the Bar strange. The idea of an independent, self-employed barrister handling a case against another such barrister who is from the same set of chambers, but who acts for the other side, is problematic for some:

> The Bar has to look at conflict in a way that it hasn't in the past anyway, because our international [name of client] in New York just don't understand the way we work and two days before I had a massive hearing … they suddenly worked out that my opponent was in my chambers … [it was a] massive problem and American clients have a real difficulty with all of that and we at the Bar have to, we explained what the position was and they've come to understand it. -Ish.
>
> (B48, head of commercial/civil set)

International clients also have difficulties accepting that a barrister, sitting as an arbitrator, might have members of her or his chambers appearing in the case. Some have set up separate arbitration companies to try and get over this difficulty: 'They won't have, you know X sitting as an arbitrator and two of my colleagues in chambers appearing in front of me, whereas I sit as a High Court judge over there and members of chambers can appear in front of me and no one minds' (B47, commercial silk/deputy High Court judge).

## VI. What Next?

Whether or not barristers like the operational aspects of direct access, this kind of instruction is likely to develop to some degree for the simple reason that many barristers need whatever work they can get. Further, the Bar has two strong selling points: they are expert advocates/specialists advisers and they are significantly cheaper than solicitors. However, direct access work requires barristers to be entrepreneurial and to develop good customer care skills as they work much more closely with the lay client. At present, not all are particularly accomplished at either or willing to spend additional time and effort on the client. Many chambers and the Bar Council now offer various types of marketing training, but it remains optional. Doing the occasional piece of direct access work does not present problems for a practitioner operating within the existing chambers model. Yet the two barristers interviewed who undertake regular and significant amounts of such work have given up court advocacy altogether so as to be able to service their clients' needs and neither works in a traditional set of chambers. In these circumstances, their distinctive and primary role as an advocate has vanished and, by their own admission, the key (or any) distinction between them and solicitors no longer applies. Some of those interviewed predicted that the Bar will shrink considerably as more barristers go in-house, engage in new models of working, say by receiving direct access instructions via an ABS, leaving only a much smaller group of specialist advocates who will work in a recognisable chambers model. However, most practitioners were very clear that conducting litigation was not something they wished to do, even with the assistance of paralegal support. As far as they are concerned, these tasks fall within the remit of a solicitor and if they had wanted to work in this way they would have become solicitors: 'I think it would be too much of a change of working method' (B5) and 'I prefer to avoid it, because it is dull administrative work' (B14) or 'the stress involved would not be worthwhile in terms of rewards' (B23).

It is hard to draw any generalised conclusions from this relatively small sample. There were a number of interviewees, from different practice areas and levels of experience, who were much more open to developing closer and more collaborative relationships with lay clients, undertaking tasks hitherto done by solicitors and operating within new structures which relied exclusively on direct client instruction. However, most of those who took part very much view their professional function as quite distinct from that of a solicitor and whilst many are prepared to undertake some direct access work, they are not currently willing to radically change their working methods or structures to enable them to develop it more fully. Thus, despite being able to operate in a wide variety of more flexible ways and the drastic reduction in work coming to the Bar, direct access work is, for the majority of participants, just an attractive bolt-on to supplement work referred via the usual channels. Few see it as an innovative and exciting new way to operate in a potentially larger market. This approach, with its clear distinction between the two branches, goes to the very root of barristers' traditional professional culture and perhaps explains the relatively slow or limited engagement with direct access work. It is also a little ironic given that courtroom advocacy plays a relatively small role in the lives of many practitioners. There are considerably fewer full hearings/trials at court. Thirty years ago, many common law early practitioners were often in court on a daily basis. During the interviews, the younger practitioners asserted that they were 'often' in court, but on further questioning, this was no more than twice a week at the most and often only for a preliminary hearing or simple application. Whether or not barristers' reluctance to engage in wider tasks continues to be sustainable, as referral work decreases, remains to be seen and the incoming generation may well be more flexible in terms of how they perceive their function and professional identity. To what extent this identity has already been affected and modified by changes in working methods, organisational culture and client contact is explored in the next chapter.

# 7

# Bar Culture

> The values of the Bar are Integrity, Excellence and Independence. They are immutable and must be jealously guarded and preserved. They are what make us what we are.
>
> Maura McGowan QC, Bar Conference, 2013

Nelken says that 'legal culture is about who we are not just what we do', linking lawyers' self-perception and sense of professional identity with their actions, organisation, ethics and customs (2004: 1). Friedman (1975) identifies it as internal legal culture. Whilst earlier sections have touched on some values of the profession, this chapter digs deeper and explores how practitioners perceive their professional identity or culture and to what degree this has evolved as a result of the increasingly commercial and managerial logics that pervade their working lives. This study identifies aspects of social interaction, which are rooted in the ways in which barristers reflect on their work and consider their institutions and professional culture. It also examines how and why they respond to change the way they do. The previous chapter illustrated why many of the barristers interviewed are reluctant to do direct access work or conduct litigation, as they likened the tasks involved and the extent of client contact with a solicitor's job, which they did not particularly want to do. This is only one example of how some view their identity, but culture emerges across multiple arenas of professional life, highlighting the interplay between professional ideology and the changes that are reshaping professional practice and situated choices (Nelson and Trubek 1992).

Culture is also dynamic, where meanings are contested and reshaped. It sometimes becomes more entrenched, in response to wider pressures and ideological shifts. Central to cultural evolution is power, which ensures its dominance and reproduction (Larson 1977; Newman 1995). Traditional professionalism, as accounted for by functionalist trait theorists and most practitioners, relies on the notion of an altruistic service ideal, guided by uniform ethical values (Abbott 1988; Francis 2005). Other more critical perspectives, considered in the opening two chapters, denounce this as a façade, masking the more self-interested motives of professionals who seek to secure their high status and rewards (Larson 1977; Abel 1988). The focus here is on how barristers themselves understand their professional culture and if and how they think it has changed. It also considers some of the emotional responses of practitioners to such changes, something that has rarely, if ever, been scrutinised in previous research studies. There is very little understanding of how barristers feel about being barristers, in the context of all the changes their professional lives have undergone. Webber (2004) considers researching legal culture to be a process of institutional feedback, often articulating what legal professionals may themselves not be able to, leaving the researcher to seek explanations for conduct, views, justifications and institutional structures. Whilst the barristers interviewed were very much able to articulate their perception of Bar culture, how it manifests in their working lives and explains their reactions to change, what follows also interrogates to what degree their perspective is reflected in the reality of their working lives. The rules of professional conduct are embodied in the BSB Code of Conduct and they reflect the basis of legal ethics and culture. They are at the foreground of the vocational training course and pupillage year, but what it means to be a barrister also includes the more informal rules and perspectives, that are traditionally reinforced in chambers, on circuit and within the Inns. Larson (1977) notes that new entrants are shaped to comply with norms and standards, effectively absorbing the culture to such a degree that it is internalised and becomes part of their subjectivity.

## I. The Development of Bar Ideology

Boon (2014) traces the historical development of the barristers' profession to explain how a distinct ideology emerged with regard to independence, neutrality, community and identity. The basis of legal culture in England and Wales emerged from the notion of a 'balanced constitution'. Citizens have core rights and freedoms, guaranteed by law and overseen by a judiciary that is independent of the state. Lawyers are deemed to be similarly independent of outside influence and to maintain control over their work. Whilst owing primary duties to their clients and to the courts in which they appear, lawyers use their expertise and autonomy to carry out their work, free from a client's assessment of a case, with legalism and procedure prevailing over wider theories of justice. From the mid-seventeenth century, the Bar's ethical rules laid out the profession's ethos of public service, stating that barristers would accept all briefs that came their way, representing all comers rather than touting for particular cases, giving rise to what is known as the 'cab rank rule' (Burrage 2006; Boon 2014).[1] This duty to accept clients irrespective of who they are or what they might have done dates back from the medieval period and reflects the principle of neutrality, one of three notions that together comprise the standard conception of the lawyer's role. The other two principles are those of partisanship, 'using all legal means in representing' the client, and, lastly, of non-accountability, 'not being morally responsible for the consequences'. Therefore, at the core of the advocate's role was the idea of independence: independence from moral judgements to represent anyone who asked and independence to decide

[1] For sceptics on the actual implementation of the cab rank rule, see Flood and Hviid (2013). The Bar's response can be found in Kentridge (2013).

how to do so, within the limits of the law and due process, in the knowledge that there would be no ramifications thereafter (Boon 2016: 2).

It was not until the growth in the provision of public funding, under the Legal Aid and Advice Act 1949, that a broader sense of public service became more prevalent in Bar ideology. As the profession expanded, with recruits from a more diverse range of backgrounds, barristers entered the 'welfare' arena, providing services on the basis of citizenship to all, as a universal right, in areas such as housing, divorce and crime, subsidised by the public coffers (Hanlon and Jackson 1999; Hanlon 2001). In such work, where the state is effectively the client or at least the paymaster, the degree of professional independence is necessarily constrained (Sommerlad 1995) and is considered in more detail below. Nonetheless, in the minds of many practitioners, independence is a strong feature of professional identity. As one criminal silk (B2) put it: 'I think that the belief in independence is so strong as to be self-fulfilling. Believing in and asserting our independence makes us independent, even if we can't always define what we're independent of.' Moreover, most if not all interviewees felt that independence fosters integrity and excellence, so these essential attributes of Bar culture intertwine. What do barristers mean by independence, integrity and excellence, how do they manifest in their professional lives and why do they think these core values differentiate them from other lawyers?

## II. Excellence, Commitment and Integrity

'Excellence' is a word that the Bar Council uses on the banner of its website's homepage, together with 'Integrity' and 'Justice' as the trilogy of ideals the profession prides itself in advancing. Rogers (2012) noted during her observational research that professional excellence was one of the characteristics promoted by the Inns on an open day for law students. Few, if any, barristers use this vocabulary when describing their professional culture, but much of what they say points to the same thing when they describe their approach to work. In keeping with functionalist trait theorists, excellence refers, in part, to the academic qualifications and training barristers acquire, and the ethical framework within which they operate. However, the notion encapsulates much more. It is something of a moral approach to or ethos about work – a commitment to work as hard and to represent a client as best they can, with full integrity, in return for the trust the client is placing in them, irrespective of their remuneration. It encompasses a professional pride in doing one's work well and the ever-present desire for this to be recognised not just by clients, but also professional peers – other barristers, solicitors and judges, who see them in action. Given the public nature of advocacy work, even the most senior practitioners feel this pressure:

> You never stop learning as a barrister. You never stop, in my view, you never stop being afraid of getting it wrong.
>
> B18, criminal barrister, 21 years' call

> When you speak to other people about what your job involves as a barrister, they find it very hard to believe that you could put yourself under that kind of pressure. They find it very hard to believe that you would go to court when you are really ill, because you know, that's the culture – that you should, unless you physically can't … I have these mixed feelings … and sometimes I play with the idea of not doing it properly, in my head as a fantasy, but when it comes to the crunch, I can't bring myself to do it. The point is that I became a barrister and I have a particular value system associated with what I think that means. What I think it means as a human being involved in the justice system, that I want to believe in.
>
> B25, circuit criminal barrister, 20 years' call

This attitude and commitment to work is a feature of professional life and identity, dictated by client demands, deadlines and court appearances, but also driven by a professional pride in being well prepared and very good in what they do. Barristers often get instructions just before a hearing, when the case has sometimes not been prepared properly (or at all) by the solicitor and they are used to working under extreme time pressures: 'I'm still very much used to getting briefs that have not been prepared and it's just a luxury when I'm doing something for good solicitors or indeed devilling or being led' (B17, civil practitioner, three years' call). Many feel that solicitors have too many other professional obligations or clients to spend sufficient time on each case. Receiving late instructions, with little time to prepare, is never an excuse not to do the work:

> I had … a burns case a couple of weeks ago that the solicitors held on to till the last minute, thinking it was going to resolve and they sent it out two days beforehand. Four experts to cross-examine. They took fright and decided they weren't going to do it themselves … I worked till 3 am both nights in between, simply because, yes, you've got a client and you need to do a decent job for the client. But the idea of going to court not having read anything and not being prepared, as some solicitors would do now – it's that ethic, it's still there (laughing). You just wouldn't do it.
>
> B32, family practitioner, 13 years' call

Yet this approach or ethos has been critiqued by some as mere ideology, a sort of fictional state of affairs, used by the profession to maintain its privileges, status and restrictive practices (Larson 1977; Abel 1988). No empirical evidence is used to support this stance. Even if it was arguably the case at the time of those critiques, this perspective rings less true in today's market. Work is scarce and many barristers desperately need repeat custom. Doing an excellent job is even more critical to build and maintain a practice.

One argument is that the modernising reform programme, much of which was imposed on the Bar, together with the vocal critics of the Bar have '[p]rovoked a reaffirmation of the old practice and ideals' to counter the 'fat cat' lawyer portrayals emanating from within the MOJ and the media. Sommerlad noted that solicitors become more entrenched in their ideology, whilst researching their reactions to change (1995: 160). However, the views expressed in the previous few extracts are very common and were voiced in similar ways by all those interviewed. Even if it was sometimes more a case of wishful thinking, this ethos remains core to the profession and it is often articulated in the rhetoric of the representative bodies. The challenges of actually maintaining and enacting this culture are less discussed. A perfectionist approach, often coupled with late instructions, can be very stressful, yet work-related stress is traditionally not readily talked about within the profession. Barristers are expected to cope with heavy workloads, much last-minute work and to perform well, without fuss and irrespective of any personal issues. One junior practitioner was struck by the reluctance of practitioners to talk about this openly, supporting Harris' assertion that, with regard to their emotional labour, practitioners are socialised into employing techniques to conceal any anxiety about their role as experts (Harris 2002; Rogers 2011):

> It's quite a stressful case ... I was open with them about how stressed out I'd been about this final hearing. I picked up the papers really late and there was a lot at stake ... and I was quite open about how I was really, really nervous about it ... The local authority's counsel became quite open about having these migraines, experiencing these migraines and relating it to stress and my opponent, she found it really uncomfortable just talking about the anxiety associated with the work and she just felt like 'Even if my boyfriend, who's another barrister, could hear me now'. It was a sign of weakness ... she was very much of the school that we have to not show it ... she found it quite uncomfortable to admit that and she felt very much that she had to preserve this façade and I found that to be quite old school.
>
> B46, family law practitioners, six years' call

In 2015, the Bar Council commissioned its first survey research on the wellbeing of its practitioners, with a sample of 2,456 barristers, 88 per cent of whom were self-employed (Positive 2015). It found that 'Rumination and self-critical perfectionism ... are at notable levels' and that practitioners were under pressure, both self-imposed and external, to strive for 'continual excellence and perfection', which although it could be a positive driver of performance was also 'strongly correlated to psychological ill-health and burnout' (Positive 2015: 3). In 2017 the Bar Council set up its first online website and support system 'Wellbeing at the Bar'. The homepage lists a whole range of work-related problems a barrister might seek support for, including excessive workload, being panicked in court, perfectionism, stress and vicarious trauma, to name but a few. This research found that barristers impose high standards upon themselves, striving for excellence and 'going the extra mile' for the client, even when some of the work is unpaid. For example, all of the criminal barristers said that they undertook work that falls under the solicitors' litigation fee (drafting of affidavits, applications under the Proceeds of Crime Act, hearsay applications and bad character applications) and were therefore not paid for it. They do so in the hope that they will get the brief if the case goes to trial. Many feel resentful about government and press portrayals of 'fat cat' lawyers being overpaid for what is perceived to be an easy job:

> I think that there are people in the Ministry of Justice, and have been people in the Ministry of Justice for a very long time, who think that being a criminal advocate is easy. It's an easy job. 'Oh, what's your problem? You just rock up at 10 o'clock in the morning, you hear a bit of evidence, you ask a few questions, you leave and go home

> at 4.30 pm' … I'm married to a barrister. It is very, very rare that on a Sunday neither of us are working on our cases … I've known my husband to get up at 3 am to work. I've known me to get up at 5 am to work, because it's not just about attending court and asking a few questions.
>
> B18, criminal barrister, 21 years' call

Barristers undoubtedly also aspire to excellence because of the spectre of public humiliation in court if they do a bad job or in some way fail their client. Fear of performing badly is a key driver to work hard: 'I'm in the firing line and I know that the buck does stop with me in terms of being the front man. As soon as you remove that culture, you've f***** it. That is what drives most barristers' (B25, criminal practitioner, 20 years' call). Many criminal practitioners feel that their goodwill has been abused and that the criminal justice system only continues to survive largely because of the amount of unrecognised unpaid work that they do – work which solicitors know they will do and do well in a bid to keep their custom: 'I think everyone does pro bono work all the time (laughing)' (B44, criminal silk, 36 years' call).

## III. Independence and Self-Employment

Independence is perceived to manifest by the very fact of self-employment: 'What I like about the job is being in chambers and the independence' (B32). A few of the interviewees rely on this perception as a reason to resist setting up an ABS:

> I feel quite strongly that the sense that barristers have, that they are sole practitioners with flexi-time … wouldn't lend itself well to a partnership structure in which they could be directed what to do … or any kind of corporate structure, whether there was a company … or some person to whom they were accountable for hours, or something like that.
>
> B36, chancery barrister, 38 years' call

By contrast, a commercial practitioner and former Bar Council officer (B13) felt that the liberalising rules under the LSA 2007 actually gave practitioners even more freedom to determine what structures and ways of operating suit them best, permitting them to adapt without losing control:

> Our aim was to make the Bar much more flexible, modern and accessible and then leave it to the Bar to find their own way. You give them the freedom, you know … all the new rules which have come in in the last four or five years have been liberalising rules, so you give chambers much greater flexibility to find their own way of trading with their own client base. So for some, it can be a Procure Co, or Supply Co … doing slightly related commercial activity, operating in different ways and that way the Bar has flexibility to evolve and grow as the market changes around it.

But, as shown in previous chapters, many are loath to engage with these new entities. Within their current structure, they can, from the beginning of their career, work as individual units, make their own professional decisions and rely on their expertise and experience unfettered by line managers, senior partners and the like. However, the interview responses reveal more contested interpretations of independence and how it manifests in daily professional life. Most conflated independence with self-employment. Some found it to be more complex:

> I think self-employed status and independence aren't quite the same thing … I can conceive of giving up self-employed status without losing the independence that makes the Bar special … I'm paying a percentage of the overheads running the place, if I just go in there and put my feet up and use the stationery … if I'm not pulling my weight, people are entitled to say to me 'Why are you only earning x and not y?' … I think that's a fair question because other people are subsidising me … so my point is that to that extent one's independence as a self-employed person is not total … so the Bar vaunts its independence but when you look at it, it is independent in important ways. It's independent in its thought.
>
> B2, criminal silk, 28 years' call

One interviewee set up an LLP, which is run as a business. Although maintaining barrister status, he gave up court advocacy and now spends his time negotiating, developing strategies, drafting documents and advising clients. Given that his role is akin to that of a solicitor, it was perhaps less surprising that he did not regard self-employed status or independence as necessary attributes to doing a good job:

> We're very much wedded to this, you know, 'You must be independent' and that this is the touchstone to everything and that actually the justice system cannot operate without people in a set of chambers being independent. I'm not actually sure that stands up … I don't think it stands up because you now see solicitors' firms doing it, you know, there are solicitor advocates doing it, they are employed within firms of solicitors … so it works in a different system.
>
> B50, corporate crime barrister, ABS

What about practitioners with 'hybrid' status, who contract their services out to solicitors for a fixed amount of hours per week, whilst still maintaining independent self-employed practice? Only one interviewee works this way. Twice a week, he is a specialist consultant in a large firm of commercial solicitors, mostly in their offices, using their computer systems and under their insurance, for a fixed hourly rate. He is overseen by a partner and attends meetings with clients and conferences where an independent barrister might have been instructed. The firm has immediate access to his services and pays more than his usual hourly rate. This parallel life, of being an independent barrister most of the week and a part-time in-house consultant for two days, provides some financial security and is testament to how flexible the independent Bar has become, allowing for both arrangements. But for those two days, the barrister represents the firm and is overseen and answerable to the partner concerned. Whilst his independence is thus constrained and he is effectively employed, there is no question in his mind that this affects the quality of his work.

The reasoning of both the above barristers is sound. Professional autonomy does not necessarily lead to excellence or ethical behaviour and the loss of it similarly does not automatically result in a lowering of standards (Francis 2005). Yet many believe that the greater the limitations on independence or professional autonomy, the higher the chances that the quality of performance is constrained. The very fact of being employed necessarily impinges on independence, not so much of thought, but on how much time they can allocate to the task in question and how work is prioritised, which in turn is linked to quality and excellence. Some criminal barristers regard going in-house, full-time for solicitors or the CPS as an arrangement that would necessarily lead to a lowering of standards. Their discretion as to when and how they went about their work would be eroded and they would be obliged to undertake too many other duties or focus their attention on getting new work to increase billable hours for the firm. Even if they retained the ability to exercise professional judgement, they would not be free to spend sufficient time to produce good-quality work. One criminal barrister (B31, six years' call) explained:

> I think it would clash with the way that I work and with the effort that I like to put into things … if they are going to the crown court and they've this number of cases and they haven't had the time to prepare them, because they are also in the police station and they are also in the office, then they are not going to have the time to sit with a brief for hours and have a conference … and do everything that they need to. And if I was in that situation, I don't think I could work like that.

Many believe that it is the less successful barristers who go in-house and that solicitors are deliberately employing inexperienced barristers, with a view to cutting costs, not attracting quality:

> In truth there are probably more barristers than there is work and I think that if you are going to go in-house, it will be run like a factory. A good barrister wouldn't go there through choice. And also a lot of these firms come at it from another point of view, 'If I can get a good barrister, who is a young bloke and I can get him for thruppence, I'm not going to pay an experienced bloke a tenner, because I don't need a tenner chap' … The in-house barristers are going to be salaried and they are going to get a set wage and a holiday. Difficult cases – I imagine you're going to get a lot of illness (laughing).
>
> B4, mixed practice, 24 years' call

Employing inexperienced barristers to work as criminal advocates is, it seems, not unusual. As law firms struggle to make legally aided work profitable, their priorities are to make savings wherever possible:

> Firms of solicitors, who have expanded into the Crown Court, are taking people on much, much more cheaply, so they are getting less experienced people in. They are getting people in who aren't as good, who haven't got much of a practice themselves and they are doing advocacy work in the Crown Court. There is a noticeable difference in Crown Court advocacy now and what it was 10 years ago, partly because of that.
>
> B3, criminal practitioner, 33 years' call

Jeffrey's (2014) review of criminal advocacy, the Bar's own research on the Bar's role within criminal justice (Rivlin 2015) and research commissioned by the SRA/BSB (Hunter et al 2018) on judicial perceptions of the quality of criminal advocates support this. They all noted that solicitor advocates and employed barristers have received considerably less training in court advocacy – a mere 22 hours – compared to the 120 days an independent barrister will undergo. They reported that they are also less prepared, less experienced and less focused in their questioning than those at the independent Bar. Many interviewees were appalled that the MOJ's proposals for price competitive tendering (PCT) and the BSB's Quality Assurance Scheme for Advocates (QASA) (both later abandoned) repeatedly referred to 'adequate' representation: 'The difficulty is that the standards are being set both in QASA and in PCT are really low. I mean PCT says that legal aid will be to provide an adequate level of representation. It doesn't say anything about a high quality or excellent one' (B2, criminal silk, 28 years' call). For a member of the Bar, this is anathema and contrary to the professional culture into which she or he has been socialised. Further, legal aid payments to criminal lawyers, in the initial government proposals in 2013, were structured so that there was a direct incentive for lawyers to get their clients to plead guilty in order to promote 'early resolution' of cases. Conceptually, this was very difficult for practitioners to digest, offending the very basis of their ethics and the rule of law:

> Lawyers, who from my experience in criminal courts have always operated with probity when it comes to things like operating within the rules of the profession, would not have been advising the client to plead guilty or not guilty on the basis of their fees … Criminal barristers often do themselves out of money, that's been my experience. But the express intention is to cut fees to the bone, with the express intention of putting financial pressure on lawyers to make defendants plead guilty … it's grotesque!
>
> B8, common law practitioner, 21 years' call

Everyone interviewed felt that the publicly funded Bar was on its last legs, with fewer barristers doing that kind of work and fewer recruits entering those areas. Practitioners are very demoralised, not just because they had fewer cases, but also because they believe standards have and will continue to drop as employed lawyers undertake more of the work. Prognosis was depressing: 'The publicly funded Bar is a dead duck. It's going to be just civil servants basically, with legal qualifications' (B14, commercial barrister, 41 years' call). For many, this marks a loss of quality that will be hard to replace: 'You are going to get counsel and the benchmark is 'adequate' and that's all money driven and it's very sad, as a whole body of excellence is going to dissolve and nobody's going to be able to stay in it' (B4, civil practice, 24 years' call). Even those who do not do criminal work sympathise with those who do, recognising its symbolic importance for the Bar as a whole:

> If you think you're in a job in which you've worked very hard and nobody's going to pay you anything and in fact the work has dried up, even though you are still very able and very experienced and you've got family commitments to meet, you can see why people have mid-life crises and this is what is, what is so tragic … the criminal Bar is the

> throbbing heart of the profession … a criminal justice system is absolutely fundamental to a healthy democracy and it's having the pips squeezed out of it.
>
> B13, head of commercial chambers

Thus, for many barristers, particularly those who have had experience of appearing against employed advocates, the fact of self-employed status, and the independence that comes with it, remains a critical contribution to maintaining high standards. Whilst it would appear that the quality of some criminal advocacy and case preparation done by employed lawyers is poor, the real point is not that they are necessarily less able, but that the structure in which they work requires them to do all manner of other things, leaving advocacy as just one of many skills/requirements of the job. For a barrister, advocacy – and the attendant preparation to do it well – is often their key task.

## IV. Independence and Excellence Constrained

Of course, the notion of independence is to some extent a fiction. Barristers owe a certain allegiance to other members of chambers, by sharing overheads and co-subsidising each other. They have obligations to other members of their practice team in terms of marketing, maintaining work and the group's reputation. They are constrained by court listings, pre-arranged conferences, roundtable meetings, procedural deadlines and so on. Despite this, many maintain that the handling of a case is largely at their discretion, even if it includes consultation or collaboration with a solicitor, and that they have no 'boss' or 'line manager'. They are also free, the rest of the time, to work where, when and how they wish. Whilst this is true on some levels, the extent to which state funding, managerial controls and regulations impinge on their independence is significant and is explored below.

## V. The Loss of State Support

With legally aided work, the reality of independence is nebulous. The autonomy of the 'social service professionalism' of such practitioners was always inevitably precarious, since their survival and prosperity was contingent on state funding. The dramatic cuts to the scope and amount of legal aid now challenge their very existence. The state is able to limit the kinds of cases lawyers can do, the way they work and the time spent on them (Sommerlad 1995; Hanlon 2001). The pay is so low for some practitioners as to degrade their skills, as their labour is not highly valued. Many of the participants' responses are similar to those of doctors who now face increased protocols, less discretion, more supervision and a feeling that their skills are undervalued by the 'modernisation' and reform of the National

Health Service (McDonald et al 2006). Some barristers said that their professional autonomy was compromised by cuts to legal aid:

> The legal aid cuts threaten the independence of the Bar because people, on the money that they're providing, can no longer afford to give a) a quality service and b) they are increasingly forced into the situation with a conflict between their personal financial interest and what would be in the best interests of their client. I think that they [the government] don't understand the psychology of a lot of criminal barristers, which is that we're not in it for the money (laughing). They don't understand that. We need money to live on, yes. That's the bottom line.
>
> B25, criminal barrister, 20 years' call

Such barristers have no corporate loyalty or targets imposed from above. Their work is something of a vocation, yet their remuneration must be sufficient, for if it is not, financial concerns begin to impinge on their approach to work and ability to do it well. Although this stance is regularly derided in the media and by MOJ statements, for many that do legal aid work, their earnings are of secondary importance: 'I think that most barristers who do publicly funded work are more concerned about justice than fees. People who choose to do that work don't go to the Bar for the money. A public service ethos must exist' (C1, Bar Council communications officer). Rogers notes 'something moralistic about the Bar's brand of ethics', which believes in 'giving to society', and she recognises that for some it remains truly meaningful (2012: 215). An experienced family practitioner (B43), specialising in local authority care cases, found that although her judgement was not directly hampered, tighter controls on expenditure might discourage barristers from pursuing the best course of action:

> Sometimes you would need to make an application to the court … but you were not fettered in the way that you are now … it doesn't change how you exercise your professional judgement, because you might still argue that you need to do this. But you know that you've not got a chance in hell of being able to get what you think is necessary in order to best represent … I would still do it [the work], but that's me. But I'm not sure whether everyone would still do it, because another person might look at it and say 'There's no chance, there's no point making this application', whereas I would say, 'I think this is necessary, I think it's worth doing it'.

One criminal practitioner (B25, 20 years' call) felt that the cuts had pushed the criminal justice system to its limits and that the government relied on the professional ethos of practitioners in order for it to survive. For him, the latest cuts to legal aid signalled a catastrophe in terms of quality: 'It's like a machine. You take out all these cogs and you're got the thing that's keeping it going still there. And then you say, "Right, it won't matter, we'll just take out the big cog" and they'll take it out and it's going to fall apart.' In May 2016, the Committee of Public Accounts did indeed declare that the criminal justice system was close to breaking point due to a lack of resources and that the MOJ had 'exhausted the scope to make more cuts without further detriment to performance' (Public Accounts Committee

2016: Summary section). One very experienced barrister found it intolerable to be instructed by the CPS, as it was driven by money, not quality:

> I feel constrained by the CPS, which is why I'm stopping working for them … because they just allocate hours, it's hopeless … the thing I'm doing … they've said 'We'll give you one hour'. I was on to them three days ago saying 'It's a 74 page [*sic*] of close-knit typing and numbers. I need at least 3.5 hours, as does my junior' … The CPS are more about making sure their budgets are OK than winning more cases.
>
> B44, criminal silk, 36 years' call

Moreover, the latest removal of or cuts to legal aid represents a threat not just to barristers' independence, but also to their role in the provision of universal justice and the counterbalance to state power:

> At the risk of appearing paranoid, I think that that represents an ideological desire to limit the ways in which the government can be held to account for its decisions. And I think you have to look at all this business in context of judicial review cuts, use of secret courts, massive increases in court fees … they say that the civil service has been hostile to the concept of an independent Bar for a very long time because it's not something that is readily controlled and quantified and box-tickable, and they want more control over it. They don't like it.
>
> B2, criminal silk, 28 years' call

The above extract represents what many barristers believe the legal aid cuts to judicial review applications mean. No fewer than 90 QCs signed a letter to the *Daily Telegraph* newspaper asserting how such cuts 'will immunise Government and other public authorities from effective legal challenge' (Arden 2013). Barristers feel that being independent of state power is essential to the rule of law and see themselves as necessary players when articulating a challenge to such power. In their view, the cuts display the government's disregard for any overreaching of its power and a disdain and dislike for the lawyers who seek redress on behalf of those who have suffered as a result of it.

## VI. Powerful Clients

What about barristers with privately paying or corporate clients, where budgetary cuts are not an issue? The independent judgement of corporate lawyers in the US has been questioned in research, where lawyers sometimes defer to powerful clients about the nature of the work they do (Heinz and Laumann 1994). Increasingly large corporate or government clients, via their in-house counsel, are instructing the Bar directly rather than going to solicitors first:

> It's now quite common that the first point of contact for a client is the Bar and there will be a discussion as to whether this can be done between the firm and the barrister or a

> barrister team or whether or not a solicitors' firm is brought in and then, quite often, it's counsel who are asked for recommendations which solicitors we'd bring in.
>
> B13, head of commercial chambers

These arrangements are relatively new and most participants did not receive instructions in this way, so it is hard to assess whether increased direct contact with powerful clients will hamper barristers' independence in their decision-making or in the nature of the advice they give. There has been some debate about this in the solicitors' profession. Lawyering in mega law firms for powerful and sophisticated corporate clients has been described as 'commercialised professionalism' (Hanlon 1999: 142), where services are tailored to satisfy the clients. The entrepreneurial tactics, sophisticated marketing and high specialisation within such firms raise questions of lawyers' ability to prioritise ethical behaviour over keeping the client happy and their own commercial gain (Francis 2005). Recent research notes the shift in the balance of power between corporate and financial institutions and their corporate or in-house lawyers, highlighting how some of the latter have an undeveloped or no sense of their independence from the client and how corporate clients seek to increase their control over their lawyers (Coe and Vaughan 2015; Vaughan and Oakley 2016; Moorhead et al 2018). Barristers have to keep clients happy and the more direct contact they have with them, the more direct demands will be made of them. One commercial practitioner noted that some clients often contact him by email directly and want immediate advice, even if he had not yet seen all the documents in a case, obliging him to devise techniques that appear to satisfy the demand without compromising his position:

> You haven't really time ... you've got to give a response ... because they want one and will go somewhere else if you don't ... you get clients, clients start emailing you as well. You guard yourself by saying 'I haven't seen the documents. It's much too early to form any sort of concluded view. There are clearly risks involved in this, although on the face of it looks good'.
>
> B14, commercial barrister, 41 years' call

It has recently become more common for outside companies to fund litigation, including group actions, often in personal injury or large commercial cases. They have a portfolio of litigation on the go at any one time, treating them like other investments. Funders have a purely financial interest in the outcome. They acquire a proportion of the damages awarded and their costs if successful and are liable for some or all of the opposing side's costs if they lose. Accordingly, they monitor the progress of the litigation carefully and require the lawyers to update them regularly as to the merits of the case and quantum estimates, so that they can make accurate risk assessments. In theory, these arrangements should be no different from any other case in terms of counsel's independence. Yet one wonders to what extent and in what ways the continual oversight by an outside, powerful commercial funder, motivated purely by profit, might constrain or influence the decision-making and handling of the case, especially if a lawyer fears a powerful client might take her or his business elsewhere.

## VII. Conditional Fee Agreements

In certain areas of civil practice, the removal of legal aid gave rise to barristers working under 'no win, no fee' conditional fee agreements (CFAs). For the first time, this gave claimant practitioners a direct financial incentive to settle cases, as only then would they guarantee being paid, potentially undermining their independent judgement of how a case should proceed: 'I would prefer, I think, not to do CFA work if the market allowed it … because it makes you less independent, automatically' (B23, specialist civil practitioner). One very senior commercial practitioner (B14) actively refuses this work: 'I avoid such arrangements, as they are too risky. I consider there would be a danger of being more inclined to encourage a client to settle in order to ensure fees get paid.' A more junior civil specialist (B12) agreed: 'I do have concerns about their impact on the independence of counsel.' Despite these reservations, some of those interviewed felt they are able to balance the competing interests in an ethical way:

> I didn't like it and to be honest I still don't like it. I still don't like the fact that you have a financial stake in the outcome of the litigation. Because I think it just gives an extra element of pressure that you shouldn't have to have. Because if you were advising a claimant whether or not to accept an offer from a defendant, you have to try to put out of your mind the fact that if you accept the offer, then you're going to get paid and you're not only going to get paid, you're going to get paid plus your uplift by the defendant … the way I do it is to be completely upfront with the client, the claimant, about it. I say 'I'm giving you this advice but I want you to understand that I am not, because I am required not to do so, taking into account the fact that I'm going to get paid, plus the uplift'.
>
> B15, specialist civil silk, 28 years' call

This conflict of interest has now been reshaped. Under the original CFA agreements, the costs risks for a defendant were hugely increased, as liability potentially included not just the basic costs of the opposing side, but also the winning legal team's 'uplift' or success fees and the costs of the after-the-event (ATE) insurance premium they had taken out to bring the action: 'It was an overloaded burden on the defendants. It made cases impossible to defend in a way that was economically sensible because defendants were paying basically treble the costs liability' (B49, specialist civil silk, 29 years' call). The controversial Jackson reforms of 2013 attempted to rebalance this, abolishing the uplift or success fee and the right to recover insurance premiums. If barristers now want a success fee, they must recover it from their clients' damages under a Damages Based Agreement (DBA) rather than from the losing party. The principle of taking fees out of one's client's award is considered to be highly distasteful and a further erosion of independence: 'You can have costs being provided for out of the award, which is totally American and basically abhorrent' (B5, civil practitioner, 28 years' call). Damages awards have been increased by 10 per cent to partially cover these costs, but lawyers are not permitted to take more than 25 per cent of any award, irrespective of what they are owed. In this new scenario, both clients and lawyers on the winning side of a case stand to lose out – perhaps more so for the lawyers, as most of those interviewed said that they would never take any of their fees out of a client's award in order to maintain a professional distance. There has been a low take-up of DBAs, perhaps because of this, though no research exists on this subject. One experienced specialist civil barrister (B20) commented: 'I do not ask for a success fee and so hope that I will be a little more dispassionate than the solicitors who do. I would find it distasteful to take money from damages.' Some instructing solicitors have told barristers that they will not send them further work if they seek to do so: 'I do a lot of work for a trade union firm. They've said "Well, you're not to take the money from the damages. You're not to take the success fee from damages" … As a matter of principle I wouldn't claim it from the client in any event' (B6, personal injury practitioner, 22 years' call).

## VIII. Managerial Reforms and Independent Regulation

Has the BSB's managerial control over chambers' activity impinged on barristers' traditional, discretionary organisational control and on the way in which practitioners work? To a certain extent, as considered in Chapters 3 and 4, the answer is inevitably yes. Recruitment and pupillage are now heavily regulated by the BSB and there are many more obligations relating to the handling of complaints and chambers' organisation. The regulator has the ability to place chambers deemed 'at risk' under its supervision in order to ensure compliance. Abiding by these rules involves much work and many view it as onerous and expensive, placing great stress on manpower and time: 'I think the BSB have gone crazy, regulatory crazy to be fair' (A8, chambers director). Where appropriate, a number of chambers who participated in this study sub-contract out some of their compliance work. Training courses on management, diversity, equality, pupil supervision and suchlike abound, and barristers and staff have to attend them. Barrister accountability has never been greater, with obligatory customer complaint procedures and independent disciplinary mechanisms in place at the Legal Ombudsman or the BSB itself:

> We only get five or six complaints a year here, I would say. Last year, for example, they were all groundless … Normally, it is found and you know, it's not looking after each other's back, it's normally found that the complaint is groundless. More often than not it's because lay clients don't understand the procedure.
>
> A5, senior clerk, common law circuit set

Many of the interviewees believe that the new regulatory framework has actively contributed to creating a culture of groundless complaints, which take a very long time to process and can be stressful for practitioners. Some perceive that lay clients are motivated by their unwillingness to pay their barristers' fees:

> It's a massive culture of complaint at the moment … you have to show your complaints procedure … you have to write it on every case that comes in, you have to point out to the solicitors that the lay client has the right to complain and 'Here's our complaint regulations' … I have to ensure that our policy is being adhered to and therefore in the initial stages, I would write to whoever the complainant is and say that the policy is x and therefore you will hear back from us in 20 days. Then I would ask the individual member, who the complaint is made against, to give an explanation. The appeal process is to the head of chambers … it was very rare but now you would get one a month … I think there is this culture, external culture where they think that if they complain they can get some money back … and you say to them 'This is nonsense' and they say 'Well I want to appeal that' and the head of chambers says 'This is nonsense, and by the way if you want to, you have to go up to the Legal Ombudsman who will confirm it's nonsense'. And they go up to the Legal Ombudsman, he confirms it's nonsense, but in the meantime you've been back, forward, back, forward … you create a system that can literally go on for months and months and months and months.
>
> A8, chambers director, multi-practice set

There is a feeling that this culture of complaint is exacerbated by the fact that the independent regulator seems unable to distinguish between patently false and genuine claims. Some barristers asserted that they have to constantly 'watch their backs' for fear of unwarranted complaints and that compliance with all the red tape involved in the complaints procedure is stressful, expensive and mostly unnecessary:

> I was on the conduct committee … people actually complain about you being nasty to them by saying nasty things about them in a case … and it's a way of trying to put pressure, bullying people to back off, making their lawyers nervous. Solicitors are getting it all the time … I fear that the culture is wrong and I think that's the culture 'Oh it's a complaint, we've got to take it seriously'. I mean it takes hours and hours to do reports on these things. You've got to go through a completely shambolic wodge of stuff and try and make some sense of it, so I think that there's the wrong – 'Oh, it's a complaint, we've got to take it seriously, we've got to deal with it, we've got to go through all the motions' … If they lose a case and you are pushing them for fees and things like that, they complain. 'Oh we don't like that, we don't think counsel cross examined for long enough', things like that … It's all got too serious and too much red tape.
>
> B14, commercial barrister, 41 years' call

Views about the BSB were mostly either negative or neutral. Many had little to do with it, though most read the regulator's emails or relied on chambers staff to do so and then report on updates on any particular matter. A few of the participants thought that the BSB did a good job and that the profession was better regulated and more accountable under its auspices. Some had fairly negative views about it because they perceived the regulator to be actively hostile to the profession or to have no real interest in or understanding of it:

> I don't think they are a particular friend of the Bar.
>
> Q: why should they be, if they are your independent regulator?
>
> I don't think they should be hostile.
>
> B43, family practitioner, 27 years' call

> It's not terribly supportive of the Bar. I don't know why.
>
> B44, Head of chambers, multi-practice set

> I think there is a feeling that it's not very efficient and not very friendly.
>
> B49, specialist civil silk, 29 years' call

> I don't think that they have got any interest whatsoever in the Bar. They say they are promoting the Bar. I mean frankly X [officer of the BSB] took a lifetime to actually say anything in favour of the Bar … they ought to be understanding of what a barrister does and how they are … I don't understand at all the way in which they think they are doing a good job. I mean it's all very well regulating something, but if you're actually regulating out of existence, you don't understand what does and doesn't make a barrister a good barrister or what is or is not a disciplinary offence.
>
> B37, criminal silk, 30 years' call

Many complained about the amount the BSB cost and how their annual subscription for practicing certificates increased after its creation. The notion of having to pay for a licence to practise a profession in which one is already qualified rankles:

> It costs me £1,500 as a silk, to buy my piece of paper which tells me I'm allowed to practice law, which is a bit mad. That goes into the Bar Council coffers and pays for the BSB … I mean if you want a career in the law, the secure place to do it is in the Regulator.
>
> B2, criminal silk, 28 years' call

A few were extremely hostile, a sentiment that was palpable at a BSB event at the Bar Conference 2013, when feelings were especially high around the time of the intention to introduce QASA (subsequently abandoned):

> Regulators make their money by regulating and so it's a self-perpetuating autocracy. The Bar Standards Board has no reason to exist other than to regulate (laughing) … the Bar Standard Board, whatever its genesis, it has become a monster of its own creation … it is just another one of the trends in all kinds of service industry … public accountability, to have quality marks, you know, you've got them for plumbers and gas fitters and everything else, so why shouldn't there be one for lawyers as well? We don't have a problem with having a quality assurance scheme as long as it does what it says on the tin … I'm paying £1,000 a year to have people tell me how to do the job I know how to do … to pay for all the f***ing bureaucrats and technocrats to administer stuff like QASA.
>
> B35, criminal barrister, 28 years' call

It is hard to assign one reason for this widespread antipathy to the regulator. Whilst all were clear that they had no issue with quality control checks in principle, many felt that the BSB's proposed QASA scheme was badly thought out, would be onerous and expensive to implement, and contained elements that were misguided. All acknowledged that more accountability was no bad thing, but many did not rate the quality of the regulation they were getting and resented the cost of it. The period of research covered a turbulent time for the Bar. Publicly funded practitioners felt beleaguered and under attack from the government and parts of the media, and many expressed discontent that the profession's own regulator was hostile at such a time. No one suggested that their disgruntlement with the BSB was because they resented external regulation per se. Most barristers were not particularly complimentary about the Bar Council either. Underlying their responses was the impression that they just wanted to be left to get on with their work and regarded the ever-increasing rules, interference, protocols and procedures as time-wasting, largely unnecessary, expensive and often imposed by an outside body that either did not understand the profession or did not care for it.

## IX. Civil Procedure and Costs Rules

The civil procedure, costs forecasting and case management rules introduced from the late 1990s onwards have asserted a control over and supervision of case progression that is radically new. For example, under the Jackson reforms in 2013, costs of civil litigation are no longer recoverable if they are reasonably incurred, but must be proportionate to the matters and money involved in the case and the financial position of each party. A costs budget must be submitted and the court will make a costs management order to control a party's budget in respect of what might be recoverable. This is but one of the many managerial controls that have been imposed on lawyers when conducting civil litigation. Some of those interviewed feel that these controls are excessive or unnecessary, time-wasting and expensive, and that the regime imposes extra work on them in the name of efficiency, yet interferes with how they would handle cases and the course of justice itself:

> There's a chancery modernisation review at the moment. I hate the word 'modernisation'. Some of the things they are doing are good, for example having docketed judges managing a case from an earlier stage. I think that's a good development, but they're now having pilot tests for fixed-term trials, so the trial has to have a fixed period and can't overrun whatever happens … The barristers mustn't give an inaccurate reading estimate for the judge, which is very difficult sometimes, and they mustn't inaccurately estimate the time, although sometimes things change. If a barrister gives an inaccurate estimate and the time taken is longer, the judge will now reduce the amount available to the parties or that particular party at the trial. There are all these silly things … these are actually proposals, pilot tested at this stage. It's rather like the new sanctions rule. Instead of the old rule whereby you couldn't cut out evidence in practice, but nowadays the courts will be ruthless and say 'The new rule is if you're late with such and such, it's out, you're not allowed it'. I mean that's, it's bad law, it's bad justice, it's bad for the reputation of the courts … it's all silly and I think they're really at risk of throwing the baby out with the bathwater,

> which is the great reputation that London still has as a legal centre, is being prejudiced by rather petty minded bureaucrats.
>
> B36, chancery practitioner, 38 years' call

Others felt that the case management systems do not address the real issues and that the courts are simply unable to cope, often because there are not enough judges: 'The Commercial Court is very full of itself about case management and how efficient it is and how cases only run when they're meant to, but they can't always provide judges.' The same commercial and chancery practitioner (B48, 29 years' call) felt that the Chancery Division was too big and 'swamped' with work: 'It dwarves the Commercial Court, because it's got all this other business … and that's the problem. It's a very broad church.' In different fields, barristers have to satisfy different managerial requirements, but many find that compliance is so time-consuming as to be time-wasting:

> We have all these new ways that we have to do things, the PLO [Public Law Outline] in family proceedings, stupid orders, and they are a complete nightmare, all these hoops that you have to go through, they are a nightmare … It's supposed to make things more efficient and I'll tell you what happens, you look at them and you think 'None of this is relevant' and you miss things that are relevant because you have to go through reams, pages of nonsense, of these new orders and everything that you have to do at each hearing and are not allowed to have the number of hearings that you might need. So you're only supposed to have your initial hearing, your CMC hearing, your IRH and your final hearing and sometimes you need more … you have a 15-page order and you have to tick all these boxes.
>
> B43, family practitioner, 27 years' call

For practitioners who think that they are already underpaid, this additional work is deeply resented, burdensome and constraining. They feel that those in charge have embarked on a seemingly endless managerial tinkering in a bid to make civil litigation cheaper, faster and more efficient, without necessarily achieving any of these things.

## X. Public Service and Pro Bono

Some of the extracts above reveal that certain barristers feel that they are not paid enough or at all for the work they do and consequently have neither the time nor the financial security to work pro bono. Most publicly (under)funded lawyers consider all their work to be in service of the public. Nonetheless, the Bar has a tradition of pro bono work. The Free Representation Unit (FRU) was set up in 1972 to provide legal representation for those appearing in social security and employment tribunals, who could not afford lawyers. Students and young practitioners, in the main, volunteered their services and continue to do so. In 1996, the Bar Pro Bono Unit was established by a barrister and now shares premises alongside the FRU and has in excess of 2,000 barristers on its books (including 250 silks). Many practitioners, especially in their early years of practice, do some pro bono work every year. The Chancery Bar Association and the Commercial Bar Association (COMBAR) also offer specialist pro bono services, in association with the Bar Pro Bono Unit. Some chambers have a stronger ethos of doing pro bono work than others and expect their members to undertake some:

> People do a lot of pro bono work … I think our chambers has always done a lot of pro bono work and traditionally it was a lot of death row work in Jamaica and the West Indies, lots of it. Now, there is a huge amount of work from the Pro Bono unit with juniors. People are expected to do it, but not everyone does it … it is part of the culture of my set, so people do a lot of pro bono work.
>
> B43, multi-disciplinary set

Other sets leave the decision of whether or not to do pro bono work to their members: 'There's not chambers policy about pro bono that I'm aware of. I think it's left entirely to those who feel that they want to do it and there are at least three or four members of chambers who I know regularly do pro bono work' (B15, mixed civil set). Demands for pro bono representation are ever-increasing as the scope of legal aid funding has narrowed. However, commitment to pro bono work varies hugely across the Bar. Not all are willing to do this work, either because they cannot afford to work for free or because they are too busy on paid cases:

> Although I've done some pro bono work in the past myself, I haven't done it for a long while, because frankly I find it difficult to afford it really at the moment as times have been harder. I encourage youngsters to do it, to get into court, but they just don't seem to have the time or inclination and the person who runs [specialist pro bono unit] is quite disappointed that our chambers haven't responded.
>
> B36, chancery set

In addition, certain chambers have charitable foundations or 'cause funds', whereby the administration automatically takes a small percentage of every practitioners' earnings, which they then distribute: 'one per cent … it's quite a lot now, well there's a lot more tenants … about £100,000 … there were certain groups that we have historically always, you know, supported … and then people make applications to us for either one-off grants or for funding' (B46, multi-disciplinary set). Others leave it to individuals to contribute what they wish or hold discrete fund-raising events. A few sets have done this for many years and have close alliances with certain charities or are open to bids for funding from others.

## XI. Discussion

A narrative of exceptionality runs through the cultural representation that the Bar collectively and its members individually project, with an oft-repeated assertion, that the combination of independence, excellence and commitment is what distinguishes them from other employed lawyers and the service they provide. In their view, it is precisely because they are self-employed and autonomous that they can provide specialist, high-quality advocacy and advisory services. Despite the incursions of managerial practices and regulatory demands, barristers feel that it is the relative freedom from corporate hierarchy, investors, target setting, cost meeting and business generating that allows them to spend the necessary time on cases to produce that quality. The fierce determination to preserve the independent Bar, to fight for legal aid to support sections of it and to prevent even more work being done by employed lawyers is motivated by the widely and strongly held belief that self-employed barristers are better and more committed specialist advocates than other lawyers.

Although independence remains a core feature of Bar ideology and culture, one wonders whether practitioners are able to admit that the cumulative effect of these recent incursions on their freedom has somewhat altered their working reality and, in turn, their professional identity and culture. The managerial reforms in the court system and of the regulator, together with legal aid cuts and CFA/DBA work, have begun to impinge on some aspects of professional autonomy. Although all would assert that their independence of thought remains unfettered, one cannot ignore the gradual erosion of discretion and control that practitioners have over the way they run their chambers and their cases. Some seemed palpably worn down by these developments, weary and nostalgic for earlier times, exhibiting reactions to the profession's modernisation, as other professionals have done in different sectors (McDonald et al 2006; Watt et al 2008). A number reminisced about how much more fun they used to have in chambers, how the camaraderie was greater and how drinks after work were more common. A few commented that there were no longer any larger-than-life 'characters' at the Bar, as practitioners were endlessly monitored or bogged down by managerial compliance. A recent survey of employed and self-employed barristers found that those in employment 'noted the lack of autonomy and reduced sense of status relative to those in the self-employed Bar' as being particular challenges. Both status and autonomy – a perceived sense of control – are correlated to psychological health and performance. Barristers still feel they have independence, even if perhaps they do not to the degree they once did, yet there has been a shift in control at the Bar. Self-employed barristers may retain more autonomy than employed ones, but the same study found that over half the sample of those at the independent Bar reported disengagement with their professional performance: 'The results are notable and a cause for concern' (Positive 2015: 3).

Commitment and excellence remain very real ideals for barristers, ideals that are ingrained via intense socialisation during their training period and thereafter within chambers. They know what is expected of them: to be well prepared, work however many hours are needed to do the job well, be good advocates in court and do the best they can for their client. Many feel that some solicitors often do not have time to commit in this way and are swayed by other considerations: 'That's what's going to happen once barristers all start going in-house … It's going to be much more about, it's not about the client, it's about "I've got to pay the office space,

I've got to pay the secretaries, we've got to pay that'" (A3, senior clerk, common law set). In the sphere of legally aided work, the majority of barristers are not prepared to accept that the current system is no longer affordable, as asserted by the state, and believe that the cuts are ideological. The persistent portrayals by the MOJ and some of the media of a profession driven by financial rewards is, in their minds, at best a failure to understand what drives and motivates them, what they care about and why they work the way they do. At worst, it is propaganda intended to disguise a neoliberal ideology that wishes to withdraw state funding for certain sections of society or those accused of crimes, irrespective of the quality and independence of representation. Many observed that the government has no issue with the commercial sector of the Bar that earns large amounts of money, contributing significantly to the state's coffers, evidenced by the three-day Global Law Summit in February 2015, during which Chris Grayling, the then Lord Chancellor, trumpeted the success of that part of the legal sector.

These interviewees may well be right, when asserting that they provide an excellent, top-quality advocacy and advisory service because of the way they have been trained and socialised. But, irrespective of whether this is true or not, many are reluctant to acknowledge and accept that, in the publicly funded sector, quality is no longer valued or deemed necessary, largely because their services are seen as too expensive. The state is not prepared to pay for such litigation and wishes to reduce the amount of it by redirecting its financial support to early dispute resolution, preferably without lawyers (MOJ 2019c). The state's stance is both ideological and pragmatic. It may be that a body of excellence and expertise will be lost in this process, but litigation has become a business and the focus is less on excellence and more on value for money. This, of course, is totally at odds with the very core of ideal-type professionalism and the Bar's own ideology and culture. It is also a state of affairs that is profoundly depressing for many practitioners, not simply because of the financial loss they have suffered and will continue to suffer, but also because they think it will result in a reduction in the quality of service and in access to justice.

Barristers have faced serious challenges in the last three decades. This once uncontested elite group has been compelled to become more modern and efficient, more commercial and competitive, more accountable and transparent, and more inclusive, all of which have encroached on their daily freedoms and created additional burdens, as the previous chapters has shown. How do these new aspects of professionalism sit in relation to their traditional self-identity? Many of the attributes now required of barristers are antithetical to their culture and traditions, which, until 30 years ago, encouraged the polar opposite approach and which remain deeply ingrained in the older generation of practitioners. The overt commercial approach, the intense competition, the marketing and managerial, administrative requirements have undoubtedly obliged them to behave differently. This chapter has highlighted some of the challenges barristers face in maintaining their core values and illustrates some of the multiple erosions, which manifest in a multitude of scenarios across the whole profession. Despite this, much of the

Bar's ideology remains intact, even if it is not or cannot fully be realised in reality. To what degree these ideals and shared values will continue depends on many things. For example, will new entrants continue to be trained and socialised into the profession as effectively, as numbers grow and people move about more? Will more practitioners change the structures within which they work and how will they, or those in hybrid practice, react to organisational control? Will powerful clients or outside funders be able to impose their will or influence practitioners? Will those in privately paying practice areas pay attention to and be involved with those who work for publicly funded areas, without splintering off into entirely self-contained sub-occupational groups with only their own interests in mind? The following and final empirical chapter considers this last point and explores to what degree practitioners think there is still one unified profession and a true Bar community.

# 8

# Community, Unity and Fragmentation

> One of your questions is 'is the Bar unified?' It's obviously not … it's a complete fiction.
>
> B49, specialist civil silk

> I think that the 'One Bar' ethos is very strong across the profession. Since being involved with the CBA and hanging out with the Bar leadership, I have been impressed by the strength of this.
>
> B2, criminal silk

The culture or ideology of the Bar was traditionally communicated and absorbed by members of the profession not just in the early years of training and practice, but throughout their careers, as practitioners spent large amounts of time grouped together in chambers, within the Inns and/or circuit community. Unlike the solicitor profession, which is much larger and more geographically spread out, the independent Bar is relatively small and, in London, mostly located within the Inns of Court. The previous chapter examined how core values are being challenged and undermined across different practice areas. The specific effects on practitioners depend on what kind of work they do and from this alone, one can see how the professional experience is not universal. This chapter considers if and how the reforms and developments over the last 30 years have affected the cohesion of the Bar community and whether, even if there is a shared professional outlook, the profession can really be perceived as unified in the light of increased specialisation and stratification. If, as some think, the Bar is fragmented, how will this impact on the continuance, reproduction and policing of shared professional norms and culture? Moreover, how can older practitioners, shaped and socialised in a very different working environment, pass on traditional culture and professional norms to new recruits who are operating in a radically different professional landscape? Is there still the opportunity for informal mutual support within chambers? Are all of the professional norms still relevant or valid?

Legal culture incorporates ethics and codes of conduct, but these are neither uniform across different branches of law nor necessarily across nation states, common law jurisdictions or continental models, though certain aspects of it can be or are imagined to be (Heinz and Laumann 1994; Newman 1995; Weeks 2004; Kurkchiyan 2005; Chambliss 2010; Boon 2014). Francis (2005) considered the potential impact of fragmentation among solicitors, noting that there was a large variety in workplaces and structures, giving rise to different, context-specific ethical choices. Is it really possible to say that there is one set of ethical norms across such a wide range of professional experiences? He further questioned how one overarching regulator could impose a set of uniform rules on a profession that was increasingly stratified and less of a collective. This chapter asks the same questions in relation to the Bar, first identifying the traditional sites of socialisation and then considering issues of unity and fragmentation.

## I. The Inns of Court and Circuits

'Traditional community' was a feature Rogers (2012) noticed that the profession used when selling itself to prospective members and it encompasses both the physical and psycho-social. The Inns of Courts' 'elegant, historical spaces', with their 'chapels, libraries, coats of arms and dining halls attest to, and reiterate, their historical connection to the Crown', giving barristers a sense of their profession's history, forming part of its central narratives and 'constitute crucial dimensions to modern self-identity, contributing to the sustenance of ontological security' (Rogers 2012: 213). The physical space and history of the Inns can play a role in identity formation:

> It's cultural too and even the younger barristers can be … very influenced by the very senior members, who have been doing it in the same way for a long time. Often, I've found that they are the ones that are most seduced by their desk, in a particular part of chambers, overlooking a particular view – that's part of the package, absolutely. It's the tradition … These people don't come in to change things. They come in because they've been brought up with the idea of a barrister.
>
> A7, Bar marketing consultant

Much professional socialisation and education took place within the Inns, and at the peak of their influence from the Tudor period until the late seventeenth century, all trainee barristers would eat, live and study there, attending regular moots, debates and readings, as outlined in Chapter 2 (Warren 1978). The communal ritual of dining was designed to prepare incoming barristers for life at the Bar and acclimatise them to the practices and norms of the profession (Boon 2014). On circuit, the community was tight-knit and its leaders would ensure that members behaved in accordance with the profession's customs and circuit rules.

A significant number of those interviewed, especially those who worked in the provinces, felt that the circuits played a lesser role than they used to and they had little to do with their local Bar community: 'Circuits are far less important than they were 20 years ago because they've lost a lot of their influence and power' (B13). A young criminal practitioner (B31) did some training with her circuit Bar, but had no other contact: 'I'm not really sure what they do other than that.' It is difficult to know the true extent of circuit influence, given the small sample of the study. By contrast, all participants thought that the Inns have made something of a revival in their pedagogic role. A number of older barristers were fairly cynical as to why. One remarked: 'They suddenly thought they might be abolished, so that's why. So they are now making themselves proactive … the advocacy stuff is very good' (B44, criminal silk, 36 years' call). The Inns and the circuits, now run all manner of CPD and new practitioner qualifying courses, including advocacy and ethics training and forensic accounting. The Inns provide a significant amount of scholarships for the BPTC, some offering accommodation to students and funding for the qualifying sessions. Dining has now become just one of the 12 activities that constitute these obligatory qualifying sessions that a student must do before call (Boon 2014). Whether it is dining, training workshops or talks, the intention is that new recruits will have an opportunity to meet older practitioners or judges and learn about the customs and traditions of the Bar: 'For example, they will have a mooting evening and that will count as one qualifying session … I probably got the most out of those qualifying sessions just by mingling really' (B17, civil practitioner, three years' call). Students come into contact with senior members of the profession before they have any real experience or knowledge of the Bar:

> You could sit on the Bar table with the judges if you'd taken part in things, so that was a great opportunity to have a chat with barristers, some of them quite senior, and some judges … I think it was more of a socialisation process … finding out what it's like, dealing with the eccentricities of senior barristers.
>
> B21, civil practitioner, three years' call

Opportunities come their way as a result of these events: 'There were a number of occasions where I was able to chat to people that I can't imagine ever having had the opportunity to chat to. I was offered a marshalling at dining by [name of judge], which was really cool' (B16, civil practitioner, 18 months' call). Whilst students and new entrants are necessarily involved in their Inn, many practitioners subsequently have little to do with them, occasionally lunching there or using the library, but nothing more. A couple of younger barristers, recipients of Inn scholarships during training, expressed regret that they no longer have the time to be involved.

However, a few of the interviewees were very engaged, using the Inns for networking and professional advancement:

> I've always been very heavily involved with my Inn … once you're on a committee … you find yourself going to other Inn events … As to what I get out of it … The more cynical motives are I think it really helps a great deal for people to see your name about and being on committees … there are quite a lot of fringe benefits. You get asked back to the private dinners with incredibly prestigious speakers and whatever, the usual benefits of committee membership, that sort of thing. And just more generally, I really enjoy meeting people from other chambers because it's very easy to think that your chambers is the only way things could possibly be done, but it isn't. It's one of the reasons why I'm a bit more alive, because I know so many people who do, say, criminal law through Middle, it's one of the reasons I am alive to all this legal aid stuff, which most of chambers are fairly oblivious about.
>
> B12, civil practitioner, four years' call

For more experienced practitioners, involvement with their Inn can be a stepping-stone to becoming a bencher, for some a prestigious position and good for their CV if they hope to become a judge: 'If you want to become a bencher, you've got to get yourself involved in advocacy', commented one criminal silk (B44). Another specialist civil mused that he would need to engage more: 'I ought to become a bencher and I've been very lazy about that. If I become a bencher I will have to do something. I'll probably do something' (B49). Yet, for many practitioners, the Inns remain a mere geographical space in which they work and perhaps take lunch. The libraries are used far less now that reports, textbooks, journals and practitioner handbooks can be found online. The current redevelopment of the Inner Temple Library, with more corporate use in mind and reduced reading spaces and desks, is evidence of this (Ames 2015).

There are obvious limitations to the notion of a united community within the four Inns. Many sets of chambers are now outside their parameters and many are outside London. The North Eastern circuit, for example, boasts 27 chambers plus two London annexes. The Northern circuit lists over 1,000 practitioners working there. The relatively new phenomenon of multi-centre sets means there are multiple barristers moving between circuits and London. Further, there are 595 sole practitioners.[1]

Not all are attracted to working in the traditional environment. One found it liberating to be outside the Inns: 'People like it. I mean I love it, because you don't have to worry about being seen by Mr Justice Bloggins, wearing your jeans or anything like that and the area is fantastic. It's by St Paul's, full of restaurants' (B44, head of multi-practice set). For some circuit practitioners, the Inns hold very little appeal. Whilst eating her qualifying dinners, one barrister felt very alienated and had no sense of shared experience:

> I used to hop on the train, run into Lincoln's Inn, eat the dinner, sign the form, jump back on the train and go to bed (laughing) … I found it very London-centric … I mean Lincoln's Inn isn't something I'm particularly interested in. I remember having to meet, what is it, you have to have an interview to show that you are a person of integrity and the judge that I spoke to … when I said I was from X, was so surprised, 'Oh do they have chambers in X?' I told him there were two and he was very surprised (laughing). So, it wasn't his fault, but I felt like I was an alien when I was there.
>
> B31, circuit practitioner, six years' call

Another London-based barrister found the experience of dining at one of the Inns to be culturally narrow and exclusive:

> My experience was I just ploughed through the dinners with friends from the BVC [Bar Vocational Course] but my most memorable experience was when my parents came and we were sat next to a judge and my Dad is very humble, but very well educated at the same time (laughing), and I think this judge was just so culturally insensitive.

[1] See https://www.barstandardsboard.org.uk/news-publications/research-and-statistics/statistics-about-the-bar/practising-barristers.html.

> But the good thing was my father really put him in his place and showed his knowledge of some African knowledge or the like and the judge was very humbled by it in the end … and my Dad was thinking, how did you manage your 12 dinners?
>
> B45, family practitioner, seven years' call

Nonetheless, a new entrant coming into the profession 25 years ago could have had almost no dealings with her or his Inn save for dining there. The extensive educational programmes and training now on offer, together with significant bursaries and an access scheme (Freer 2018), make their contribution to a new entrant's professional socialisation not insignificant.

## II. Specialist Bar Associations

The specialist Bar associations have, over the last 20 years, become more numerous and influential. These associations have an educational function and each barrister interviewed was a member of at least one, and often more, if only to attend events and get CPD points. Some are signed up with broader specialist associations, servicing the whole legal profession. These are seen as a good way of keeping up to date on developments in any particular area, networking and marketing. Many associations invite junior representation on their committees, broadening the range of voices, and all are represented on the Bar Council. They also have a wider function when consulted by the Bar Council or government bodies, to represent their members on issues directly affecting their practice area or those concerning the profession as a whole. However, their role goes beyond representation, as specialist associations play an important part in supporting and approving professional development. As mentioned in Chapter 3, if a new area of specialism arises, a group of practitioners might lobby the Bar Directories to recognise it, whilst setting up an association to legitimise it further.

The CBA has become fairly militant in the face of endless cuts to legal aid funding and has taken on a more trade union style of leadership and representation. It mobilised large numbers of the profession to go on strike and to implement a 'no returns' policy, in protest at the legal aid reforms: 'Those are areas that are largely funded by the state and they are under massive, and one might feel rather unfair pressure, so they've got a really strong reason to get down to their Bar association and start demonstrating' (B28, specialist Bar association chair). This politicisation of barristers and their professional associations is indicative of just how threatened parts of the profession feel by the legal aid cuts and how such a threat can inspire ideological entrenchment and unity:

> The Bar is a conservative profession … but people have become more radical in the last two years, because they have suffered constant pay cuts and finally the penny is dropping that there's no negotiating with the Lord Chancellor. He is an ideologue. He is a result merchant politician.
>
> B35, criminal circuit practitioner, 28 years' call

In the face of government challenge, significant groups within the profession have collaborated to present a strong and united voice of resistance: 'I think in the past couple of years, I think that the CBA have been very assertive ... I think that the publicity has helped ... It might manipulate things, one way or the other, a little' (B18, criminal practitioner, 21 years' call).

These associations support and benefit the wider Bar community in other ways. For example, the CBA sought and received support and funding from other Bar associations to fund judicial review proceedings relating to legality of the QASA proposals. COMBAR has also worked to benefit the whole of the civil Bar:

> COMBAR has had a negotiation with the City of London Law Society, and produced standard terms and that was a very important piece of work, which everyone else has used ... they've actually drafted some terms and they've persuaded the City solicitors to use them and so everybody else is leapfrogging on that and using those terms. So that's an area that they've actually in some ways been more useful than the Bar Council itself, because the Bar Council's terms were too pro barrister so the solicitors refused to use them, but the Combar have managed to get a compromise that it seems solicitors are prepared to use. So that's an example of bringing something of real benefit, not just to their own members.
>
> B28, specialist civil silk, Bar association chair

Many of the barristers interviewed had nothing or little directly to do with the overarching representative body, the Bar Council, and many had either no view or thought that it was ineffectual, pointless and lacked good leadership. Yet almost all were members of at least one specialist Bar association, bringing them into contact with practitioners in similar practice, to collaborate on issues of continuing education, representation and protest.

## III. Chambers

The collegiality of chambers life was touched on in Chapter 3 and is considered in more detail here, as chambers is perhaps the most significant site of professional socialisation. Unlike Northern Ireland and Scotland, where there is no chambers system, most practitioners in England and Wales are part of a set (Morison and Leith 1992). A new entrant will spend a year in pupillage in chambers, attached to a number of supervisors who are tasked with training them. The regulator prescribes many aspects of this apprenticeship year, yet much of what the pupils observe and experience is less easily classified, but no less influential in terms of professional identity formation. The guidance offered by supervisors will go well beyond satisfying the BSB's requirements, which are viewed by some as a mere box-ticking exercise. Many supervisors develop lasting relationships with their pupils: 'A nicer man you couldn't have met and welcoming and he invited me to his home for supper with his family and made a point of making sure I knew, if I ever needed help, he was always there for me. It was incredible' (B33, criminal circuit practitioner, six years' call). In this environment, pupils will absorb what they see as normal standards of behaviour, learn what is expected of them, how to present themselves and behave in chambers, to solicitors, clients and in court (Harris 2002; Rogers 2011). It is in chambers that the subtleties and complex interaction related to getting and keeping work takes place (Morison and Leith 1992). It is in chambers that pupils see the mix of confidence and anxiety of practitioners as they navigate their professional lives (Rogers 2011). It is also within (and across) chambers that professional and social friendships are formed, tales recounted, matters complained about and legal analysis debated. For a newcomer, this camaraderie can be very supportive: 'It is very personable and I feel very at home here, very at ease and even as a pupil, I felt as much at ease as you can as a pupil' (B17, civil practitioner, three years' call).

The Bar commissioned research on wellbeing in the profession, which found that: 'The deepest level of support within the self-employed Bar is reported as coming from others within chambers … Often individuals form close bonds when they share adverse or challenging situations or events – the challenge and emotions associated becoming the relationship glue' (Positive 2015: 3). In spite or because of growing numbers in sets, efforts are made to maintain a sense of community: 'There is still sort of a collegiate atmosphere. We still have chambers' tea every day' (B15, specialist civil silk, 28 years' call). Mentoring schemes now exist in chambers to tackle the problem of newcomers getting lost amongst the large membership. It is deemed important for new members to get to know and seek guidance from older ones:

> We've created mentoring systems in chambers, so they've always got people to talk to higher up … all the youngsters have a mentor, someone who's maybe two – one, two, three years above them and then senior members of chambers are told – there are some people you wouldn't send youngsters to because they would just depress them – but senior members of chambers are expected to make themselves available and it works. You start them off with mentoring and a collegiate atmosphere and they gradually, they know the people they go to see. And it works.
>
> B13, head of commercial chambers

In fact, unofficial mentoring has always existed at the Bar and it continues to be common practice for barristers to go into each other's rooms and discuss legal or procedural points, exchange ideas or ask for help from their colleagues. This is not something they perceive to be as common in solicitors' firms, so is yet another example of how barristers view their particular organisational set-up to be different (and better):

> I think it's extraordinary given the fact that these are all self-employed people, who've got incredibly busy practices and if you talk to solicitors and junior solicitors and they say 'Oh the difficulty is I never know, I can never discuss anything with anyone and I really worry about my work' and you think 'Well that's ridiculous, you're presumably in

a team, in a firm, where everyone is PAYE, so surely it's in everyone's interest to assist you', when here I think it's remarkable the time that people are prepared to give up and without any sort of sense of 'Ugggh (sigh) not you again'.

B21, civil practitioner, three years' call

However, not all are convinced that the atmosphere is really that cosy and take a more pragmatic view of barristers' self-employed status within chambers:

They are competing against each other. Even within the teams you are competing against each other. Some people are actually against each other on a day-to-day basis in court, aren't they? But that's why 'teams' is the wrong word I think, 'practice groups' is probably a better phrase, because you're not working as a team really … I think most people at the Bar are selfish. They only see themselves in terms of their own practice. They want what's best for them. They can say one thing in a meeting and then be completely different in the way they behave, in using resources and what they want to be done.

B41, family practitioner, mixed set, 30 years' call

The profession, its structure and practitioners' self-employed status necessarily make barristers individualistic and competitive, and a number of interviewees were prepared to discuss this aspect more frankly. Some have had bad experiences within chambers, where there was no sense of fellowship when it was put to the test, belying the veneer of collegiality. One barrister recounted how his chambers dissolved and his 'team' found another set to join as a group of specialists. The receiving chambers would only agree on the condition that they did not bring along their junior members, as it would bring too much competition for their own juniors. His team had no issue with leaving them in the lurch:

Eventually the team found a 'buyer' in X chambers, but they didn't want anyone young, they didn't want any of the bottom three or four of us, which included me, because we were too junior, you see. The head of chambers said we had a long tail, 'We don't want lots of juniors'. That's the most anti-competitive element, because I was then in a position of having to be in sheltered practice, because you have to spend the first three years, post pupillage, you have to be in a practice with more senior members, so I had to find somewhere or I wouldn't be able to practise as a barrister.

B9, sole practitioner, eight years' call

Obviously, some sets have a friendlier atmosphere than others, but the chambers ideal of community and support is not always reflected in reality:

In a lot of barristers' chambers you have egomaniacs all trying to run the show and fighting and all that. We were, here, very fortunate. We had these people who … wanted chambers to work quietly, efficiently, be a nurturing place and not be a place where they acted out their own egotistical fantasies, which you do find, I think.

B36, chancery practitioner, 38 years' call

Research into wellbeing at the Bar (Positive 2015) found that chambers remain the most significant site for professional community, identity formation and socialisation. Many barristers will have spent a year as a pupil in the set they end up joining, will spend some time working there (even if they might not have a designated desk), might sit on one of the committees and participate to some extent in the running of chambers, will attend the annual meeting, chambers parties and be part of the marketing seminars. Many will be pupil supervisors and all will be a member of at least one practice group. So a set of chambers remains, in its modernised form, a critical site for the formation of collegial relations and the absorption of Bar culture. However, a number of interviewees commented that the growing trend to work from home impacts negatively on chambers community and professional socialisation, as people see less of each other, losing '[t]he professional camaraderie and more pertinent, the means by which barristers acquire knowledge and information from colleagues' (B36, chancery practitioner). For him, there is a risk that chambers become 'hollowed-out organisations'. Another expanded on this point:

> There are fewer interactions between colleagues. That's bad for fostering the Bar ethos. I hear reports of counsel behaving badly in court – personal rudeness to one another and to judges – which is the sort of thing that traditionally would have been ironed out by regular contact with other members of chambers.
>
> B2, criminal silk, 28 years' call

These two barristers observed the adverse effects of working from home or within very large, overpopulated sets of chambers. The impact of traditional communal, informal governance can be reduced or ineffective, undermining traditional Bar values, behaviour and potentially practitioner status.

## IV. A United Bar or an 'Imagined Community'?

Much of the rhetoric emanating from the Bar Council on its website or at its annual conferences presents a united profession. In the period of public conflict with the Ministry of Justice, it is perhaps not surprising that the profession has in some ways united and became more entrenched in its ideology. At the 2013 annual conference, in the opening speeches, the conference chairman referred to it as 'one Bar, with shared values', and the then Chairman, Maura McGowan QC, reiterated the point: 'We are One Bar, the whole is greater than the sum of its parts. Every section of the Bar works to support the others' (McGowan 2013: 4). The then Lord Chief Justice, who spoke at the close of the day, was perhaps more circumspect: 'The Bar of England and Wales is, or should be, one cohesive profession' (Cwmgiedd 2013). He then highlighted two aspects that gave him cause for concern in relation to the profession's unity: first, the increased concentration of the legal profession in London and in specialist areas in particular; and, second, the marked difference in income between those practitioners who are privately paid and those doing legally aided work.

Hunter (2003a) draws on Anderson's notion of an 'imagined community', sustained by Hobsbawm's idea of 'invented traditions', in her analysis of how the

Bar's structure and culture in Australia necessarily excludes women from fitting in and advancing their careers. In that context, she challenges the idea of a real community. This study applies the concept when considering whether, in the minds of practitioners, the 'one Bar' rhetoric holds up under examination. When talking of a given national group, Anderson recognises that not everyone knows everyone else, yet 'in the minds of each lives the image of their communion' (Anderson 1991: 6). With reference to the Australian Bar community, Hunter (2003a: 119) asserts that 'acculturation processes' reinforce this notion. To what degree is the culture of the profession in England and Wales sufficiently strong, uniform and relevant in barristers' minds to bind practitioners in different locations, with different practice areas and clients together in a true community? Whilst most barristers seemed to strongly identify with the shared values of independence, integrity and commitment, the idea of community, which necessarily implies unity of some sort, provoked a very different view from a number of interviewees.

## V. The 'Private/Public Divide'

Many practitioners highlighted the huge differences in the day-to-day experiences and income between those carrying out privately funded work and those who undertake publicly funded work:

> It's quite a different market, I mean the Bar is split into two, you've got two almost identifiable different markets … The Bar is absolutely schismatic. You've got the privately funded Bar and specialist Bar, which are doing very well. You've got the publicly funded Bar which is under huge stress, because you've got a monopsony buyer, the state, who sets the rates, legal aid rates, and is determined to reduce the rates and now a barrister will do a case for less than they would have done 20 years ago … it's very different now. You need to almost analyse these questions twice, once for the publicly funded Bar, once for the privately funded Bar.
>
> B13, commercial barrister, former Bar Council officer

> There are incredibly different Bars. No, I wouldn't say it was one Bar at all, no. It doesn't feel like a united Bar … the impression I get is that the commercial and civil bar, there's a lot of talking about how we understand the vulnerability of the criminal Bar and it's an outrage but I'm not sure juniors at x chambers, say, and all those places, really have any idea what it must be like to be in Banbury Mags earning £26 or whatever they get.
>
> B19, civil practitioner, 15 years' call

Until about 25 years ago, most practitioners started their careers in general common law practice and specialised much later on, if at all (Morison and Leith 1992). The majority did some legally aided work, particularly in their early years of practice:

> The Bar has completely fragmented, that was the point I was going to make and it really has become obvious … whereas we were all part of an overall club, and everybody did

> everything. Not everybody, but lots of people did everything. You know, I did jury trials, I did all that stuff.
>
> B48, commercial silk, 28 years' call

As most barristers are now specialists, a junior will rarely stray out of a particular area of work and might never experience broader practice or do publicly funded work. This can lead to a complete lack of understanding of what some other practitioners do, how they think and the problems they face, making support for each other challenging. Their interests do not always intersect:

> I'm now on COMBAR, so I get to see quite a lot of what's going on behind the scenes over things like legal aid cuts and what the Criminal Bar want the rest of the Bar to do to support them and the conflict is quite difficult … they want us to go on strike, they want us to boycott the government's global law summit next year as a protest, whereas the commercial Bar doesn't want to do that.
>
> B48, commercial silk, 28 years' call

The same barrister highlighted how wide the gulf is between those in different types of practice:

> When I said we're fragmented, it is not so much that there are political divisions, but what became clear to me – I had a meeting … with circuit leaders, criminal circuit leaders … it became obvious to me in that meeting, that I was the only person in that meeting who understood both sides of what everyone was doing, because I do commercial work and because I used to be a circuit practitioner and I know all these guys. The criminal Bar have no idea what happens in commercial sets. The things they were saying about how this would affect the practices of young barristers in all sets, including commercial sets, were just nonsense. They're miles apart in terms of what people are doing now and they haven't a bloody clue what happens on circuit in the criminal sets or in the mixed law sets … It was really shocking … in the old days we all knew what we were doing.

Practitioners might share the same ethos in abstract terms, yet their working culture is situated in very different contexts and subject to distinct professional interests and relationships with solicitors/clients, with markedly dissimilar incomes and practice security.

Practitioners liken specialist practice areas to different 'bubbles' of experience, with practitioners sheltered from the experience of those in other areas of work: 'I think there are bubbles. My area of work … it's a relatively small number of people who are doing a lot of the cases, it's very nice to know those people and so on, but I don't have many dealings with people who do other areas of law' (B28, specialist silk, 25 years' call). For many, the only means of finding out what other areas of practice are like is by either reading media accounts or by learning second-hand from friends:

> I think there are so many bubbles within the Bar and if you're in a specialist bubble, you don't really know what's going on outside it. I mean I only hear about the criminal bar very tangentially. I don't really know anyone who practices at the criminal Bar, but

> I hear about things from my roommate, because she's married to a circuit judge and he sits in [place] and does crime … And equally I don't know what's going on with the big boys in the commercial sets. That's a different world, you know. Unless you've got a specific friend there, you don't know.
>
> B20, specialist civil practitioner, 38 years' call

Many interviewees recognised the difference in lived experience and also the complexity of the problem: 'It's a profession of individuals. You'll get people in our chambers, for whom it's the most wonderful ivory tower and they're delighted to be there and they really don't want to look outside at the town' (B13, commercial set). However, the same commercial practitioner points to commitment by those who strive to keep the profession unified:

> The leadership at the Bar Council predominantly comes from the commercial and specialist Bars, year in, year out. People are really interested in what the Bar as a whole is doing and are prepared to give up an enormous amount of time because they feel they ought to and it's the right thing to do. That's quite common across the Bar, you don't see that across the solicitors profession. There is still a strong collegiate atmosphere across the Bar, that we're one Bar, even though everybody recognises the publicly funded Bar has almost been carved off to an entirely different economic market. Yes, there are lots of people who just go on gently, plodding away in their nice easy furrows and they don't think of what's going on elsewhere, but there are also lots of other people who are interested.

Some criminal practitioners definitely felt supported by some of the specialist Bar associations and privately paid practitioners during the protracted dispute with the MOJ over legal aid reforms:

> I don't think the Bar is fragmented, but of course people deal with their own lives and their own world, and there must be swathes of barristers who don't really understand what's happening to publicly funded work. But I think there are many who are very engaged with it, through social media and are keeping up to date with it, or because they have friends who are criminal barristers or family practitioners or whatever, so I don't think that it's fragmented in that sense … if you've got any involvement in any of the professional bodies then that would be a way, or if you were in a mixed set you would overlap … We were helped by our non-publicly funded colleagues. They did sign our petitions, they did get behind us, they did spread it out to their friends.
>
> B18, criminal practitioner, 21 years' call

The commercial and specialist Bars continue to grow and prosper, and whilst the Lord Chief Justice commended those practitioners for doing pro bono work, he warned the profession that more is needed to maintain unity. Pro bono work is a start:

> [It assists] the profession with two distinct halves … it begins to address the means of providing cohesion through an understanding on the part of the privately funded sector of the reality of the issues faced by the publicly funded sector. But it is only a small step. Much greater steps to assist those planning on or embarking on a career in

> the publicly funded sector of the Bar to ensure that that sector attracts those that can provide independent advocacy of a high quality … the privately funded sector has its part to play in the changed circumstances which now exist and must do so not only in ways I have mentioned but in many others, if the Bar is to maintain its cohesion as one Bar.
>
> (Cwmgiedd 2013)

The current reality is that fewer new entrants are attracted to the publicly funded Bar, as they are unable to make a reasonable living (or in the early years enough to survive). From the early days of legal aid provision, there were signs of a splintered community, yet as barristers have been compelled to specialise earlier and more, and given the low rates of pay, many now do no legal aid work at all. There is a much clearer separation of the sectors: the publicly funded one, which is underpaid, effectively 'degraded' and in decline, and the more prosperous, privately paid group. The Bar now comprises two distinct markets, distinguished by the stratification of their client groups, rendering them in turn divided.

## VI. Changing Chambers

It is not merely the 'private/public' Bar divide that can undermine the idea of community. Whereas before practitioners would commonly spend their entire careers in one set of chambers, now it is not uncommon to move, sometimes multiple times, as sets have become more specialist or have struggled to maintain levels of work in a particular area. Many interviewees had moved chambers at least once. Between the original fieldwork in 2013/14 and the follow-up interviews in 2018/19, just under one-third of the participant barristers moved sets, three of them twice. Two clerks moved in the same period, both of them twice. The old sense of chambers being a second family seems to have gone:

> I'm afraid, it's less of a club now and it's more of a business and people are leaving and coming all the time. That's a new thing, the extent of the movement, I think. There was always one or two but it was frowned upon, because I think chambers then and certainly these chambers, it was all a club.
>
> B19, 15 years' call, common law set

People move for different reasons. Some because sets are disbanding because a key group leave and survival for the rest is no longer viable: 'We've done reasonably well picking up people here and there from other sets of chambers that have been dissolving to make up for departures. Lots of chambers are [dissolving]. People move and … that will increase over the next five years' (B20, specialist civil set, 38 years' call). Others move because they are unhappy with the developments within their own chambers: 'We had merged with another set of chambers twice and so we had a completely new structure … At that time there was very much a move to mega-sized sets' (B18, criminal practitioner, 21 years' call). As sections of the Bar become more specialised, practitioners move as they feel their career trajectory has better prospects elsewhere:

> It was my idea to leave and x came with me, because we were both family specialists … there was no solidity to return things to. I just felt that [name] and I were the only ones. There wasn't any progression, career progression, so it wasn't as if there wasn't any work. It was just that I felt that we were stuck at a level of work.
>
> B39, family practitioner, 24 years' call

The trade press' announcements indicate that chambers regularly acquire new members at all levels of experience, evidencing a fairly recent trend that being in one set 'for life' is a thing of the past. Work insecurity and competition oblige barristers to be pragmatic about moving and focus less on loyalty or attachment to any particular set.

## VII. Women at the Bar

The remit of the fieldwork was to get a broad overview of how the reforms and their effects were reshaping the profession. As a result, issues of diversity and inclusion were not specifically put to participants. However, some of them spontaneously commented on the experiences of women at the Bar. Their observations are included here, as they act as indicators of what areas need more qualitative research, which can provide a greater understanding of the experiences of being a female barrister and what might be done to improve them. Since 2000, woman have qualified as barristers in equal numbers to men (Bar Council 2015a) and the gender split of pupils is, with annual variations, more or less equal (BSB 2019b). A number of older, male practitioners felt this was reflected in their chambers' demographic: 'There are many more women too, which is good … if you look at most chambers from the bottom up you'll find the proportion of women in the bottom half is quite high and that's the future isn't it?' (B36, chancery chambers) or 'If you look at the profile [of chambers] at the top, it's sort of, entirely misogynistic top, but out of our seven entrants this year, three were women' (B13, commercial chambers). However, the attrition rate is high, which neither commented on.

Hunter (2003b) exposes a common problem at the Bar in Australia, where although the intake of women had increased, many leave the profession after they start families and therefore are less likely to progress than men. This problem persists at the Bar in England and Wales. Until recently, the structure and culture of the profession made no provision either for maternity leave or for women to have a reasonable practice on return from having taken time off (BSB 2016). The percentage of women at the Bar steadily decreases as they progress in their careers (Bar Council 2015b) and the latest figures show that only 37.4 per cent of practitioners and 15.8 per cent of QCs are women (BSB 2019a). The Association of Women Barristers, founded in 1991, declares on its website that: 'Little has really changed for women at the Bar although misleading statistics indicate that there have been minor, cosmetic, advances which lull the unwary into a false sense of security.' One practitioner related how she was not expected to return when she left to have children:

> I had about three months off … I was the first woman in these chambers. I was the first woman to get married … first woman to have one child, first woman to have two children, first woman to have three children … every single time they thought I would leave and what's more, they thought I ought to leave and there was no maternity policy at all.
>
> B37, criminal silk, 30 years' call

When women did take time off, there was no concession in chambers regarding the payment of rent or chambers dues during that period. Another woman, who had three children, noted distinct hostility from male members of chambers in terms of accommodating any time off:

> I didn't negotiate anything. I got nothing … I was paying chambers dues on any fees I had in … [I was away] three months, six weeks, three months … but I remember it being suggested in [name of chambers] that we might have a three month break from chambers dues if we were having a baby and [name of barrister] hit the roof, absolutely hit the roof.
>
> B39, family practitioner, 24 years' call

Some women convert to solicitor status, which gives them more flexibility, security of employment and sick/maternity benefits. Those who return to the Bar find that their work has all but disappeared: 'There wasn't much of a practice at the other end … I'm sure it's better, it couldn't really be worse, could it?' (B37, criminal silk, 30 years' call). Despite some progress (maternity policies), in reality male members of chambers and clerks feel that the longer a woman is away, the harder it is to keep her solicitors loyal. Her practice will inevitably diminish and a focused and combined effort on her part, together with the clerks, must be made to rebuild it:

> In the old days [the clerk] probably didn't like having women at all because they all get pregnant at 30 and go away, but now we are very keen … they do [come back] and we're keen to get them in before the end of their maternity leave, not full time, but just try and get them back into the swing of things and get them to meet their solicitors. Because even if you have gone on maternity leave, whatever the statute and the laws are, you've been out of the loop for 12 months and solicitors tend to forget you, so it's quite important you get them back in … we try and encourage that and then it was always take time to get your practice back, your practice is not going to be the same when you come back after 12 months.
>
> B44, head of multi-practice set

Since chambers now pay their pupils, it is not in their interests to lose that investment when female practitioners leave to have children and fail to return. One commercial barrister described how his chambers make a concerted effort to encourage them to return:

> We haven't lost a single one and very, very proud of the fact … we adopt the policy that if they want absolutely anything from us under the sun, they can have it … have a year

> off, and 'I don't want to pay my room rent', fine ... There is a very, very strong set of instructions to the clerks that you look after the young women ... we've had one woman who was very ill and took nearly 18 months off, and she came back part-time and you get people who say 'I want to take a year off and I want to work mainly for home' and 'I'm going to be very picky about my cases' and that's actually fine ... generally the instructions to the centre is that 'You've got to look after these people, you've got to keep their practice going, you've got to bend over backwards, clerks. If it means you've got to go out to them, visit them in their homes and go through their practice with them every so often, get out there.' But when you think of the amount of effort we spend in recruiting these youngsters. it's hundreds and hundreds of thousands of pounds and if you then lose them 10 years on because they go and have a baby, because they feel that chambers isn't looking after them, what a ridiculous ... (tails off).
>
> B13, head of commercial set

Nonetheless, focus group research indicates that one of the main challenges women face is finding the balance between childcare and work, and the success of this depends largely on the kind of chambers they are in and the attitudes of the clerks (Bar Council 2015b; BSB 2016). One criminal practitioner (B31, six years' call) commented that in the last few years, her practice had begun to develop nicely: 'I was in court every day, I was getting more instructions from other clients ... my defence practice started growing and I began to defend serious sexual offences.' When she was re-interviewed five years later, things had changed. She had a baby. After returning from a year's maternity leave, there was almost nothing left:

> The trading standards work that I was getting had disappeared ... the trials that I would have done went to other barristers who now continue to work for them. I haven't pursued this because I know that, in reality, I can't work for them while I have a young family. The trials necessitated 70-hour working weeks, living in hotels in cities away from home ... my defence practice also disappeared.

This practitioner was obliged to re-invent herself. She has now started to cultivate and develop a prosecution and regulatory practice, and has had to increase the amount of marketing she did. It may well be that some areas of practice are more difficult to maintain during absences. The profession's structure, working hours and attitudes make it very difficult for women to progress unless they take much less time off, delegate most (if not all) of their parenting duties and are supported by their clerks. The recent initiative of HMCTS to impose more 'flexible' or extended hours in some civil and family courts has caused many to object to this discriminatory reform: it will negatively affect women at the Bar who also have childcare commitments, which they already juggle with their professional lives. Holding court hearings before and after school hours will make childcare arrangements impracticable and expensive (Brunner 2017; HMCTS 2018).

Expectations of female practitioners have changed considerably in the last 30 years, making them more demanding: 'I'd had some time off with my first child and then I spoke to my clerk ... and said I wanted to work part-time. So he looked at me, laughing, and said "Well you know that never works, don't you?" And I said "Well, I tell you what, that's what I'm going to do"' (B30, criminal circuit practitioner, 18 years' call). Despite initial reluctance, this clerk became more cooperative:

> I was frequently being led in a number of fairly long cases … I did a lot of the prep quite flexibly and then I would take out chunks of a couple of months to go and do the trials and then have a rest. Have a number of months off, so it was rather nice and flexible … what was interesting is that of my cohort of pupils … three-quarters of us were female and at least started by doing crime and I think all of us have gone on to have children and all of us did part-time … I was always contacted by the clerks who said, 'Would you like to do x? Would you like us to put your name forward?' … I have to say chambers have been always fabulous.
>
> B30, criminal circuit practitioner, 18 years' call

Younger female practitioners are more insistent and have higher expectations, contesting, as their solicitor counterparts have done, the traditional structures and cultures of the profession (Sommerlad 2002). One interviewed was astonished that it was only in 2013 that the Bar Council sourced a local nursery crèche, at reduced rates for barristers. However, this small innovation was short-lived and the arrangement ended four years later (Connelly 2017).

Hunter (2003a) took the view in her study of the Bar in Australia that the masculine cultures of the Bar are so embedded that women are not even conscious of any systemic discrimination. Women are at best either 'honorary blokes' or outsiders with a potential to disrupt hegemonic masculinity. None of those who spoke of their experiences as women practitioners seemed unaware of systemic obstacles; on the contrary, as indicated in some of the extracts above, they were very aware of them. One interviewee volunteered that her clerk wanted her to have a family law and not a criminal practice, which she resisted:

> I looked very young the first day that I walked in. The senior clerk … burst out laughing and said that there was no way that I was going to be briefed to do crime because of how I looked, but I maintained that position and there were a number of years early on where there wasn't a great deal of work … I just said 'I'm not doing family', which is essentially what the debate was about. 'We can sell you doing family.' So I then, as I got more senior, I began to do a bit more prosecuting and I think that was the saving grace really.
>
> B30, criminal circuit practitioner, 18 years' call

Another female criminal practitioner spontaneously reflected that she thought male barristers were able to market to male solicitors more easily because of their gender: 'It's easier for the men to do it because they can go out and play golf or they can go to the football and things like that' (B31, circuit practitioner, six years' call), a view repeated in Bar Council focus group research (Bar Council 2015b). Whilst there has been some recent research on women's views and experiences at the Bar, more qualitative in-depth studies are needed. In this way, the causes of the ongoing and new obstacles women face in their career progressions can the identified and possible solutions can be fashioned, whether by reshaping the profession's structure or the outmoded patriarchal attitudes of those running chambers, instructing solicitors or the government's reforming bodies.

# VIII. Discussion

The above accounts reveal complex, often contradictory views about the Bar's unity and community. Elements of professional community undoubtedly remain. Some of the newer entrants insisted that they feel they are part of a chambers family, despite the increase in numbers and competitive pressures. The Inns and specialist Bar associations have become more proactive and relevant in areas of training and continuing education, bringing together either students or groups of specialists with shared interests. Students and pupils continue to have contact with older practitioners and judges, through qualifying sessions, advocacy or other training, mooting events or dining. Pupil supervision, although more prescribed, continues to play a critical role in early profession identity formation and there is evidence that socialisation processes continue, for some, to instil a sense of belonging. The ongoing reproduction of the profession, with many of its traditional characteristics, continues (Rogers 2011; Pirie and Rogers 2013). In practitioners' own minds, the profession's cultural ideals or distinguishing characteristics remain similar and identifiable across the Bar, and it could be that despite their varied daily lived experiences and incomes, 'what it means to be a barrister' is a remarkably constant and unifying notion.

Yet, when considering the reality of their daily lives, many of those interviewed think that the profession is fragmented and clearly not unified, with a distinct divide between the privately and publicly paid practitioners in terms of their markets and lived experience. There is a growing sense of a winners/losers dichotomy. With the increase in specialist areas, there are further divisions within the private client sector of the Bar, as specialised groups become more isolated from one another. As chambers move out of the Inns and practitioners move more frequently between sets, the traditional unity within the Inns and within chambers is under strain. Diversity remains an issue, and whether or not women and non-traditional entrants feel truly part of the Bar community and thrive as they should is a matter for further specific research. The profession's own survey research (BSB 2016) revealed that much must be done to improve the experiences of female practitioners. The legal aid dispute attracted support from privately funded practitioners and some of the professional associations. However, there is a disconnect between, for example, the interests of the criminal Bar and those of the commercial Bar, evidenced by the latter's reluctance to boycott the Global Law Summit in 2015. Outside the summit, an alternative protest event was held, highlighting the division in the Bar community and their different interests, even if a number of speakers attending the official summit did speak in support of the legally aided Bar and against the cuts (*Law Society Gazette* 2015).

The reality therefore seems to be that the profession is only truly united by cultural ideals (which are themselves shifting) and by its regulatory and representative bodies and their rhetoric. Given that practitioners experience and apply their professional culture in context-specific arenas and that these in themselves are so very varied, the profession's unity appears even more illusory. The small, homogeneous Bar, comprised of practitioners undertaking a broad range of work in the early years and sharing much in the way of daily professional experiences, even as their practices become more specialised, no longer exists. The notion of shared interests in the intimate setting of a small set of chambers is a thing of the past. These multiple fragmentations have the potential to diminish levels of socialisation and oversight, but more importantly, they challenge the very idea of universal professional norms and ethical rules across such a heterogeneous and stratified group.

# 9

# Conclusion

## *A New Bar, with a New Kind of Barrister?*

The aim of this book was to identify, from interview and observational research, how barristers have responded to the reforms their profession has undergone in the last 30 years. The research sought to understand, from practitioners' perspectives, how their working lives have been affected and how their ideology, culture and professionalism have been reconstituted as a result. The changes have been significant, as have the qualities and skills a practitioner needs in order to succeed in a career at the Bar. The impact of such changes has reshaped the profession in multiple ways and has also reconfigured the Bar's relationship with the state, the consumer and the market. The state has cast doubt on some areas of the profession's legitimacy and utility by imposing cuts to public funding, breaking its monopoly of audience rights and introducing a programme of reform that envisages early dispute resolution for many civil cases, without the need for traditional litigation and courtroom advocacy. Managerial oversight and accountability, the profession's freedom to innovate and the onus on its practitioners to adapt and compete in the marketplace are all evidence of neoliberal policies and practices in action. The Bar is now a competitive business and its practitioners are selling their services. Whilst training, credentials and expertise persist as recognisable features of traditional professionalism, much more is required of a barrister these days. A barrister's relationship with her or his consumer has undergone a radical reversal. The balance of power has shifted away from the once controlling and respected professional in favour of the client, forcing barristers to adapt and evolve. A practitioner must have commercial and marketing skills, and adopt flexible and more transparent methods of charging and working. The traditional service ethic has to be counterbalanced by a need to make money in a no longer protected and highly competitive marketplace. Drawing on barristers' own experiences and observations and in keeping with Abbott's thesis (1988), there is much evidence in this book of professional adaptation and development in the last 30 years in response to these changes and the challenges they have stirred up.

Barristers have discovered and colonised new areas of work, have created professional associations to legitimise and support them, and have become adept at acquiring expertise in micro-specialist areas to make them indispensable in the market and distinguish them from solicitors when differences between their tasks have radically diminished. They have adopted commercial practices within their organisational structures and whilst there are variations, often due to differential resources, the chambers model has evolved. Staffing structures, governance, division of labour and self-presentation have been modernised to cater for this brave new world of work in which barristers find themselves. Chambers are larger, are run as collectives by committee and are steered by managerial and business expertise. There have been significant developments in marketing and branding, even though some practitioners still struggle with the notion of having to sell their services and dislike doing so.

Yet, as Abbott also theorised, jurisdictional disputes and unsettlements can also lead to professional degradation. The Bar's work boundaries have been redrawn and, combined with cuts to public funding, both winners and losers have emerged. The differences across the Bar, in terms of day-to-day work experiences, have increased, creating stratifications across the profession in terms of client type, income and status. Together with an abundance of specialised sub-groups, this has weakened the existence of a true Bar community and identity. What does this all mean in the context of the debates about professionalism? Barristers' working lives now vary hugely, across practice areas, geographical location, chambers and level of experience. Any attempts at overarching statements in some kind of grand narrative about all barristers' professionalism should be read in the light of this. Professionalism is essentially an ideological construct and a shifting one at that. It is a concept that is contingent on, for example, state support, market forces or legitimacy. It is dynamic and under constant renegotiation, and, as Paterson (1996: 140) noted, is 'a set of dispositions lawyers use to interpret their situations and orient their choices', linking it to their working culture and in turn to how that culture is reproduced and transformed. Whilst the profession shares a strong sense of identity and barristers themselves subscribe to a narrative of exceptionality in their working ethos, the actual experiences that shape a practitioner's ideology can be very different in the light of all these differences.

Traditional professionalism is shifting or evolving to accommodate change, and in some areas of practice, that change is very different in terms of degree or substance. In broad terms, the new, evolving professionalism means less autonomy in the running of chambers and the running of cases, and more external oversight and accountability. The client is now very much at the centre of the professional dynamic, exerting pressure on the provider to supply value-for-money services. The Bar has made a commercial turn in terms of both how chambers are run and how practitioners seek work. One can run through features of traditional professionalism and see how they have persisted or are being eroded, and indeed many parts of the book do just that in the context of specific areas of practice or organisational features. One can see that some developments are common to most practitioners, but vary in degree, such as the size of chambers membership and how these collectives are now run. However, others changes, such as the effect of working under CFAs or the levels of pay, are practice-specific. The overall effect of these diverse and unevenly experienced changes and their consequences has resulted in a fragmented profession.

Expertise and high-quality, bespoke legal services offered by the Bar are valued according to who is paying for them. These are rewarding and exciting times for highly specialised practitioners, who are largely (but not always) funded by private or corporate clients. Those with burgeoning practices in successful chambers have the means, as a group, to employ outside, expert support to manage and strategise their course in this new marketplace. Being specialist experts, they have the power, the reputations and the leverage to be enterprising and innovate far more easily than those in publicly funded practice. This is evident in many aspects of their working lives: the higher fees which they can command, the increase in recruitment at all levels, the modernisation of the buildings in which they work, the levels and sophistication of their staff and technical support in chambers, their marketing strategies and the low levels of chambers dues they have to pay to fund all of these. Their practices are now steered by commercial concerns, but remain steeped in the traditional ethos of providing high-quality work, seemingly marrying the two with relative ease. In these instances, professionalism has evolved without standards of professional conduct or status being compromised. These barristers have operationalised aspects of enterprise to adapt their traditional ways of working, whilst retaining their cherished self-employed status and the relative freedom that comes with it. Some feel they have more in common with corporate or specialist solicitors than other parts of the Bar in terms of client base and the commercial approach. But, unlike solicitors, they remain free from partnership structures, line manager oversight and targets, thus retaining more autonomy than most lawyers. They have been flexible and in many cases have adapted successfully to outside reforms. This is the Bar that the British state is proud to promote as part of the best legal system in the world. This is not to say that individual practitioners at the criminal or family Bar, for example, have not also adjusted their outlook and practices, innovated and diversified. Some of these practitioners and those in more generalist sets have also shown initiative and commercial clout, have consolidated into large sets, regrouped, specialised and have developed sustainable practices.

However, for many at the Bar, whether they be generalists, non-finance family practitioners, those who work in housing and other social welfare areas, who bring or defend small claims or whose practice areas (such as crime) are mostly dependent on state funding, their legitimacy as expert barristers has been devalued. Whilst barristers in these practice areas have been socialised into believing that their services are essential to preserving the rule of law and are of an unmatched quality, those with the power (and the money) no longer prioritise these factors. The state, sometimes the media and possibly the public do not always view them as being necessary players in the delivery of legal services and justice. Their identities have been intensely recharacterised by a hostile state, drawing on a variety of discursive resources. The arguments used to denigrate this section of the Bar are various and multiple. They are seen as expensive and greedy, providing an old-fashioned and outdated service, their fees in legally aided cases are a drain on the public purse, sometimes encouraging unnecessary litigation and often representing underserving clients. Do we really need them when small claims could be resolved online at a fraction of the cost, without lawyer interference? Those accused of committing crimes can be represented by other, cheaper, in-house lawyers or public defenders who are directly employed by the state and who will incentivise them to enter early guilty pleas and reduce public expenditure on trials. Do some of these clients even deserve public funding? Couples going through divorces can represent themselves, even if this means hearings take much longer to process through the courts. Does it really matter if these alternative options and case outcomes provide clients with services that are 'good enough' rather than excellent?

The government's intentions seem clear. The Briggs Report (2016) never recommended a presumption that online courts would replace existing ones. Yet, despite little progress being made in the unrolling of the HMCTS reform programme at the time of writing, many of the lower courts have already been sold and their staff dispensed with, providing a much reduced and often inadequate service in those buildings that remain. Many courts do not have enough judges or staff to hear cases. Many are in a state of disrepair. Chronic underfunding has put the whole system in jeopardy (The Secret Barrister 2018; *The Times* 2019; Ames 2019a; Bowcott 2019b). Despite recent increases in levels of legal aid and CPS pay for those doing criminal work, most barristers in this field continue to be grossly underpaid and are thus devalued as professionals. Numbers coming into these parts of the profession are declining, either because chambers will not recruit as there is not enough work or because newly qualified barristers are put off by the lack of a secure income at reasonable levels. State intervention and the neoliberalisation of the profession has shattered this part of the Bar and the status of its practitioners, and, aside from barristers themselves, no one seems to mind if this means that a whole body of excellence in the form of existing and future practitioners will be lost. For many practitioners, this viewpoint seems inexplicable, foolhardy and profoundly sad.

What are the implications of the profession's fragmentation? Some sections of the Bar will shrink considerably, with existing practitioners leaving for more secure positions in-house and new ones choosing to enter more prosperous practice areas. This is already happening. Those who remain to do criminal, family or other publicly funded work, will carry on, sometimes by consolidating into big groups or mega-sets, absorbing overheads with large numbers. Adopting a more enterprising approach, many have and will continue to market themselves in specialist sub-groups, to include an assortment of better-paid regulatory work or will acquire specific niche specialist expertise. At the junior end, it will be difficult to get enough work and some predict that only those with other incomes will be able to work in those areas. This shift towards narrow specialism is likely to be the norm across the whole Bar, leading to a 'narrower vision' (Wright Mills, cited in Johnson 1972: 16) and an even more fragmented profession. These new divisions have the potential to affect levels of professional socialisation and control over practitioners and the ability to ensure compliance with ethical standards. One can go further and question, as Francis (2005) did in relation to solicitors, whether it is really possible to have one overarching regulatory code to cater for such different contexts of work and types of clientele or for chambers that vary hugely in size and in the type and degree of staff support they employ. Can one set of ethics effectively apply to the enormously different daily experiences and challenges that practitioners face?

Those in specialist or commercial practice will continue to provide a bespoke, expert advisory and advocacy service at a considerably cheaper rate than solicitors because of their self-employed status and chambers structure. There is little evidence to suggest that they will be a serious threat to corporate solicitor practices in terms of poaching large commercial cases. Few, if any, have the necessary structural support, experience or inclination to run such cases and many lack the desire to undertake, or even oversee, all the attendant, administrative and more mechanical tasks usually done by solicitors, their paralegals and clerks. The lack of entities and ABSs to date supports this. So the professional development, as Abbott envisages, has to be viewed in the context of the profession in question's self-identity, culture and ideology. Legislation and the regulatory body may well have paved the way for new working structures and new tasks, yet if this goes against the very core of existing, ingrained ideology, there may be little interest in developing them. For example, there is ongoing resistance by some to developing new ways of running chambers or adopting new entrepreneurial practices. Many seem reluctant to do much direct access work or to set up any form of entity or ABS. Almost none of the barristers interviewed for this book had any interest in conducting litigation. As Dingwall (2014 [1983]) and Burrage (2006) noted, barristers have primarily always been interested in maintaining their independent status as specialist advisors and advocates. Anything that challenges this and/or introduces more administrative tasks, historically done by solicitors, or threatens their autonomy is seen as undesirable and to be avoided. In light of this, asserting and acquiring a legal claim to carry out certain work/tasks is but the first process in Abbott's professional development thesis. The practitioners then have to culturally adapt to the idea of carrying out those tasks before undertaking them. External forces may well require them to adapt, but only a few have really engaged with direct access work and one wonders how many barristers would willingly undertake any if the market were less competitive. What Abbott (1988) has perhaps understated is the complex, deep-seated aspects of professional identity and culture that actively hinder or slow development even when the profession itself, or part of it, is under enormous strain. If the proposed opportunities do not make sense to the practitioners in the context of their perceived function, they are less likely to be explored or developed, even if it results in professional decline. Barristers on the whole do not want to work like solicitors, even if the reforms permit this. Collecting evidence, being at the coalface of client interaction, sorting through large amounts of documents or carrying out many of the administrative tasks associated with litigation and client care detract from their real job as specialist advisors and advocates.

Some individual barristers, across practice areas, have shown commercial flair, adaptive skills and remarkable resilience during what many perceive as a sustained attack on the profession. Others have found it difficult to adapt, perhaps because of the limited options for change within their practice areas or due to their inability to engage with the need to be more commercial and promote themselves, or both. Older practitioners retain a strong memory of 'how things were', some lamenting the changes, and a certain melancholy permeates many of the interviewees' accounts, as they cling nostalgically to a past where their status was respected, legitimation was not needed, work was plentiful and remuneration was sufficient. This nostalgic idealisation of the past is not surprising in those who are disillusioned by the reform agenda and unable to make it work to their advantage in their own professional lives. As stated in earlier chapters, others have noted the same dynamic amongst doctors in the NHS, where a loving reconstruction of the past and collective nostalgia was used to maintain a sense of professional continuity, create a form of resistance to modernisation and combat anxiety at the changes that were imposed (McDonald et al 2006; Watt et al 2008). The devaluation of some barristers' services has been profoundly unsettling for a significant portion of those interviewed, as it undermines their traditional professional identities. Aside from the personal consequences, many worry about how new members will be socialised with the same high standards and sense of professional community.

Few, if any, have been prepared for this evolving professional landscape. Even newer members failed to realise that skills in marketing and branding, and using digital platforms, organisational management and strategy would be necessary. Are law students being trained properly in these new essential abilities so that they can prosper at the Bar? The skill set they now need includes a host of new and different proficiencies. Processes of entry into the profession are expensive, lengthy, arduous and not for the faint-hearted. The financial risks and debts incurred to qualify place a considerable burden on students. The aspiring barrister must also demonstrate greater academic achievement, social and entrepreneurial skills, and be prepared to wait longer before securing a pupillage. Once in practice, a barrister must be enterprising, self-improving and commercially astute, with the ability to envisage and deploy new business opportunities. A barrister must be polished, confident and mobilise contacts, whilst fighting to get and keep work, be creative in carving out new specialisms and exploit IT, social media and marketing tools in order to do so.

The barristers who took part in this study were aware that things have changed irreversibly and will continue to do so, and there was a notable *fin de siècle* feeling across much of the publicly funded Bar and amongst some of the older practitioners. By contrast, some in specialist and commercial practice are energised by the possibilities the changes have created. The speed of change in a profession that is noted for its resistance to change and the multi-layered nature of the changes are striking. Traditional professional values are being reshaped and have inevitably shifted in line with the new discourses of innovation, enterprise and commercialism. Being flexible, resilient, adaptable and enterprising are essential attributes if the next generation of barristers wishes to survive and flourish in this new professional landscape.

# APPENDIX

## List of Anonymised Interview Participants

**Barristers**

| | Practice | Status | Where in practice | M/F | Call | Years of call at time of interview |
|---|---|---|---|---|---|---|
| B1 | Civil mix | Junior | London | M | 1988 | 24 |
| B2 | Crime | QC | London/NE Circuit | M | 1986 | 26 |
| B3 | Crime | J | Circuit | M | 1979 | 33 |
| B4 | Civil mix | J | London | M | 1988 | 24 |
| B5 | Civil mix | J | Circuit | M | 1986 | 26 |
| B6 | Civil – PI | J | Circuit | M | 1990 | 22 |
| B7 | Crime | J | Circuit | M | 1984 | 28 |
| B8 | Mix | J | London | M | 1991 | 21 |
| B9 | IP/Civil | J | London (sole) | M | 2004 | 8 |
| B10 | Family | QC | London | M | 1987 | 25 |
| B11 | Civil/Comm | J | London | M | 2011 | 18 months |
| B12 | Civil/Comm | J | London | F | 2008 | 4 |
| B13 | Commercial | QC | London | M | 1986 | 27 |
| B14 | Commercial | J | London | M | 1972 | 41 |
| B15 | Civil – PI | QC | London | M | 1985 | 28 |
| B16 | Civil | J | London | F | 2012 | 1 |
| B17 | Civil | J | London | F | 2010 | 3 |
| B18 | Crime | J | Circuit/London | F | 1992 | 21 |
| B19 | Civil/Comm | J | London | M | 1998 | 15 |
| B20 | Civil Clin neg | J | London | F | 1975 | 38 |
| B21 | Civil Prof neg | J | London | F | 2010 | 3 |
| B22 | Civil | Pupil | London | F | 2013 | |

*(continued)*

***(Continued)***

| | Practice | Status | Where in practice | M/F | Call | Years of call at time of interview |
|---|---|---|---|---|---|---|
| B23 | Civil Prof neg | J | London | M | 2006 | 7 |
| B24 | Civil/Fam | J | Circuit | M | 1982 | 31 |
| B25 | Crime | J | Circuit | M | 1993 | 20 |
| B26 | Civil | J | Circuit | M | 1988 | 25 |
| B27 | Civil – Chanc | J | Circuit | M | 1973 | 40 |
| B28 | Civil Prof neg | QC | London | M | 1988 | 25 |
| B29 | Crime | J | Circuit | M | 1975 | 38 |
| B30 | Crime | J | Circuit | F | 1995 | 18 |
| B31 | Crime | J | Circuit | F | 2007 | 6 |
| B32 | Fam/Crime | J | Circuit | F | 2000 | 13 |
| B33 | Crime/Reg | J | Circuit | M | 2007 | 6 |
| B34 | Fam/Mix | J | Circuit | M | 2010 | 3 |
| B35 | Crime | J | Circuit | M | 1985 | 28 |
| B36 | Chancery | J | London | M | 1975 | 38 |
| B37 | Crime | QC | London | F | 1983 | 30 |
| B38 | Civil | J | London | M | 1986 | 27 |
| B39 | Family | J | Circuit | F | 1989 | 24 |
| B40 | Family | Pupil | Circuit | M | 2013 | |
| B41 | Family | J | Circuit | M | 1983 | 30 |
| B42 | Family | J | London | F | 2003 | 10 |
| B43 | Family | J | London | F | 1986 | 27 |
| B44 | Crime | QC | London | M | 1977 | 36 |
| B45 | Family | J | London | F | 2006 | 7 |
| B46 | Family | J | London | F | 2007 | 6 |
| B47 | Civil | J | London | F | 2011 | 2 |
| B48 | Comm/Civil | QC | London | M | 1985 | 28 |
| B49 | Civil prof neg | QC | London | M | 1984 | 29 |
| B50 | Crime | J | London | M | 1994 | 20 |
| B51 | Civil prof neg | J | London | M | 2017 | 1 |

**Non-barrister participants**

| | Profession | M/F | Where in practice | Area of expertise | Years of experience in this role |
|---|---|---|---|---|---|
| C1 | Bar Council communications officer | M | | | 3 |
| C2 | Legal blogger | F | | | 3 |
| | | | | | |
| S1 | Solicitor | F | Circuit | Family law | 22 |
| S2 | Solicitor (partner) | M | London | Family law | 24 |
| | | | | | |
| A1 | Chambers administrator | F | Circuit | Mixed set | 21 |
| A2 | Chambers manager | F | London | Civil | 2 |
| A3 | Senior clerk | M | London/ Circuit | Mixed set | 28 |
| A4 | Deputy senior clerk | F | Circuit | Mixed set | 20 |
| A5 | Senior clerk | M | Circuit | Mixed set | 40 |
| A6 | Second clerk | F | Circuit | Criminal | 26 |
| A7 | Marketing consultant | F | Both | Family | 3 |
| A8 | Chambers director | M | London | Mixed set | 25 |

# BIBLIOGRAPHY


Abbott, A (1988) *The System of Professions* (Chicago, University of Chicago Press).

Abel, R (1986) 'The Decline of Professionalism?' 49 *Modern Law Review* 1.

——. (1987) 'England and Wales: A Comparison of the Professional Projects of Barristers and Solicitors', in R Abel and P Lewis (eds), *Lawyers and Society, Vol 1: The Common Law World* (Berkeley, University of California Press).

——. (1988) *The Legal Profession in England and Wales* (Oxford, Basil Blackwell).

——. (2004a) *English Lawyers between Market and State: The Politics of Professionalism* (Oxford, Oxford University Press).

——. (2004b) 'The Professional is Political' 11 *International Journal of the Legal Profession* 131.

Abel-Smith, B and Stevens, R (1967) *Lawyers and the Courts: A Sociological Study of the English Legal System 1750–1965* (London, Heinemann).

——. (1968) *In Search of Justice: Law, Society and the Legal System* (London, Penguin).

Ackroyd, S (1996) 'Organization Contra Organizations: Professions and Organizational Change in the United Kingdom' 17 *Organization Studies* 599.

Ackroyd, S and Muzio, D (2007) 'The Reconstructed Professional Firm: Explaining Change in English Legal Practices' 28 *Organization* 729.

Aldridge, A (2015) 'Atkin Chambers Raises Pupillage Award to £72,500 – The Highest at the Bar by Far', *Legal Cheek*, 24 September, www.legalcheek.com/2015/09/atkin-chambers-raises-pupillage-award-to-72500-the-highest-at-the-bar-by-far.

Allen, K, Quinn, J, Hollingworth, S and Rose, A (2013) 'Becoming Employable Students and the "Ideal" Creative Workers: Exclusion and Inequality in Higher Education Work Placements' 34 *British Journal of Sociology of Education* 431.

Ames, J (2015) 'Campaigners Bid to Block Development Plans That Would "Devastate" Inner Temple Library', *Legal Cheek*, 24 August, www.legalcheek.com/2015/08/campaigners-bid-to-block-development-plans-that-would-devastate-inner-temple-library.

——. (2019a) 'Justice System is on Brink of Collapse, Warns Senior Judge', *The Times*, 21 June, www.thetimes.co.uk/article/justice-system-is-on-brink-of-collapse-warns-senior-judge-m6tcjbtw0.

——. (2019b) 'Clouds Hang over Future of Bar after Anniversary', *The Times*, 11 July, www.thetimes.co.uk/article/clouds-hang-over-future-of-bar-after-anniversary-clt73p76c.

Anderson, B (1991) *Imagined Communities: Reflections on the Origin and Spread of Nationalism* (London, Verso).

Arden, A (2013) 'Proposals to Limit Legal Aid for Judicial Review Will Undermine the Rule of Law' *Daily Telegraph*, 23 May, www.telegraph.co.uk/comment/letters/10084925/Proposals-to-limit-legal-aid-for-judicial-review-will-undermine-the-rule-of-law.html.

Arthurs, H and Kreklewich, R (1996) 'Law, Legal Institutions and the Legal Profession in the New Economy' 34 *Osgoode Hall Law Journal* 1.

Ashley, L (2010) 'Making a Difference? The Use (and Abuse) of Diversity Management at the UK's Elite Law Firms' 24 *Work, Employment and Society* 711.

Asthana, A (2017) 'Number of Legal Aid Providers Falls 20% in Five Years, Figures Show', *The Guardian*, 17 September, www.theguardian.com/law/2017/sep/19/number-of-legal-aid-providers-falls-20-in-five-years-figures-show.

Bach Commission (2017) *The Right to Justice: The Final Report of the Bach Commission*. Fabian Policy Report, www.fabians.org.uk/wp-content/uploads/2017/09/Bach-Commission_Right-to-Justice-Report-WEB.pdf.

Baker, J (2000) *An Introduction to English Legal History*, 4th edn (London, Butterworths).
Baksi, C (2014a) 'Ministry Ticked off over Barrister Earnings Claim', *Law Society Gazette*, 18 March, www.lawgazette.co.uk/practice/ministry-ticked-off-over-barrister-earnings-claim/5040420.article.
——. (2014b) 'Civil Legal Aid: Access Denied', *Law Society Gazette*, 7 April, www.lawgazette.co.uk/law/civil-legal-aid-access-denied/5040722.article.
——. (2014c) 'Practitioner Bodies Berate "Face-Saving Bar Deal', *Law Society Gazette*, 28 July, www.lawgazette.co.uk/law/practitioner-bodies-berate-face-saving-bar-deal/5042083.article.
Bar Council (2007) *Entry to the Bar Working Party Final Report*, www.barcouncil.org.uk/media/164103/finalreportneuberger.pdf.
——. (2012) *Bar Barometer: Trends in the Profile of the Bar*, https://www.barcouncil.org.uk/media/177469/bar_barometer_nov_2012_web_upload_higher_res.pdf.
——. (2014a) 'Bar Council Response to the Justice Select Committee's Inquiry into the Impact of Changes to Civil Legal Aid under the Legal Aid, Sentencing and Punishment of Offenders Act 2012', www.barcouncil.org.uk/media/290903/bc_response_to_justice_select__committee_changes_to_civil_legal_aid_under_the_legal_aid__sentencing_and_punishment_of_offenders_act_2012.pdf.
——. (2014b) *Bar Barometer: Trends in the Profile of the Bar*, https://www.barcouncil.org.uk/media/285116/barometer_report_112pp_tuesday_3.pdf.
——. (2015a) *Momentum Measures: Creating a Diverse Profession*, www.barcouncil.org.uk/media/378213/bar_council_momentum_measures_creating_a_diverse_profession_summary_report_july_2015.pdf.
——. (2015b) *Snapshot: The Experience of Self-Employed Women at the Bar*, https://www.barcouncil.org.uk/media/379529/snapshot_-_the_experience_of_self_employed_women_at_the_bar.pdf.
——. (2018) *LASPO Five Years on: Bar Council Submission to the Ministry of Justice LASPO Post-Implementation Review*, www.barcouncil.org.uk/media/687865/laspo_pir_submission_bar_council_final.pdf.
Bathmaker, A, Ingram, N and Waller, R (2013) 'Higher Education, Social Class and the Mobilisation of Capitals: Recognising and Playing the Game' 24 *British Journal of Sociology of Education* 723.
BBC (2017) 'Employment Tribunal Fees Unlawful, Supreme Court Rules', *BBC News*, 26 July, https://www.bbc.co.uk/news/uk-40727400.
——. (2018) 'Legal Aid Lawyers Win £23m Fee Rise after Strike', *BBC News*, 24 November, https://www.bbc.co.uk/news/uk-46328004.
——. (2019) *Out of Office*, episode 3, Radio 4, 19 April, 11.08 am.
Becker, PH (1993) 'Common Pitfalls in Published Grounded Theory' 3 *Qualitative Health Research* 254.
Bentham, M (2013) 'Legal Aid Cuts "Disaster" for Black Londoners, Warns Lawyer for Stephen Lawrence's Family', *Evening Standard*, 20 May, http://www.standard.co.uk/news/uk/legal-aid-cuts-disaster-for-black-londoners-warns-lawyer-for-stephen-lawrences-family-8623319.html.
Bindman, D (2018) 'Shared Office Space Will Give Barristers Pay as You Go London Base', *Legal Futures*, 25 May, https://www.legalfutures.co.uk/latest-news/shared-office-space-will-give-barristers-pay-as-you-go-london-base.
Boon, A (2010) 'Professionalism under the Legal Services Act 2007' 17 *International Journal of the Legal Profession* 195.
——. (2014) *The Ethics and Conduct of Lawyers in England and Wales*, 3rd edn (Oxford, Hart Publishing).
——. (2016) 'The Legal Professions' New Handbooks: Narratives, Standards and Values' 19 *Legal Ethics* 207.
Boon, A and Flood, J (1999) 'Trials of Strength: Advocacy and Litigation as a Contested Terrain' 33 *Law & Society Review* 595.
Boon, A, Flood, J and Webb, J (2005) 'Postmodern Professions? The Fragmentation of Legal Education and the Legal Profession' 32 *Journal of Law and Society* 473.
Boon, A and Levin, J (2008) *The Ethics and Conduct of Lawyers in England and Wales*, 2nd edn (Oxford, Hart Publishing).
Bourdieu, P (1986–87) 'The Force of Law: Toward a Sociology of the Juridical Field' 38 *Hastings Law Journal* 814.

——. (1990) *The Logic of Practice* (Cambridge, Polity Press).

Bowcott, O (2013) 'Catholic Church Says Legal Aid Cuts Will Harm Human Trafficking Victims', *The Guardian*, 22 May, https://www.theguardian.com/law/2013/may/22/catholic-church-legal-aid-trafficking.

——. (2014a) 'Grayling Agrees Legal Aid Truce with Barristers over Complex Fraud Trials', *The Guardian*, 8 July, https://www.theguardian.com/law/2014/jul/08/grayling-legal-aid-truce-barristers-complex-fraud-trials.

——. (2014b) 'Legal Aid Residence Test "Discriminatory and Unlawful", High Court Rules', *The Guardian*, 15 July, https://www.theguardian.com/law/2014/jul/15/legal-aid-high-court-residence-test-discrimination-grayling.

——. (2015) 'Barristers Threaten to Walk out over Legal Aid Cuts', *The Guardian*, 21 May, https://www.theguardian.com/law/2015/may/21/barristers-threaten-walk-out-legal-aid-cuts.

——. (2016a) 'Michael Gove in U Turn over Legal Aid Fund', *The Guardian*, 28 January, https://www.theguardian.com/politics/2016/jan/28/michael-gove-in-u-turn-over-legal-aid-fund.

——. (2016b) 'Qualifying as a Barrister "May Cost Students up to £127,000"', *The Guardian*, 23 February, https://www.theguardian.com/law/2016/feb/23/qualifying-barrister-may-cost-new-students-127000.

——. (2019a) 'Criminal Barristers in England and Wales Vote for National Walkout', *The Guardian*, 7 June, www.theguardian.com/law/2019/jun/07/criminals-barristers-in-england-and-wales-vote-to-stage-national-walkout.

——. (2019b) 'Family Courts "Running up a down Escalator" Due to Increase in Cases', *The Guardian*, 3 July, www.theguardian.com/law/2019/jul/03/family-courts-running-up-a-down-escalator-due-to-increase-in-cases.

——. (2019c) 'Legal Advice Centres in England and Wales Halved since 2013/14', *The Guardian*, 15 July, www.theguardian.com/law/2019/jul/15/legal-advice-centres-in-england-and-wales-halved-since-2013-14.

Briggs, Lord Justice (2015) *Civil Courts Structural Review: Interim Report*, Judiciary of England and Wales, www.judiciary.uk/wp-content/uploads/2016/01/ccsr-interim-report-dec-15-final1.pdf.

——. (2016) *Civil Courts Structural Review: Final Report*, Judiciary of England and Wales, www.judiciary.uk/wp-content/uploads/2016/07/civil-courts-structure-review-final-report-jul-16-final-1.pdf.

Brunner, K (2017) 'Western Circuit Women's Forum: Observations on Extension of Court Sitting Hours', *Western Circuit Women's Forum*, https://westerncircuit.co.uk/wp-content/uploads/2019/01/WCWF-Flexible-Hours-Response.pdf.

BSB (Bar Standards Board) (2015a) *The Pupillage Handbook* (London, Bar Standards Board).

——. (2015b) *Future Bar Training*, https://www.barstandardsboard.org.uk/uploads/assets/e85659f2-9dce-453c-9cc1ce640677c227/fbttripleconsultationjuly2015.pdf.

——. (2016) *Women at the Bar*, www.barstandardsboard.org.uk/media/1773934/women_at_the_bar_-_full_report_-_final_12_07_16.pdf.

——. (2017a) *Exploring Differential Attainment at BPTC and Pupillage*, www.barstandardsboard.org.uk/media/1910429/differential_attainment_at_bptc_and_pupillage_analysis.pdf.

—— (2017b) *Provision of Legal Services by Barristers*, https://www.barstandardsboard.org.uk/uploads/assets/c551bdf1-4c2e-404c-b7a11b802f31a2c3/deliverymodelsreport-finaldraftapproved-1.pdf.

——. (2019a) *Diversity at the Bar 2018*, https://www.barstandardsboard.org.uk/uploads/assets/1fda3d4b-c7e3-4aa8-a063024155c7341d/diversityatthebar2018.pdf.

——. (2019b) *Review of Pupillage Advertising and Selection Criteria*, https://www.barstandardsboard.org.uk/uploads/assets/9a37ecd0-3458-4c5e-b9467a56f236aed1/reviewofpupillageadvertisingandselectioncriteria.pdf.

——. (2019c) BPTC *Key Statistics: An Analysis of Students over Three Academic Years*, https://www.barstandardsboard.org.uk/uploads/assets/7a20eb3e-b152-4777-9e821417bf596eed/bptckeystatisticsreport2019.pdf.

Burrage, M (1997) 'Mrs Thatcher against the "Little Republics": Ideology, Precedents, and Reactions' in T Halliday and L Karpik (eds), *Lawyers and the Rise of Western Political Liberalism*' (Oxford, Clarendon Press).

——. (2006) *Revolution and the Making of the Contemporary Legal Profession: England, France and the United States* (Oxford, Oxford University Press).

CAB (Citizens Advice Bureau) (2014) 'Nowhere to Turn: Citizens Advice Speaks out on Impact of Legal Aid Cuts', 8 July, www.citizensadvice.org.uk/about-us/how-citizens-advice-works/media/press-releases/nowhere-to-turn-citizens-advice-speaks-out-on-impact-of-legal-aid-cuts.

Cape, E and Moorhead, R (2005) *Demand Induced Supply? Identifying Cost Drivers in Criminal Defence Work: A Report to the Legal Services Commission* (London, Legal Services Research Centre, Legal Services Commission).

Carr-Saunders, A and Wilson, P (1933) *The Professions* (Oxford, Clarendon Press).

Lord Carter of Coles (2006) *Legal Aid: A Market-Based Approach to Reform*, https://webarchive.nationalarchives.gov.uk/20081205143452/http:/www.legalaidprocurementreview.gov.uk/docs/carter-review-p1.pdf.

*Chambers Student* (2019) 'A Preliminary Warning', www.chambersstudent.co.uk/the-bar/a-career-at-the-bar/a-preliminary-warning.

Chambliss, E (2010) 'Measuring Law Firm Culture' 52 *Studies in Law, Politics and Society*, Special Issue: *Law Firms, Legal Culture and Legal Practice* 1.

Clarke, J (2004) 'Unsettled Connections: Citizens, Consumers and the Reform of Public Services' 7 *Journal of Consumer Culture* 159.

Clarke, J, Cochrane, A and McLaughlin, E (1994) 'Introduction: Why Management Matters' in J Clarke, A Cochrane and E McLaughlin (eds), *Managing Social Policy*' (London, Sage).

Clementi, D (2004) *Review of the Regulatory Framework for Legal Services in England and Wales: Final Report*, available at: http://www.avocatsparis.org/Presence_Internationale/Droit_homme/PDF/Rapport_Clementi.pdf.

Coe, C and Vaughan, S (2015) *Independence, Representation and Risk*, Independent Report, Solicitors Regulation Authority, https://sra.org.uk/sra/how-we-work/reports/independence-report.page.

Connelly, T (2017) 'Bar Council Ditches London Nursery Crèche for Barristers' Babies', *Legal Cheek*, 13 October, www.legalcheek.com/2017/10/bar-council-ditches-london-nursery-scheme-for-barristers-babies.

——. (2018) 'Revealed: 2,089 Wannabe Barristers Submit 14,516 Applications for Just 224 Pupillage Spots', *Legal Cheek*, 12 February, www.legalcheek.com/2018/02/revealed-2089-wannabe-barristers-submit-14516-applications-for-just-224-pupillage-spots.

Cook, A, Faulconbridge, J and Muzio, D (2012) 'London's Legal Elite: Recruitment through Cultural Capital and the Reproduction of Social Exclusivity in City Professional Service Fields' 44 *Environment and Planning* A 1744.

Cooper, D, Hinings, B, Greenwood, R and Brown, J. (1996) 'Sedimentation and Transformation in Organizational Change: The Case of Canadian Law Firms' 17 *Organizational Studies* 623.

Cordrey, T (2016) 'How to Gold-Plate Your Pupillage Gateway Application', *Legal Cheek*, 7 March, www.legalcheek.com/lc-careers-posts/how-to-draft-a-winning-pupillage-gateway-application.

Counsel (2015) 'Solicitors' Association of Higher Court Advocates', *Counsel Magazine*, December, 9.

Cross, M (2016) 'Transforming Justice: Digital Courts Get Green Light in £1bn Initiative', *Law Society Gazette*, 15 September, https://www.lawgazette.co.uk/news/transforming-justice-digital-courts-get-green-light-in-1bn-initiative/5057639.article.

Crouch, C (2011) *The Strange Non-death of Neoliberalism* (Cambridge, Polity Press).

Cwmgiedd, Lord Chief Justice (2013) 'Bar Conference Speech', 2 November, www.judiciary.uk/wp-content/uploads/JCO/Documents/Speeches/lcj-bar-conference-02112013.pdf.

Dent, M and Whitehead, S (eds) (2002) *Managing Professional Identities: Knowledge, Performativity and the 'New' Professional* (Abingdon, Routledge).

Dingwall, R (2014 [1983]) 'Introduction' in R Dingwall and P Lewis (eds), *The Sociology of the Professions: Lawyers, Doctors and Others* (New Orleans, Quid Pro Books).

Evetts, J (2011) 'A New Professionalism? Challenges and Opportunities' 59 *Current Sociology* 406.

——. (2012) 'Professionalism in Turbulent Times: Changes, Challenges and Opportunities', paper given at *Propel International Conference*, Stirling, 9–11 May, www.yumpu.com/en/document/read/12242124/full-paper-professionalism-in-turbulent-times-changes-propel.

——. (2013) 'Professionalism: Value and Ideology' 61 *Current Sociology* 778.

——. (2014) 'The Concept of Professionalism: Professional Work, Professional Practice and Learning' in S Billet, C Harteis and H Gruber (eds), *International Handbook of Research in Professional and Practice-Based Learning* (New York, Springer).

——. (2015) 'Professionalism, Enterprise and the Market: Contradictory or Complementary?' in H. Sommerlad, S Harris-Short, S Vaughan and R Young (eds), *The Futures of Legal Education and the Legal Profession* (Oxford, Hart Publishing).

Faulconbridge, J and Muzio, D (2008) 'Organizational Professionalism in Globalizing Law Firms' 22 *Work, Employment and Society* 7.

Fenhalls, M (2019) 'Sharp Fall in Criminal Prosecutions Shames Our Country', *The Times*, 18 July, www.thetimes.co.uk/article/the-sharp-fall-in-criminal-prosecutions-shames-our-country-9bnfz5vcx.

Fitzgibbon, F (2013) 'Short Cuts' 35 *London Review of Books* 32.

——. (2015) 'Quality Control of Advocacy: Response' *Counsel Magazine*, December, 30.

Flood, J (1981) 'Middlemen of the Law: An Ethnographic Inquiry into the English Legal Profession' 2 *American Foundation Research Journal* 377.

——. (1983) *Barristers' Clerks: The Law's Middlemen* (Manchester, Manchester University Press).

——. (1996) 'Megalawyering in the Global Order: The Cultural, Social and Economic Transformation of Global Legal Practice' 3 *International Journal of the Legal Profession* 169.

——. (2003) 'Response to the Bar Council and Bar Standards Board Responses to the Flood-Hviid Report on the Cab Rank Rule for the Legal Services Board', https://ssrn.com/abstract=2258707 or http://dx.doi.org/10.2139/ssrn.2258707.

——. (2011) 'The Re-landscaping of the Legal Profession: Large Law Firms and Professional Re-regulation' 59 *Current Sociology* 507.

Flood, J, Boon, A, Whyte, A, Skordaki, E, Abbey, R and Ash, A (1998) *Reconfiguring the Market for Advocacy Services: A Case Study of London and Four Fields of Practice*, report for the Lord Chancellor's Advisory Committee on Legal Education and Conduct.

Flood, J and Hviid, M (2013) *The Cab Rank Rule: Its Meaning and Purpose in the New Legal Services Market* (London, Legal Services Board).

Flood, J and Whyte, A (2008) *Straight There No Detours: Direct Access to Barristers*, Summary Report for A2B Day).

Fouzder, M (2015) 'Criminal Bar Votes Overwhelmingly for Direct Action', *Law Society Gazette*, 21 May, https://www.lawgazette.co.uk/law/criminal-bar-votes-overwhelmingly-for-direct-action/5048944.article.

Fournier, V (2000) 'Boundary Work and the (Un)Making of the Professions' in N Malin (ed), *Professionalism, Boundaries and the Workplace* (London, Routledge).

Francis, A (2005) 'Legal Ethics, the Marketplace and the Fragmentation of Legal Professionalism' 12 *International Journal of the Legal Profession* 173.

——. (2011) *At the Edge of Law: Emergent and Divergent Models of Legal Professionalism* (Farnham, Ashgate).

Francis, A and Sommerlad, H (2009) 'Access to Legal Work Experience and its Role in the (Re)Production of Legal Professional Identity' 16 *International Journal of the Legal Profession* 63.

Freer, E (2016) 'Professional Associations, Agency, Motivation and Change: The Case of Social Mobility and the Bar', PhD thesis, Keele University.

——. (2018) *Social Mobility and the Legal Profession: The Case of Professional Associations and Access to the English Bar* (Abingdon, Routledge).

Freidson, E (2001) *Professionalism: The Third Logic* (Cambridge, Polity Press).

Friedman, L (1975) *The Legal System: A Social Science Perspective* (New York, Russell Sage Foundation).

Gane, N (2012) 'The Governmentalities of Neoliberalism: Panopticism, Post-panopticism and beyond' 60 *Sociological Review* 611.

Garth, B (2013) 'Crisis, Crisis Rhetoric and Competition in Legal Education: A Sociological Perspective on the (Latest) Crisis of the Legal Profession and Legal Education' 24 *Stanford Law and Policy Review* 503.

Gorman, E (2015) 'Getting Ahead in Professional Organizations: Individual Qualities, Socioeconomic Background and Organizational Context' 2 *Journal of Professions and Organizations* 122.

Granville Stafford, A (2015) 'Pioneering Work' *Counsel Magazine*, August, 10.

Grey, C (1994) 'Career as a Project of the Self and Labour Process Discipline' 28 *Sociology* 479.

Gummesson, E (1997) 'Relationship Marketing as a Paradigm Shift: Some Conclusions from the 30R Approach' 35 *Management Decision* 267.

Hanlon, G (1997) 'A Profession in Transition? Lawyers, the Market and Significant Others' 60 *Modern Law Review* 798.

——. (1998) 'Professionalism as Enterprise: Service Class Politics and the Redefinition of Professionalism' 32 *Sociology* 43.

——. (2001) 'The State-Lawyer Relationship in England and Wales' in J van Hoy (ed), *Legal Professions: Work, Structure and Organization* (New York, JAI Press).

Hanlon, G and Jackson. J (1999) 'Last Orders at the Bar? Competition, Choice and Justice for All: The Impact of Solicitor-Advocacy' 19 *Oxford Journal of Legal Studies* 555.

Harris, L (2002) 'The Emotional Labour of Barristers: An Exploration of Emotional Labour by Status Professionals' 39 *Journal of Management Studies* 553.

Harris, L and Piercy, N (1998) 'Barriers to Marketing Development in the Barristers' Profession' 18 *Service Industries Journal* 19.

Harris, L and O'Malley, L (2000) 'Maintaining Relationships: A Study of the Legal Industry' 20 *Service Industries Journal* 62.

Hazell, R (ed) (1978a) *The Bar on Trial* (London, Quartet Books).

——. (1978b) 'Independence and Fusion' in R. Hazell (ed), *The Bar on Trial* (London, Quartet Books).

——. (1978c) 'Clerks and Fees' in R Hazell (ed), *The Bar on Trial* (London, Quartet Books).

——. (1978d) 'Introduction to the Bar' in R Hazell (ed), *The Bar on Trial* (London, Quartet Books).

——. (1978e) 'Pupillage' in R Hazell (ed), *The Bar on Trial* (London, Quartet Books).

Heinz, J and Laumann, E (1994) *Chicago Lawyers: The Social Structure of the Bar*, revised edn (Evanston, Northwestern University Press).

Hill, L (2003) 'Publicity Rules of the Legal Profession with the UK' 20 *Arizona Law Journal of International and Comparative Law* 323.

Hill, M (2015) 'The Advocate', *Counsel Magazine*, December, 16.

HMCTS (Her Majesty's Courts and Tribunals Service) (2018) *Flexible Operating Hours Pilots: Prospectus for Civil and Family Court Pilots*, https://assets.publishing.service.gov.uk/government/uploads/system/uploads/attachment_data/file/756624/HMCTS_Flexible_Operating_Hours_-_Prospectus.pdf.

Hughes, E. (1994) *On Work, Race and the Sociological Imagination*, L Coser (ed) (Chicago, University of Chicago Press).

Hunter, G, Jacobson, J and Kirby A (2018) *Judicial Perceptions of the Quality of Criminal Advocacy* (London, Institute of Criminal Policy Research/Birkbeck), http://eprints.bbk.ac.uk/22949/1/Judicial%20perceptions%20of%20criminal%20advocacy.pdf.

Hunter, R (2003a) 'Women Barristers and Gender Difference in Australia' in U Schultz and G Shaw (eds), *Women in the World's Legal Professions* (Oxford, Hart Publishing).

——. (2003b) 'Women in the Legal Profession: The Australian Profile' in U Schultz and G Shaw (eds), *Women in the World's Legal Professions* (Oxford, Hart Publishing).

Hynes, S (2012) *Austerity Justice* (London, Legal Action Group).

Ilex Professional Standards, BSB and Solicitors Regulation Authority (2013) *The Future of Legal Services Education and Training Regulation in England and Wales: Final Report* (London, IPS, BSB and SRA).

Jacobs, K (2003) 'Class Reproduction in Professional Recruitment: Examining the Accounting Profession' 14 *Critical Perspectives on Accounting* 569.

Jeffrey, B (2014) *Independent Criminal Advocacy in England and Wales* (London, Ministry of Justice).

Johnson, T (1972) *Professions and Power* (London, Macmillan).

Kennedy, H (1978) 'Women at the Bar' in R Hazell (ed), *The Bar on Trial* (London, Quartet Books).

Kentridge, Sir S (2013) 'The Cab Rank Rule: A Response to the Report Commissioned by the Legal Services Board', https://www.barcouncil.org.uk/media/203452/sir_sydney_kentridge_crr_response.pdf.

Kritzer, H (1991) 'Abel and the Professional Project: The Institutional Analysis of the Legal Profession' 16 *Law and Social Inquiry* 529.

——. (1999) 'The Professions are Dead, Long Live the Professions: Legal Practice in a Postprofessional World' 33 *Law and Society Review* 713.

Kurkchiyan, M (2005) 'Researching Legal Culture in Russia' in R Banakar and M Travers (eds), *Theory and Method in Socio-legal Research* (Oxford, Hart Publishing).

Lane, C, Potton, M and Littek, W (2002) 'The Professions between State and Market: A Cross-national Study of Convergence and Divergence' 4 *European Societies* 235.

Larson, M (1977) *The Rise of Professionalism: A Sociological Analysis* (Berkeley, University of California Press).

Law Society (2014) *The Justice Select Committee Inquiry into the Impact of the Changes to Civil Legal Aid under the Legal Aid, Sentencing and Punishment of Offenders Act 2012, Submission by the Law Society* (London, Law Society).

*Law Society Gazette* (2015) 'Global Law Summit – as it Happened', 26 February, http://www.lawgazette.co.uk/law/global-law-summit-as-it-happened/5046961.fullarticle.

Legal Action Group (2013) *Civil Legal Aid: The Secret Legal Service?* (London, Legal Action Group).

Legal Services Board (2012) *Market Impacts of the Legal Services Act 2007: Baseline Report (Final) 2012* (London, Legal Services Board).

Lemmings, D (2004) 'Ritual, Majesty and Mystery: Collective Life and Culture among English Barristers, Serjeants and Judges, c.1500–1830' in W Wesley Pue and D Sugarman (eds) *Lawyers and Vampires: Cultural Histories of Legal Professions* (Oxford, Hart Publishing).

Maclean, M (2015) 'New Ways to Seek Legal Information and Advice on Family Matters in England and Wales: From Professional Legal Services to Google and Private Ordering' in M Maclean, J Eekelaar and B Bastard (eds), *Delivering Family Justice in the 21st Century* (Oxford, Hart Publishing).

Maclean, M and Eekelaar, J (2009) *Family Law Advocacy: How Barristers Help the Victims of Family Failure* (Oxford, Hart Publishing).

——. (2016) *Lawyers and Mediators: The Brave New World of Services for Separating Families* (Oxford, Hart Publishing).

Mason, M and Vaughan, S (2017) 'Sexuality at the Bar: An Empirical Exploration into the Experiences of LGBT+ Barristers in England & Wales', University of Westminster School of Law Research Paper, https://ssrn.com/abstract=3043790 or http://dx.doi.org/10.2139/ssrn.3043790.

McDonald, R, Waring, J and Harrison, S (2006) 'At the Cutting Edge? Modernization and Nostalgia in a Hospital Operating Theatre Department' 40 *Sociology* 1097.

McGowan, M (2013) The Bar in Society: A Vital Force for Good', speech to the Annual Bar Conference, 2 November, https://www.barcouncil.org.uk/media/235752/chairman_of_the_bar_speech_for_bar_conference_2013.pdf.

McLaughlin, E (2007) *The New Policing* (London, Sage).

McNay, L (2009) 'Self as Enterprise: Dilemmas of Control and Resistance in Foucault's *The Birth of Biopolitics*' 26 *Theory, Culture and Society* 55.

Mikecz, R (2012) 'Interviewing Elites: Addressing Methodological Issues' 18 *Qualitative Inquiry* 482.

Miller, P and Rose, N (1990) 'Governing Economic Life', 19 *Economy and Society* 1.

——. (2008) *Governing the Present: Administering Economic, Personal and Social Life* (Cambridge, Polity Press).

MOJ (Ministry of Justice) (2016a) *Transforming Our Justice System*, https://assets.publishing.service.gov.uk/government/uploads/system/uploads/attachment_data/file/553261/joint-vision-statement.pdf.

——. (2016b) *Legal Aid Statistics in England and Wales: April to June 2016*, Ministry of Justice Statistics bulletin, www.gov.uk/government/uploads/system/uploads/attachment_data/file/556216/legal-aid-statistics-bulletin-apr-to-jun-2016.pdf.

——. (2019a) *Civil Justice Statistics Quarterly, January to March 2019*, National Statistics, www.gov.uk/government/statistics/civil-justice-statistics-quarterly-january-to-march-2019.

——. (2019b) *Criminal Justice Statistics Quarterly, December 2018*, National Statistics, www.gov.uk/government/statistics/criminal-justice-system-statistics-quarterly-december-2018.

——. (2019c) *Post-implementation Review of Part 1 of the Legal Aid, Sentencing and Punishment of Offenders Act 2012 (LASPO)*, Ministry of Justice, February, https://assets.publishing.service.gov.uk/government/uploads/system/uploads/attachment_data/file/777038/post-implementation-review-of-part-1-of-laspo.pdf.

Moorhead, R (1998) 'Legal Aid in the Eye of the Storm: Rationing, Contracting and a New Institutionalism' 25 *Journal of Law and Society* 365.

Moorhead, R, Vaughan, S and Godhino, C (2018) *In-House Lawyers' Ethics: Institutionalised Logics, Legal Risk and the Tournament of Influence* (Oxford, Hart Publishing).

Morison, J and Leith, P (1992) *The Barrister's World and the Nature of Law* (Buckingham, Open University Press).

Muzio, D (2004) 'The Professional Project and the Contemporary Re-organisation of the Legal Profession in England and Wales' 11 *International Journal of the Legal Profession* 33.

Muzio, D and Flood, J (2012) 'Entrepreneurship, Managerialism and Professionalism in Action: The Case of the Legal Profession in England and Wales' in M Reihlen and A Werr (eds), *Handbook of Research on Entrepreneurship in Professional Services* (Cheltenham, Edward Elgar).

Muzio, D and Kirkpatrick, I (2011) 'Introduction: Professions and Organizations – a Conceptual Framework' 59 *Current Sociology* 389.

Nelken, D (2004) 'Using the Concept of Legal Culture' 29 *Australian Journal of Legal Philosophy* 1.

Nelson, R and Trubek, D (1992) 'Arenas of Professionalism: The Professional Ideologies of Lawyers in Context' in R Nelson and D Trubek (eds), *Lawyers' Ideals/Lawyers' Practices* (Ithaca, Cornell University Press).

Newman, J (1995) 'Gender and Cultural Change' in C Itzin and J Newman (eds), *Gender, Culture and Organizational Change: Putting Theory into Practice* (Abingdon, Routledge).

Newman, J and Clarke, J (1994) 'Going about Our Business? The Managerialization of Public Services' in J Clarke, A Cochrane and E McLaughlin (eds), *Managing Social Policy* (London, Sage).

Nicolson, D (2005) Demography, Discrimination and Diversity: A New Dawn for the British Legal Profession?' 12 *International Journal of the Legal Profession* 201.

O'Malley, L and Harris, L (1999) 'The Dynamics of the Legal Market: An Interaction Perspective' 33 *European Journal of Marketing* 874.

Osiel, M (1989/90) 'Lawyers as Monopolists, Aristocrats, and Entrepreneurs' 103 *Harvard Law Review* 2009.

Palihawadana, D and Barnes, B (2004) 'Client Loyalty and Defection in the Corporate Legal Industry' 24 *Services Industries Journal* 101.

Parsons, T (1939) 'The Professions and Social Structure' 17 *Social Forces* 457.

Paterson, A (1996) 'Professionalism and the Legal Services Market' 3 *International Journal of the Legal Profession* 136.

Peacock, L (2014) 'Legal Aid Cuts Will Help Public School Boys Get to the Top, Says Top Female Judge', *The Telegraph*, 18 April, http://www.telegraph.co.uk/women/womens-business/10772365/Britains-most-senior-female-judge-Legal-aid-cuts-will-help-public-school-boys-get-to-the-top.html.

Peck, J (2008) 'Remaking Laissez-Faire' 32 *Progress in Human Geography* 3.

——. (2010) *Constructions of Neoliberal Reason* (Oxford, Oxford University Press).

Pfadenhauer, M (2006) 'Crisis or Decline? Problems of Legitimation and Loss of Trust in Modern Professionalism' 54 *Current Sociology* 565.

Pike, G and Robinson, D (2011) *Barristers' Working Lives: A Biennial Survey of the Bar 2011* (London, General Council of the Bar/Bar Standards Board).

Pinto, A (2015) 'International Work' *Counsel Magazine*, December, 20.

Pirie, F and Rogers, J (2013) 'Pupillage: The Shaping of a Professional Elite' in J Abbink and T Salverda (eds), *The Anthropology of Elites: Power, Culture and the Complexities of Distinction* (New York, Palgrave Macmillan).

Positive (2015) *Wellbeing at the Bar: A Resilience Framework Assessment* (London, General Council of the Bar).

Prest, W (1986) *The Rise of Barristers: A Social History of the English Bar 1590–1640* (Oxford, Clarendon Press).

Public Accounts Committee (2016) *Efficiency in the Criminal Justice System*, www.publications.parliament.uk/pa/cm201617/cmselect/cmpubacc/72/7202.htm.

Reed, M (2018) 'Elites, Professions, and the Neoliberal State: Critical Points of Intersection and Contention' 5 *Journal of Professions and Organization* 297.

Rivlin, G (2015) *Criminal Justice, Advocacy and the Bar* (London, General Council of the Bar).

Rogers, J (2010) 'Shadowing the Bar: Studying an English Professional Elite' 36 *Historical Reflections* 39.

——. (2011) 'Pupillage: The Making of the Barristers' Profession', PhD thesis, Oxford University.

——. (2012) 'Representing the Bar: How the Barristers' Profession Sells itself to Prospective Members' 32 *Legal Studies* 202.

——. (2014) 'Feeling Bad and Being Elite: A Comparative Analysis of the Anxieties and Uncertainties of Aspiring Barristers' 13 *Comparative Sociology* 30.

Rose, N (1999) *Governing the Soul: The Shaping of the Private Self*, 2nd edn (London, Free Association Books).

——. (2014) 'Civil Justice Council Slams Government's Court Fee Reforms', *Litigation Futures*, 13 February, https://www.litigationfutures.com/news/civil-justice-council-slams-governments-court-fee-reforms.

——. (2016) '6 Pump Court Becomes First Major Set to Create BSB Entity', *Legal Futures*, 16 September, http://www.legalfutures.co.uk/latest-news/exclusive-6-pump-court-becomes-first-major-set-create-bsb-entity.

——. (2018) 'Co-op: We're Now the UK's Largest Probate Providers', *Legal Futures*, 14 September, https://www.legalfutures.co.uk/latest-news/co-op-were-now-the-uks-largest-probate-provider.

Rozenberg, J (2017) 'Justine Online: Just as Good?', Gresham College Lecture, Museum of London, 22 February.

——. (2019) *The Online Court: Will IT Work?* (Guildford, Legal Education Foundation).

Saks, M (2012) 'Defining a Profession: The Role of Knowledge and Expertise' 2 *Professions and Professionalism* 1.

Schraer, R (2019) 'Could Barristers Earn More Working in McDonalds?', *BBC News*, 27 February, www.bbc.co.uk/news/uk-47372265.

The Secret Barrister (2018) *Stories of the Law and How it's Broken* (London, Macmillan).

Shiner, M (2000) 'Young, Gifted and Blocked! Entry to the Solicitors' Profession' in P Thomas (ed), *Discriminating Lawyers* (London, Cavendish Publishing).

Shiner, M and Newburn, T (1995) *Entry into the Legal Profession: The Law Student Cohort, Year 3* (London, Law Society).

Simons, M and Masschelein, J (2008) 'The Governmentalization of Learning and the Assemblage of a Learning Apparatus' 58 *Educational Theory* 391.

Singh, R (2013) 'The Unity of Law or the Dangers of Over-specialisation', Society of Legal Scholars Centenary Lecture, University of Birmingham 28 November, http://www.birmingham.ac.uk/schools/law/events/2013/sls-2013-lecture.aspx.

Slingo, J (2019) 'Criminal Bar Strikes Deal on Higher Fees', *Law Society Gazette*, 12 June, https://www.lawgazette.co.uk/news/criminal-bar-strikes-deal-on-higher-fees/5070587.article.

Smith, K (2006) 'Problematising Power Relations in "Elite Interviews"' 37 *Geoforum* 643.

Smith, V (2010) 'Enhancing Employability: Human, Cultural and Social Capital in an Era of Turbulent Unpredictability' 63 *Human Relations* 279.

Solicitors Regulation Authority (2019) 'Regulated Populated Statistics', www.sra.org.uk/sra/how-we-work/reports/statistics/regulated-community-statistics/data/higher_rights_of_audience.

Sommerlad, H (1995) 'Managerialism and the Legal Profession: A New Professional Paradigm' 2 *International Journal of the Legal Profession* 159.

——. (2002) 'Women Solicitors in a Fractured Profession: Intersections of Gender and Professionalism in England and Wales' 9 *International Journal of the Legal Profession* 213.

——. (2007) 'Researching and Theorizing the Process of Professional Identity Formation' 34 *Journal of Law and Society* 190.

——. (2011) 'The Commercialisation of Law and the Enterprising Legal Practitioner: Continuity and Change' 18 *International Journal of the Legal Profession* 73.

——. (2015) 'The "Social Magic" of Merit: Diversity, Equity, and Inclusion in the English and Welsh Legal Profession' 83 *Fordham Law Review* 2325.

Stanley, C (1991) 'Enterprising Lawyers: Changes in the Market for Legal Services' 25 *Law Teacher* 44.

Strauss, A and Corbin, J (2015) *Basics of Qualitative Research Techniques and Procedures for Developing Grounded Theory*, 4th edn (Los Angeles, Sage).

Suddaby, R and Greenwood, R (2005) 'Rhetorical Strategies of Legitimacy' 50 *Administrative Science Quarterly* 35.

Suddaby, R and Muzio, D (2015) 'Theoretical Perspectives on the Professions' in L Empson, D Muzio, J Broschak and B Hinings (eds) *The Oxford Handbook of Professional Service Firms* (Oxford, Oxford University Press).

Susskind, R (2000) *Transforming the Law: Essays on Technology, Justice and the Legal Marketplace* (Oxford, Oxford University Press).

——. (2010) *The End of Lawyers? Rethinking the Nature of Legal Services* (Oxford, Oxford University Press).

——. (2013) *Tomorrows Lawyers: An Introduction to Your Future* (Oxford, Oxford University Press).

Susskind, R and Susskind, D (2015) *The Future of the Professions. How Technology Will Transform the Work of Human Experts* (Oxford, Oxford University Press).

Sutton Trust (2018) '"Pay as You Go?" Internship Pay, Quality and Access in the Graduate Jobs Market', www.suttontrust.com/research-paper/internships-pay-as-you-go.

Thomas, R, Darroch, J and Galvin, W (2001) 'Marketing and Service Orientation in New Zealand Law Firms' 19 *Marketing Intelligence & Planning* 103.

Thompson, J (2005) 'The New Visibility' 22 *Theory, Culture and Society* 31.

*The Times* (2019) 'Cuts to Justice Leading to Breakdown of Rule of Law, Says Former Judge', 23 May, https://www.thetimes.co.uk/article/cuts-to-justice-leading-to-breakdown-of-rule-of-law-says-former-judge-mx3bdtrgc.

Vaughan, S and Oakley, E (2016) '"Gorilla Exceptions" and the Ethically Apathetic Corporate Lawyer' 19 *Legal Ethics* 50.

Vickers, J (2001) *Competition in the Professions* (London, Office of Fair Trading).

Vickerstaff, A (2000) 'Legal Sector Marketing: A Contested Case' 38 *Management Decision* 354.

Wagner, A (2014) 'Don't Be Fooled by the "Concessions", There is Still a Real Threat to Judicial Review', *UK Human Rights Blog*, 6 February, https://ukhumanrightsblog.com/2014/02/06/dont-be-fooled-by-the-concessions-there-is-still-a-real-threat-to-judicial-review.

Walters, M (2018) 'Pupil Barristers to Get up to 50% More under New Minimum Salary', *Law Society Gazette*, 7 December, www.lawgazette.co.uk/law/pupil-barristers-to-get-up-to-50-more-under-new-minimum-salary/5068598.article.

Warren, N (1978) 'The Inns of Court' in R Hazell (ed), *The Bar on Trial* (London, Quartet Books).

Watt, I, Nettleton, S and Burrows, R (2008) 'The Views of Doctors on Their Working Lives: A Qualitative Study' 101 *Journal of the Royal Society of Medicine* 592.

Webb, J (2004) 'Turf Wars and Market Control: Competition and Complexity in the Market for Legal Services' 11 *International Journal of the Legal Profession* 81.

——. (2015) 'The LETRs (Still) in the Post: The Legal Education and Training Review and the Reform of Legal Services Education and Training – A Personal (Re)View' in H Sommerlad, S Harris-Short, S Vaughan and R Young (eds), *The Futures of Legal Education and the Legal Profession* (Oxford, Hart Publishing).

Webber, J (2004) 'Culture, Legal Culture and Legal Reasoning: A Comment on Nelken' 29 *Australian Journal of Legal Philosophy* 27.

Weeks, J (2004) *Unpopular Culture: The Ritual of Complaint in a British Bank* (Chicago, University of Chicago Press).

Wesley Pue, W (1997) 'Lawyers and Political Liberalism in Eighteenth and Nineteenth Century England' in T Halliday and L Karpik (eds), *Lawyers and the Rise of Western Political Liberalism* (Oxford, Clarendon Press).

Wilkinson, S and Kitzinger, C (2013) 'Representing Our Own Experience: Issues in "Insider" Research' 37 *Psychology of Women Quarterly* 251.

Woo, K and Leelapanyalert, K (2014) Client Relationship Marketing Practices: An Exploratory Study of the Legal Industry' 13 *Journal of Relationship Marketing* 286.

Wood, D (2010) *Review of Pupillage Report of the Working Group* (London, Bar Standards Board).

YouGov/London Economics (2018) 'Consumer Behaviour and Attitudes towards Price and Service Transparency', https://www.barstandardsboard.org.uk/uploads/assets/59164f2f-1816-4620-babc5cbf573bf8f6/pricetransparencyresearchreport-final.pdf.

Zander, M (1968) *Lawyers and the Public Interest: A Study in Restrictive Practices* (London, Weidenfeld & Nicolson).

——. (1988) *A Matter of Justice: The Legal System in Ferment* (Oxford, Oxford University Press).

——. (1990) 'The Thatcher Government's Onslaught on the Lawyers: Who Won?' 24 *International Law* 753.

Zimdars, A (2010) 'The Profile of Pupil Barristers at the Bar of England and Wales 2004–2008' 17 *International Journal of the Legal Profession* 117.

# INDEX

*Note*: Alphabetical arrangement is word-by-word, where a group of letters followed by a space is filed before the same group of letters followed by a letter, eg 'social values' will appear before 'socialisation'. In determining alphabetical arrangement, initial articles and prepositions are ignored.


**Abbott, A,** 6, 8–9, 10, 11, 13–15, 35, 90, 149–50, 153
**Abel, R,** 2, 9, 11, 21, 36, 73, 95
**Abel-Smith, B,** 21
**ABS,** *see* **Alternative Business Structures**
**Absolute Barrister,** 55
**academic credentials:**
pupillage selection, 70, 71, 73
**academic excellence:**
pupillage selection, 71
**academic qualifications:**
excellence acquired, 109
**access schemes:**
Inns of Court, 134
**access to justice,** 128
detrimental impact, Bar Council, 28
**Access to Justice Act 1999 (AIA),** 27, 28
**accountability,** 26
barristers, 128
chambers, 13, 44
costs, 13
court procedures, 13
customer service, 13
legal profession, 13, 32
professionalism, 12, 150
recruitment, 13
regulation, 121
success qualities, 1
training, legal profession, 13
**accountancy profession,** 26
**accountants:**
attorneys' competition from, 22
bankruptcy work, 21, 22
insolvency work, 21
solicitors' competition from, 22
**accounting, forensic,** 132
**accounts, chambers,** 37
**Ackroyd, S,** 11
**ad hoc committees, chambers,** 36
**adaptability,** 154
**adaptive skills,** 153
**administration managers, chambers,** 44
**Administration of Justice Act 1985,** 25
**administrative tasks, chambers,** 36
**administrators, chambers,** 36, 44, 46
**admiralty courts:**
proctors in, 17
**admission,** 22
**advancement mechanisms, pupillage,** 61
**advertising:**
Bar, ban lifted, 25
by barristers, ban lifted, 75
direct access, 104
forbidden, barristers, 36
getting work, 78
pupillage, 67
services provided by barristers, 104
solicitors, 25
*see also* marketing
**advocacy:**
as barrister defining feature, 18
potential, pupillage selection, 72
representation function separation from, 16
service:
bespoke, specialist Bar, 153
direct access and, possibility of doing both, 100
skills:
pupillage selection, 72
success qualities, 1
solicitors, *see* solicitors
training:
Inns of Court and circuits, 132
**advocates:**
barristers' independent status as, 153
in College of Civilians, 17–18
in Doctors' Commons, 17–18
expert, 105

independent, 16
solicitors training in court advocacy and, 115
**Advocates' Graduated Fee Scheme (AGFS),** 31
**advocatus,** 16–17
**after-the-event (ATE) insurance,** 120
**AGFS (Advocates' Graduated Fee Scheme),** 31
**AIA (Access to Justice Act 1999),** 27, 28
**alerters, chambers,** 85
**Alexander QC, Robert,** 25
**Alternative Business Structures (ABS),** 32
Bar Standards Board licensing, 52
barristers, 32
chambers, 52–54, 56
independence as reason to resist setting up, 112
solicitors, 32
Solicitors Regulation Authority licensing, 52
**alternative dispute resolution,** 33
**altruistic motives, professionals,** 23
**Ames, J,** 11
**analytical skills,** 1
**Anderson, B,** 138–39
**Anglo-American modes of professionalism,** 6
**annexes opened by chambers,** 54
**anti-competitiveness:**
Bar advocacy in higher courts deemed, 24
**apprenticeships:**
Inns of Court, 18
Serjeants-at-Law, 17
years, chambers, 135
**Arbitration Act 1889,** 21
**arbitration companies:**
separate formed by chambers, 105
**arbitrators,** 21, 105
**argument:**
skills or potential, pupillage selection, 72
**Aristotle,** 73
**Association of Women Barristers,** 143–44
**associations, professional,** ***see*** **professional associations; specialist Bar associations**
**ATE (after-the-event) insurance,** 120
**attorneys:**
briefs, barristers' preparation delegated to, 20
Common Bench, 17
in common law courts, 17
accountants, competition from, 22
auctioneers, competition from, 22
conveyancing monopoly, 20
debt collectors, competition from, 22
etiquette rules, 20
evidence, barristers' preparation delegated to, 20
Inns of Chancery, 18
litigation initiation monopoly, 20
merged with solicitors, 18
regulation, 20
training, 20
**auctioneers,** 22
**Australian Bar:**
community, 139
women, 143, 146
**authorised bodies,** 32
**autonomy:**
barristers, 151
employed barristers' lack of, 127
legal profession, 10, 13–14
professional, 114, 117

**Bach Commission,** 28
**backstage location, chambers,** 41–43
**balance of power shifts,** 119
**balanced constitution notion,** 108
**BAME students, pupillage,** 59, 73
**Bankruptcy Courts:**
solicitors as advocates in, 21
**bankruptcy work:**
accountants, 21, 22
**Bar:**
advertising ban lifted, 25
advocacy in higher courts, 24, 25, 27
aristocracy, route into, 19
associations, *see* specialist Bar associations
bespoke, high-quality legal services offered by, 151
chambers within Inns policy changed, 25
commercial, *see* commercial Bar
community, 130, 135, 147, 150
as competitive business, 149
consumers at heart of system, 23
Courts and Legal Services Act 1990, 26–27
criminal, *see* criminal Bar
critical studies on, 24
culture, 107–108, 130
absorption, 138
civil procedure and costs rules, 124–25
commitment, 109–12
conditional fee agreements, 120–21
development of Bar ideology, 108–109
excellence, 109–12, 116
ideals, 147
independence, 112–16
independent regulation, 121–24
integrity, 109–12
managerial reforms, 121–24

powerful clients, 118–20
pro bono, 125–26
public service, 125–26
self-employment and independence, 112–16
state support loss, 116–18
discretionary judgement as feature of, 55
distinguishing characteristics, 147
early origins, 16–18
ethical rules, 108
expertise offered by, 151
family, 151, 152
fragmentation, 130, 139–40, 147–48
General Council, *see* Bar Council
gentleman's profession, status and distinction, 19–20
governance, 22–23, 24
high-quality, bespoke legal services offered by, 151
identity weakened, 150
ideology, 108–109, 127, 129, 130
in Inns of Court, 130
independence, 19, 127
independent regulation imposition, 1
junior members of Inns, 18
knowledge as feature of, 55
legal aid and growth, 23
liberties, 18–19
loss of monopoly on higher court audience rights, 1
marketisation, 13
mentoring, unofficial, 136
Ministry of Justice and, dispute between, 6
monopoly on higher court audience rights, 9
narrow specialism, shift towards, 152
neoliberal, independent regulation and the Legal Services Act 2007, 31–33
organisational structure liberalising rules, 1
privately funded, 139–142
privileges, 18–19
Pro Bono Unit, 29, 125–26
professional life at, 55–56
public funding withdrawal, 1
public interest, serving, 23
publicly funded, 115, 129, 139–42
restrictive practices challenges, 24
Royal Commission on Legal Services 1979, 24
self-government, 19
Senate, 22, 25
small, homogeneous, of early years, 147–48
solicitors challenging advocacy of, 9
specialist, 141–42
status as feature of, 55
structure challenges, 24
traditional characteristics reshaped by commercial and organisational logics, 13
unity, 147
wellbeing, research on, 136, 137–38, 147
in wider political and economic world, 6–7
women, 143, 147
childcare and work balance, 145
flexible or extended hours, HMCTS initiative, 145
maternity leave, 143–46
work boundaries redrawn, 150
**Bar Committee,** 21, 22
**Bar Council,** 21
access to justice detrimental impact, 28
barristers little or nothing to do with, 135
direct access, 94, 103
discipline powers, 22
etiquette powers, 22
'Excellence', word used on website homepage, 109
Fair Recruitment Guide, 67
'Integrity', word used on website homepage, 109
International Committee, 54, 104
'Justice', word used on website homepage, 109
marketing training, 89, 105
Monopolies Commission, 24
Pupil Equality Monitoring Toolkit, 67
regulation and representation functions separation, 32
representation, 32, 22
Soft Skills Development Course, 89
specialist Bar associations represented on, 134
Subconscious Bias, 67
united profession, rhetoric presenting, 138
'Wellbeing at the Bar' online website and support system, 111
wellbeing survey research, 111
**Bar Directories:**
chambers' marketing target, 51
**Bar Mark,** 46
**Bar of England and Wales,** *see* **Bar**
**Bar Professional Training Course (BPTC),** 59
mini-pupillages during, 62
scholarships, Inns of Court, 132
self-promotion not covered, 79
work experience prerequisite to get on, 63

**Bar Standards Board (BSB),** 32
ABS entities licensing, 52
chambers regulation, 38
Code of Conduct, 108
customer complaints procedures, 121
disciplinary mechanisms, 121
Equality and Diversity Rules, 67
hostile views about, 123
legal services at the Bar study, 95, 104
LLP licensing, 53
managerial control over chambers' activities, 121
managerial reforms, 127
negative views about, 122–24
neutral views about, 122–24
pupillage regulation, 121, 135
Quality Assurance Scheme for Advocates (QASA), 115, 123–24, 135
recruitment regulation, 121
regulator, 22–23
research, 2
risk-based supervision approach to regulation of chambers, 46
views about, 122–24
**Barristers Direct,** 55
**Barristers Online,** 55
**Barristers' Clerks, Institute of (IBC),** 45, 48
**behaviour:**
ethical, 114
malleable self-regulating subjects shaping and normalising, 13–14
**benchers:**
Inns of Court stepping-stones to becoming, 133
**bespoke advocacy and advisory services,** 33, 153
**bespoke legal services offered by Bar,** 151
**bias, conscious and unconscious, pupillage,** 69, 73
**Billy Bot,** 55
**blogs,** 82
**Boon, A,** 27, 108
**boundary shifts,** 9
**BPTC,** *see* **Bar Professional Training Course**
**branded websites, sets,** 79
**branding:**
chambers, 50–52
developments in, 150
online, 79–83
sets, chambers, 50–52
skills, 154
**briefs:**
barristers' preparation delegated to solicitors and attorneys, 20
**Briggs Report (2016),** 152
**BSB,** *see* **Bar Standards Board**
**budgets:**
costs, 124
marketing, chambers, 46–47, 83
**Burrage, M,** 8, 9, 19, 21, 78, 153
**bursaries:**
Inns of Court, 134
**business:**
chambers as, 48–50, 57
commercialism, chambers, 43–47
competitive, Bar as, 149
directors, chambers, 47
expertise, chambers steered by, 150
legal profession as, 32
litigation as, 128
managers, chambers, 43–44
plans, chambers, 48
strategies, barristers, improving, 104

**cab rank rule,** 108
**CAB (Citizens Advice Bureaux),** 28
**career,** 1
**Carr-Saunders, A,** 7
**Carter of Coles, Lord,** 29
**cases:**
family law, 2, 29
less autonomy in running of, professionalism, 150
management, 13, 124–25
**cause funds, chambers,** 126
**CBA,** *see* **Criminal Bar Association**
**CEO (chief executive officers), chambers,** 47
**CFA,** *see* **conditional fee agreements**
**chambers:**
accountability, 44
accounts, 37
ad hoc committees, 36
administration managers, 44
administrative tasks, 36
administrators, 36, 44, 46
alerters, 85
Alternative Business Structures, 52–54, 56
annexes opened, 54
apprenticeship years, 135
arbitration companies, separate, 105
backstage location, 41–43
Bar and Ministry of Justice, effect of dispute between, 6
Bar Standards Board:
regulation, 38
managerial control over activities, 121

barristers:
  decision-making led by, 55
  hot-desking, 42
  information technology, 42
  rooms, 41
  working from home, 42
  views on chambers as business, 49
branding, 50–52
as business, 48–50, 57
business commercialism, 43–47
business directors, 47
business expertise, steered by, 150
business managers, 43–44
business plans, 48
cause funds, 126
changing, 142–43
charitable foundations, 126
chief executives, 44, 47
chief operating officers, 44
clerks, 36, 40
  direct access, 103–104
  fees clerks, 37
  junior, 37
  management training, 44, 47–48
  super clerks, 47–48
  teams, 48
  traditional model, 55
  unaccountable for brief allocation, 78
  views on chambers as business, 49–50
  workloads increased, 46
clients:
  conferences, 37
  service and satisfaction, 41
  visiting, catering to, 43
collegiality, 12–13, 43, 55, 135–38
commerce focus, 55
commercial managers, 47
commercialism, business and management, 43–47
committees, 46
community, 136, 137–38, 142
competition, 76
compliance focus, 55
conferences, 37, 41, 83
constitutions, 44
cost sharing, 37
customer care focus, 55
customer-centred professional service, 48
decision-making, 44, 55
direct access, 103–104
directors, 39, 44, 47
discrimination policies, 46
divisions of labour, 44
dues, 47
educational background, shared, 38
efficiency focus, 55
enterprise concept, 55
entertainment, 85
experiences, shared, 38
fair selection policies, 46
fees clerks, 37
front stage location, 41–43
General Chambers Meetings, 36
general common law practices, 37
geographical addresses, 37
global, going, 52–54
group bids, 84
growth, and rise of specialist teams, 38–41
heads of chambers, 44
hierarchy, 37
higher number of barristers in, 40
hollowed-out organisations, risks of becoming, 138
hot-desking, 42, 43
information technology liberated barristers from working in, 42
junior clerks, 37
juniors, 44
lawyers abroad, alliances with, 54
lectures targeted at solicitors, 83
less autonomy in running of, professionalism, 150
limited companies, 54
limited liability partnerships, 53–54
location, front stage, backstage and chambers as virtual space, 41–43
logos, 51–52
loyalty to, 39
management commercialism, 43–47
management plans, 48
managerial control over activities, Bar Standards Board, 121
managerial expertise, steered by, 150
managerial interference, independence from, 56
managers, 44–45
manuals, 46
market closure, 37
market-oriented, 79
marketing:
  Bar Directories target, 51
  budgets, 46–47, 83
  consultants, 51
  managers, 44

specialists, 85
teams, 83
training, 105
maternity policies, 46
members shaped and controlled by environment, 37
membership, 36, 38
mentoring schemes, 136
Ministry of Justice and Bar, effect of dispute between, 6
model evolved, 150
movement out of Inns, 147
new commercialism, business and management, 43–47
new ways of running, resistance to, 153
newsletters, 85
North Eastern circuit, 133
office space acquisitions, 54
online chambers, 55
online presence, 51
open door practice, 43
organisation accountability, 13
outside Inns of Court, 37
overcrowding, 37
paralegals, alliances with, 99
physical space within, 41
practice development, 44, 47
practice managers, 48
professional socialisation, 37, 135, 138
pupillage, 67, 68, 135–36
reception areas, 41
receptionists, 37
recruitment policies, 46
regulation, 46
relationship marketing models, 79
rents, commercial, 38
run as collectives by committees, 150
self-employed practitioners, 36
self-employed status within, 137
seminars targeted at solicitors, 83–84
sets:
common law rebranded, 51
branded websites, 79
branding, 50–52
merging, 38
mixed disciplinary, 51
movement between, 147
moves out, 43
multi-disciplinary, 51
shared interests, 148
size, 38
small shared interests in, fragmentation, 148
showroom common parts, focus on, 43
solicitors, small firms, alliances with, 99
specialists, 37
Bar Associations, 40–41
recognition, 40
teams, 38–41
strategic overviews, 49
strategy, 47, 55
structure, 37
support, 137
support staff, 37, 40
traditional model, 34, 35–38
or something new, 55–57
trainees, 48
training, 38, 105, 135
transparency, 44
typing services, 37
unity within under strain, 147
virtual chambers, 55
virtual space, 41–43
vocational training, shared, 38
waiting areas, 41
web analytics, 80
websites, 51, 79
work culture, shared, 38
work unevenly or unfairly distributed within, 78
working from home impact, 138
written constitutions, 44
**Chancery Bar Association,** 126
**Chancery Court,** 17
**charging methods,** 149
**charitable foundations, chambers,** 126
**Charles II, King,** 18
**Chicago School of Sociology,** 8
**chief executive officers (CEO), chambers,** 47
**chief executives, chambers,** 44
**chief operating officers, chambers,** 44
**childcare,** 145
**circuits:**
advocacy training, 132
community, 130
continuing professional development courses, 132
customs, 131
ethics training, 132
forensic accounting, 132
importance loss, 131
new practitioner qualifying courses, 132
North Eastern, chambers, 133

Northern, 133
rules, 131
tight-knit community, 131
**Citizens Advice Bureau (CAB),** 28
**citizenship:**
service provision on basis of, 109
**City of London Law Society:**
Commercial Bar Association standard terms for solicitors, 135
**civil claims:**
inquisitorial style without lawyers, 76–77
**civil legal aid, scope of,** 28
**civil procedure, costs,** 124–25
**civil service reforms,** 26
**Civilians, College of,** 17–18
**Clashfern, Lord Mackay of,** 26
**Clementi, David,** 31
**clerks:**
barristers, 20
chambers, *see* chambers
Inns of Court, 18
**Clerksroom,** 55
**clients:**
at centre, professionalism, 150
chambers, *see* chambers
direct access, 100–102
direct instructions to barristers, 21, 75, 77
international work, 104–105
lay, *see* lay clients
powerful, *see* powerful clients
professionals, *see* professionals
repeat, solicitors as, 77
trust, professionals, 23
**CLSA (Courts and Legal Services Act 1990),** 26–27
**codes of conduct:**
Bar Standards Board, 108
legal culture incorporation, 130
**collaborative lawyering,** 33
**collectives:**
chambers run by committees as, 150
**College of Civilians,** 17–18
**collegial governance,** 10
**collegiality, chambers,** 12–13, 43, 55, 135–38
**collegiate professions,** 12, 35
**COMBAR,** *see* **Commercial Bar Association**
**commerce focus, chambers,** 55
**commercial approach:**
barristers, 128
solicitor profession, 10
**commercial astuteness:**
success qualities, 1
**commercial Bar,** 140
bespoke expert advisory and advocacy service, 153
interests, criminal Bar disconnect, 147
pupillage, 60
**Commercial Bar Association (COMBAR):**
City of London Law Society standard terms for solicitors, 135
pro bono services, 126
**commercial branch professions,** 11
**commercial concerns,** 151
**commercial flair,** 153
**commercial funders,** 119–20
**commercial logics:**
Bar traditional characteristics reshaped by, 13
**commercial managers, chambers,** 47
**commercial orientation,** 13
**commercial practices,** 150
**commercial skills,** 149
**commercialisation,** 8, 11, 12
**commercialised professionalism,** 88, 119
**commercialism,** 10, 43–47, 154
**commitment,** 109–12, 126, 127
**Committee of Public Accounts,** 117–18
**committees:**
ad hoc, chambers, 36
chambers, 46
**Common Bench,** 17
**common law:**
courts, 17
development, 16
emergence, 16
expansion, 16
general practices, chambers, 37
rebranded sets, chambers, 51
**Common Pleas, Court of,** 17
**community:**
Australian Bar, 139
Bar, 130, 135, 147, 150
chambers, 136, 137–38, 142
circuits, 130, 131
ideology, 108
imagined, 138–39
Inns of Court, 130, 131, 133
professional, 147
splintered, 142
traditional, Inns of Court, 131
united, Inns of Court, limitations, 133
**companies, limited, chambers,** 54
**Compensation Courts,** 21
**competition,** 26
barristers, 76, 128

chambers, 76
injection into legal services market, 12
legal profession, 32, 33
markets opened up to, professionals, 11
monopolies opened up to, professionals, 11
outside profession, 76
promotion, legal profession, 13
for pupillage places, 58–59, 60–61, 66
self-employment, 137
**competitive approach, professions,** 8
**competitive business, Bar as,** 149
**competitive tendering,** 115
**complaints:**
culture, 122
customer complaints procedures, 121
direct access clients, 102
groundless, 121–22
**compliance:**
chambers focus, 55
managerial, 127
**conditional fee agreements (CFA),** 28, 76, 120–21, 127
**conduct,** *see* **codes of conduct; professional conduct**
**conferences, chambers,** 37, 41, 83
**confidence:**
lack in marketing, 90
**conflict:**
professionalism as dynamic, resulting from, 9
**conscious bias, pupillage,** 73
**constant scrutiny,** 6
**constitution of professionalism,** 6
**Constitutional Affairs Select Committee,** 29
**constitutions, chambers,** 44
**consultants:**
marketing, chambers, 51
**consumerism,** 10, 11
**contentious matters:**
solicitor intervention required, 21
**contingent forces:**
professions development dependant on, 9
**continuing professional development (CPD):**
accredited events, solicitors, 83, 84
courses, Inns of Court and circuits, 132
professionals, 11
seminars accredited for, 83
**control:**
Inns of Court, 18–19
organisational, 129
**conveyancers:**
in common law courts, 17
licensed, 25
**conveyancing:**
fees reduction, Law Society, 25
monopoly, solicitors, 20, 24–25
**corporate clients:**
control of lawyers increasing, 119
**corporate institutions:**
corporate or in-house lawyers and, balance of power shifts, 119
**corporate sector:**
legal profession, global presence, 32–33
**costs:**
accountability, legal profession, 13
budgets, 124
civil procedure, 124–25
forecasting, 124
management orders, 124
sharing, chambers, 37
*see also* fees
**County Courts Act 1846,** 20, 21
**courses,** *see* **training**
**Court of Common Pleas,** 17
**courts:**
chronic underfunding, 152
digital, 33
ecclesiastical, proctors in, 17
higher, *see* higher courts
issue fees, 75–76
Magistrates, 21
online, 76–77
procedures accountability, legal profession, 13
system, managerial reforms, 127
**Courts and Legal Services Act 1990 (CLSA),** 26–27
**CPD,** *see* **continuing professional development**
**CPS,** *see* **Crown Prosecution Service**
**criminal advocates:**
inexperienced barristers employed to work as, 114–16
**criminal Bar,** 151
CPS pay increases, 152
interests, commercial Bar disconnect, 147
legal aid increases, 152
neoliberalisation, 152
state intervention, 152
**Criminal Bar Association (CBA):**
assertiveness, 135
militancy, 134
QASA legality judicial proceedings, 135
strike action, 30–31, 134
trade union style of leadership and representation, 134

**criminal cases, legal aid,** 6
**criminal defence work:**
  direct access, 98
**criminal law work:**
  diversifying, 86–87
  pupillage, 60
  solicitors, 27, 76
**criminal lawyers:**
  legal aid payments to, 115
**criminal legal aid,** 6, 29–31
**criminal prosecutions,** 76
**critical thinking:**
  skills or potential, pupillage selection, 72
**Crown Prosecution Service (CPS):**
  barristers' secondments to, 87
  budget cuts, 76
  criminal Bar pay increases, 152
  instruction by, 118
  prosecution fees, 31
**cultural assumptions:**
  surrounding professionals as persons to trust, 26
**cultural capital:**
  cultivation to improve employability, 62
  of pupillage applicants, 73
**cultural factors:**
  pupillage applicants' employability, 66
**cultural ideals,** 147
**cultural life:**
  Inns of Court centres of, 18
**culture:**
  Bar, *see* Bar
  of complaints, 122
  dynamic, 107
  evolution, power central to, 107
  legal, *see* legal culture
  professional, 10, 107, 154
  professionalism developing, 6
**customer care:**
  chambers focus, 55
  skills, direct access requiring, 105
**customer-centred professional service:**
  chambers, 48
**customer complaints,** 121
**customer-focus,** 1
**customer service:**
  accountability, legal profession, 13
  solicitor profession, 10
**customs, circuits,** 131
**CVs, pupillage,** 59, 61–63, 66
**Cwmgiedd, Lord Thomas of,** 138
**Damages Based Agreements (DBA),** 120–21, 127
**debates about professionalism,** 150
**debt collectors:**
  competition from, 22
**debts, students,** 154
**decision-making:**
  chambers, 44, 55
  powerful clients, direct contract hampering, 119
**decline, professional,** 10
**defensiveness about marketing,** 90
**degradation, professional,** 150
**Department of Trade and Industry (DTI):**
  Restrictive Trade Practices Policy Review 1988, 25
**devaluation of services,** 154
**development, professional,** 9, 10, 134, 153
**digital courts,** 33
**digital platforms,** 154
**Dingwall, R,** 153
**dining, Inns of Court,** 41, 131, 132, 133–34
**direct access,** 94–95
  advertising, 104
  advocacy services and, possibility of doing both, 100
  attitudes to, 95
  barristers' schedules not always allowing availability, 99
  Bar Council, 94, 103
  as bolt-on supplementing work referred through usual channels, 106
  chambers, 103–104
  clients, 100–102
  criminal defence work, 98
  fees, 96–97
  future development, 105–106
  instructing solicitors not always aware, 104
  marketing, 79
  offending solicitors, 102–103
  private family work, 103
  public awareness, 103–105
  research on, 2
  seminars:
    human resources officers or consultants invited, 104
  suitability, 97–100
  turning work away, 101
  working well, examples of, 99
**Direct Professional Access,** *see* **direct access**
**directors:**
  chambers, 39, 44, 47
**discipline,** 22, 121

**discretion, legal profession,** 10
**discretionary judgement:**
as feature of Bar, 55
**discrimination:**
policies, chambers, 46
**dismissal:**
barristers, 22
**dismissiveness of marketing,** 90
**disputes:**
containment and avoidance, 33
jurisdictional, 20–22, 150
resolution, 33, 128
**diversification:**
getting work, 79, 85–88
**diversity,** 147
training, 67, 121
**division of labour,** 16, 21–22
chambers, 44
modernised, 150
profession links, 7
**Doctors' Commons,** 17–18
**DTI,** *see* **Department of Trade and Industry**
**dual capacity:**
in getting work, 87–88
as self-employed and employed practitioners, 32
**dues, chambers,** 47
**Durkheim, Émile,** 7, 23
**dynamic culture,** 107
**dynamic professionalism,** 9, 150

**ecclesiastical courts, proctors in,** 17
**economic gains:**
professionalism, concerns, 24
**economic hostility,** 11
**economic policies, neoliberal,** 8
**economic world:**
wider, Bar in, 6–7
**education:**
elite, pupillage selection focus, 69–70
Inns of Court, *see* Inns of Court
shared background, chambers, 38
specialist Bar associations' function, 134, 147
*see also* pupillage; training
**Eekelaar, J,** 2
**efficiency:**
barristers, 128
chambers focus, 55
solicitor profession, 10
**elegant spaces, Inns of Court,** 131
**elite education:**
pupillage selection focus, 69–70
**employability,** 62, 66
**employed barristers:**
autonomy, lack of, 127
status, reduced sense of, 127
training in court advocacy and, 115
**employed practitioners:**
self-employed practitioners and, barristers' dual capacity as, 32
**employment structures:**
legal profession, less secure, 33
**Employment Tribunals:**
fees, 76
**enterprise:**
chambers, 55
concept, 1, 55
culture, 1 88, 151
principles blurred, 12
pupillage selection requirement, 73–74
traditional professional values reshaped in line with, 154
entertainment, chambers, 85
**entrenchment, ideological,** 134
**entrepreneurship,** 26
direct access requiring, 105
practices, resistance to adoption, 153
promotion, legal profession, 13
rhetoric, professional relationships, 1
students, managing employability, 66
**environment:**
chambers members shaped and controlled by, 37
**equality:**
pupillage applicants' employability issues, 66
training, 67, 121
**Equality and Diversity Rules:**
Bar Standards Board, 67
**ethics:**
behaviour, 114
framework, excellence, operated within, 109
legal, BSB Code of Conduct reflecting, 108
legal culture incorporation, 130
one set for all experiences, 153, 153
rules, Bar, 108
training:
Inns of Court and circuits, 132
values, 107
**etiquette:**
powers, Bar Council, 22
rules, 20
**evidence:**
barristers' preparation delegated to solicitors and attorneys, 20

**excellence,** 126, 127
academic qualifications and training acquired, 109
aspiration to, 112
Bar culture, 109–12, 116
continual, pressure in striving for, 111
ethical framework operated within, 109
as ethos about work, 109
external pressure to strive for, 111
as moral approach to work, 109
professional autonomy not necessarily leading to, 114
self-imposed pressure to strive for, 111
technical, 91, 93
value for money focus rather than, 128
word used on website Bar Council homepage, 109
**exclusivity loss, professionals,** 12
**experiences:**
chambers shared, 38
ethics, one set for all, 153
transparency, 80
**expert advisory service:**
bespoke, specialist Bar, 153
**expert advocates:**
barristers as, 105
**expertise:**
business, chambers steered by, 150
managerial chambers steered by, 150
micro-specialist, 149–50
offered by Bar, 151
transparency, 80
**extended hours:**
HMCTS initiative, women at the Bar and, 145
**external oversight:**
professionalism, 150
replacing professional self-regulation, 11
**external pressure:**
to strive for excellence, 111
**external regulation:**
professionalism, 12
**external supervision:**
replacing professional self-regulation, 11

**face-to-face interviews,** 2–3, 155–57
**Fair Recruitment Guide, Bar Council,** 67
**fair selection policies, chambers,** 46
**Falconer, Lord,** 29
**family Bar,** 151, 152
**family justice system,** 29
**family law:**
cases, 2, 29
seminars in field of, 83–84
specialising, 86
**family work:**
private, 103
pupillage, 60
**Faulconbridge, J,** 50, 56
**feedback, institutional,** 108
**fees:**
barristers, 30, 104
constant scrutiny, 6
court issue, 75–76
cuts, 30
direct access, 96–97
Employment Tribunals, 76
fixed, 80, 96
hourly, 80, 96
prosecution, CPS, 31
solicitors, 30, 96–97
success, 120–21
upfront information demands, 80
uplift, 120–21
*see also* costs
**fees clerks, chambers,** 37
**filtering criteria:**
pupillage selection, 73
***fin de siècle* feeling:**
for publicly funded Bar, 154
**financial institutions:**
corporate or in-house lawyers and, balance of power shifts, 119
**financial risks, students,** 154
**fixed fees,** 80, 96
**fixed-term trials,** 124–25
**flexibility,** 154
**flexible hours:**
HMCTS initiative, women at the Bar and, 145
**flexible methods of charging,** 149
**flexible working,** 79, 88
**Flood, J,** 2, 12, 21, 27, 78, 95, 96, 97, 100, 102
**forecasting costs,** 124
**forensic accounting,** 132
**Foucault, Michel,** 66
**fragmentation:**
Bar, 130, 139–40, 147–48
legal profession, 151, 152
shared interests in small sets of chambers, 148
solicitors, 130–31
**franchising, legal aid,** 28
**Francis, A,** 9, 130–31, 152–53
**Free Representation Unit (FRU),** 125

**free surgeries,** 104
**Freer, E,** 2, 69
**Freidson, E,** 7–8, 10, 11
**Friedman, L,** 107
**FRU (Free Representation Unit),** 125
**functionalist trait theorists,** 107, 109
**funders,** 119–20, 129
**funding:**
loss, Citizens Advice Bureaux, 28
public, *see* public funding
pupillage, 58
state, 151–52
**further educational qualifications:**
pupillage, 63–64

**GDL (Graduate Diploma in Law),** 59, 62
**General Chambers Meetings,** 36
**General Council, Bar,** *see* **Bar Council**
**generalists,** 38
**gentleman's profession:**
Bar as, status and distinction, 19–20
**geographical addresses:**
chambers, 37
**geographical spaces**
Inns of Court as mere, 133
**getting work:**
advertising, 78
barristers and solicitors, 77–78
commercialised professionalism, 88
diversification, 85–88
dual capacity, 87–88
flexible working, 88
high visibility, 79–83
hybrid status, 87–88
individual initiatives, 85–88
market-oriented models deployment, 89
new marketeers, 75–93
new practice areas, 85–88
online branding, 79–83
recommendations, 92
relationship building, 88–90
relationship marketing deployment, 89
reputation, 93
secondments in law firms, 87
self-promoting barristers, 78–79, 87, 90
services, promotion of, 78
social media, 79–83
solicitors and barristers, 77–78
specialism, 85–88
technical excellence, 91, 93
*see also* marketing
**global accounting firms:**
legal services by, 33
**Global Law Summit,** 128, 140, 147
**globalisation:**
chambers going global, 52–54
legal profession corporate sector presence, 32–33
legal services, 12
reshaping professionalism, 12
**goals, personal,** 90
**Gove, Michael,** 30
**governance:**
Bar, 22–23, 24
collegial, 10
modernised, 150
new modes, 13–14
**government:**
indirect mechanisms of, 14
of internal world, 13
**graduate degrees,** 64, 65
**Graduate Diploma in Law (GDL),** 59, 62
**Gray's Inn:**
specialists, 37
**Grayling, Chris,** 30, 128
**Green Papers:**
legal profession 1989, 26
**groundless complaints,** 121–22
**groups:**
bids, chambers, 84
marketing in, 79, 83–85

**Hanlon, G,** 10–11
**Harris, L,** 50, 78, 111
**Hazel, R,** 23, 37
**heads of chambers,** 44
**hearings, virtual,** 33
**Heinz, J,** 10–11
**Her Majesty's Courts and Tribunals Service (HMCTS),** 12, 145
**hierarchy:**
chambers, 37
Inns of Court, 18
**high-quality legal services offered by Bar,** 151
**high-quality work ethos,** 151
**high street retailers:**
legal services by, 33
**high visibility:**
getting work, 79–83
**higher courts:**
audience rights, Bar loss of monopoly on, 1
Bar advocacy in, 24, 25, 27
solicitors' advocacy in, 27
**historical spaces:**

Inns of Court, 131
**HMCTS (Her Majesty's Courts and Tribunals Service),** 12, 145
**Hobsbawm, Eric,** 138
**hollowed-out organisations:**
risks of chambers becoming, 138
**home working,** *see* **working from home**
**hostility, economic and ideological,** 11
**hot-desking, chambers,** 42, 43
**hourly fees,** 80, 96
**Hughes, Everett,** 8
**human resources officers or consultants:**
direct access seminar invitations, 104
**Hunter, R,** 138–39, 143, 146
**hybrid status:**
in getting work, 87–88
organisational control, 129
practitioners, 113–14
**hyper-specialisation,** 56

**IBC (Institute of Barristers' Clerks),** 45, 48
**ideal-type professionalism,** 10
**ideals, cultural,** 147
**identity:**
formation role, Inns of Court, 131
ideology, 108
professional, *see* professional identity
work, to improve employability, 62
**ideology:**
Bar, 108–109, 127, 129, 130
community, 108
concepts, 150
entrenchment, 134
hostility, 11
identity, 108
independence, 108
neutrality, 108
professionalism, 6, 150
shifting concept, professionalism as, 150
unity, 134
**imagined community,** 138–39
**in-house lawyers:**
corporate institutions and, balance of power shifts, 119
**inclusivity, barristers,** 128
**independence,** 126–27
Bar culture, 112–16
constrained, 116
as core feature of Bar ideology and culture, 127
idea of, 108–109
ideology, 108
legal aid cuts threat to, 118
legal profession, 10
limitations on, 114
powerful clients, direct contract hampering decision-making, 119
professional identity feature, 109
as reason to resist setting up ABS, 112
specialist advisors and advocates, status as, 153
**independent advocates,** 16
**independent professions:**
obliged to justify existence, 12
**independent regulation,** 1, 121–24
**indirect mechanisms:**
of government and self-government, 14
**individual autonomy:**
legal profession, 10, 13–14
**individual initiatives:**
getting work, 85–88
**individual marketing,** 79
**influences:**
powerful clients, 129
**information technology,** 33, 42
**inner barristers,** 17
**Inner Temple:**
Library, 133
**innovation:**
success qualities, 1
traditional professional values reshaped in line with, 154
**Inns of Chancery:**
attorneys, 18
**Inns of Court:**
access schemes, 134
admission regulations, 22
advocacy training, 132
apprenticeships, 18
Bar in, 130
Bar Professional Training Course scholarships, 132
benchers, stepping-stones to becoming, 133
bursaries, 134
chambers:
movement out of, 147
outside, 37
*see also* chambers
clerks, 18
community, 130
continuing professional development courses, 132
control, 18–19
cultural life, centres of, 18

decline in seventeenth century, 18
dining, 41, 131, 132, 133–34
education, 131, 134, 147
educational centres, 18, 19
elegant spaces, 131
ethics training, 132
forensic accounting, 132
hierarchy, 18
historical spaces, 131
identity formation role, 131
influence, 18–19
internal powers, 19
libraries, 41
as mere geographical spaces, 133
mooting, 132
networking, 132
new entrants, 132
new practitioner qualifying courses, 132
pedagogic role revival, 131–32
political life, centres of, 18
professional advancement, 132
pupils, supervision, 147
reluctance by some to move outside, 41
Royal Courts of Justice proximity, 41
self-perpetuating oligarchies of benchers, 22
Serjeants-at-Law, 18
social life, centres of, 18
socialisation, 131, 132, 147
students, 132, 147
symbolic ritual, 18
traditional community, 131
training, 18–19, 134, 147
united community, limitations, 133
unity within under strain, 147
*see also* Gray's Inn; Inner Temple; Lincoln's Inn

**inquisitorial style:**
civil claims without lawyers, 76–77
**insolvency work, accountants,** 21
**Institute of Barristers' Clerks (IBC),** 45, 48
**institutional feedback,** 108
**instructing solicitors:**
not always aware of direct access, 104
**instructions, late,** 110–11
**insurance, after-the-event (ATE),** 120
**integrity:**
Bar culture, 109–12
**intellectual approach:**
pupillage selection, 71
**intellectual rigour:**
pupillage selection, 73
**interests:**
shared, in sets in chambers, 148
**internal powers, Inns of Court,** 19
**internal reforms, legal profession,** 25–26
**International Committee, Bar Council,** 104
**international work,** 104–105
**internet:**
visibility, marketing, 79
*see also entries beginning with* online
**internships,** 63
**interviews:**
pupillage selection stage, 71–73
**invented traditions,** 138–39

**Jackson reforms,** 76, 120, 124
**James II, King,** 18
**Jeffrey, B,** 115
**Judicature Acts,** 18, 22
**junior clerks, chambers,** 37
**juniors:**
chambers, 44
members of Inns, 18
**jurisdictional disputes,** 20–22, 150
**justice:**
universal, roles in provision of, 118
word used on Bar Council website homepage, 109
**Justice Select Committee,** 28

**King's Bench court,** 17
**King's Counsels,** 17
in common law courts, 17
**Kirkpatrick, I,** 34–35
**'know-how' providers, legal,** 33
**knowledge:**
as feature of Bar, 55
new areas of, professions creation attempts, 9
self-contained areas of, professions creation attempts, 9

**labour, division of,** *see* **division of labour**
**Larson, M,** 108
**LASPO (Legal Aid, Sentencing and Punishment of Offenders Act 2012),** 5–6, 28
**late instructions,** 110–11
**Laumann, E,** 10–11
**law firms:**
becoming managerial professional businesses, 34
**law internships,** 63
**Law Society:**
access to justice detrimental impact, 28
conveyancing fees reduction, 25

legal aid budget removed from control of, 25
solicitors' advertising ban relaxed, 25
**law students,** *see* **pupillage; students**
**lawyers:**
abroad, chambers' alliances with, 54
corporate clients, control of, 119
criminal, legal aid payments to, 115
peripatetic, 17
*see also* advocates; attorneys; barristers; solicitors
**lay clients:**
barristers redirecting to solicitors, 95–96
collaborative relationships developing, 106
**LBGT+ practitioners,** 2
**leases:**
auctioneers drafting, 22
**leasing agencies,** *see* **legal leasing agencies**
**lectures targeted at solicitors,** 83
**legal advice:**
inability to access, 30
**legal aid:**
budget control of Legal Aid Board, 25
civil, scope of, 28
criminal, 6, 29–31
cuts to, 116–18, 127
ideological, 128
politicisation of barristers and professional associations, 134–35
threat to independence, 118
dispute, 6, 147
effects on profession, 10, 28–30, 75–76, 103, 116
franchising, 28
growth of Bar and, 23
increases, criminal Bar, 152
payments to criminal lawyers, 115
procurement review, 29
professional autonomy compromised by cuts to, 117
public law cases, 6
residence test, 30
*Transforming Legal Aid* consultation paper (2013), 6, 29–31
**Legal Aid Act 1988,** 25
**Legal Aid and Advice Act 1949,** 109
**Legal Aid Board:**
legal aid budget control of, 25
**Legal Aid Efficiency Scrutiny Committee,** 25
**Legal Aid, Sentencing and Punishment of Offenders Act 2012 (LASPO),** 5–6, 28
**legal culture,** 107
BSB Code of Conduct reflecting, 108
codes of conduct incorporation, 130
emergence from balanced constitution notion, 108
ethics incorporation, 130
**legal ethics:**
BSB Code of Conduct reflecting, 108
**legal 'know-how' providers:**
legal services by, 33
**legal leasing agencies:**
legal services by, 33
**legal management consultants:**
legal services by, 33
**Legal Ombudsman,** 121
**Legal Practice Management Association (LPMA),** 45
**legal practitioners:**
in common law courts, 17
**legal process outsourcers:**
legal services by, 33
**legal profession:**
accountability, 13, 32
Alternative Business Structures, 32
authorised bodies, 32
autonomy, 10
bespoke advocacy and advisory services, 33
as business and profession, 32
case management accountability, 13
commercial orientation, 13
competition, 32, 33
promotion, 13
restriction, Office of Fair Trading, 31
corporate sector, global presence, 32–33
costs accountability, 13
court procedures accountability, 13
Courts and Legal Services Act 1990, 26–27
customer service accountability, 13
discretion, 10
employment structures, less secure, 33
entrepreneurship promotion, 13
fragmentation, 151
implications, 152
governance, new modes, 13–14
Green Papers 1989, 26
independence, 10
individual autonomy, 13–14
information technology impact, 33
legal services market liberalisation, 33
liberalisation, 13
loss of monopolies and internal reforms, 25–26

market freedoms, 13
marketing resistence, 78
'more for less challenge', 33
organisational structure, 10
as profession and business, 32
professional culture, 10
recruitment accountability, 13
reform calls, 23–25
regulation increased, 13
restrictive practices, 24
self-regulation, 10
supervision:
risk assessment approach, 32
surveillance increased, 13
theoretical framing research, 6–7
training accountability, 13
transparency, 32
unity illusory, 147–48
**legal professionalism,** 35
**legal qualifications,** 1
**legal reasoning:**
skills or potential, pupillage selection, 72
**legal representation:**
inability to access, 30
**legal services:**
bespoke, offered by Bar, 151
competition injection, 12
by global accounting firms, 33
globalisation, 12
high-quality, offered by Bar, 151
by high street retailers, 33
by legal 'know-how' providers, 33
by legal leasing agencies, 33
by legal management consultants, 33
by legal process outsourcers, 33
liberalisation, 12
managerial reforms, 12
market liberalisation, 9, 33
by online legal services, 33
**Legal Services Act 2007,** 27, 32
**Legal Services Board (LSB),** 31, 32
**legal work:**
state funding withdrawal for many types of, 9
**legally aided work,** 139
**legitimacy:**
professionalism contingent on, 150
**Leith, P,** 2, 43
**liberalisation,** 12, 13
**liberties:**
Bar, 18–19
**libraries:**
Inns of Court, 41, 133
**Licensed Access,** *see* **direct access**
**licensed conveyancers:**
solicitors' competition with, 25
**limitations:**
on independence, 114
**limited companies, chambers,** 54
**limited liability partnerships (LLP)**
chambers, 53–54
**Lincoln's Inn:**
specialists, 37
**LinkedIn,** 81
**litigation:**
barristers conducting, 77, 94, 105–106
as business, 128
funders, 119–20
initiation monopoly, 20
value for money focus, 128
**Living Wage Foundation,** 58
**LLP,** *see* **limited liability partnerships**
**logos, chambers,** 51–52
**loyalty to chambers,** 39
**LPMA (Legal Practice Management Association),** 45
**LSA (Legal Services Act 2007),** 27, 32
**LSB (Legal Services Board),** 31, 32

**Mackay of Clashfern, Lord,** 26
**Maclean, M,** 2
**Magistrates Courts:**
solicitors as advocates in, 21
**management:**
from above, 35
commercialism, chambers, 43–47
consultants, legal, 33
marketing led by, 79
objectives, 35
orders, costs, 124
organisational, 154
plans, chambers, 48
training, 44, 47–48, 121
*see also entries beginning with* managerial
**managerial administrative requirements,** 128
**managerial approach:**
professions, 8
**managerial compliance,** 127
**managerial concerns, career,** 1
**managerial control, professionalism,** 12
**managerial expertise:**
chambers steered by, 150

**managerial interference:**
independence from, chambers, 56
**managerial professional businesses:**
law firms becoming, 34
**managerial reforms:**
Bar culture, 121–24
Bar Standards Board, 127
court system, 127
legal services, 12
reshaping professionalism, 12
**managerialisation,** 11
**managerialism:**
legitimacy increased by critics of professionalism, 11
new, 26
principles blurred, 12
**managers:**
administration, chambers, 44
business, chambers, 43–44
chambers, 44–45
commercial, chambers, 47
duties, chambers, 44–45
marketing, chambers, 44
**manuals, chambers,** 46
**market allocation of resources,** 25–26
**market closure, chambers,** 37
**market forces:**
professionalism contingent on, 150
**market freedoms:**
legal profession, 13
**market liberalisation:**
legal services, 9, 33
**market logics:**
law firms becoming managerial professional businesses, 34
**market model:**
enshrining key elements of professionalism in, 32
**market monopolies:**
professions exercise of power to obtain, 7
**market-oriented chambers,** 79
**market-oriented models:**
deployment in getting work, 89
**marketeers, new,** 75–93
**marketing,** 75
advertising, *see* advertising
attitudes to, 90–93
Bar Directories target, chambers, 51
barristers, 104, 128
budgets, chambers, 46–47, 83
chambers, *see* chambers
consultants, chambers, 51
defensiveness about, 90
developments in, 150
direct access work, 79
dismissiveness of, 90
diversifying practices, 79
flexible working, 79
in groups, 79, 83–85
individual, 79
initiatives, 79
internet visibility, 79
lack of confidence, 90
legal profession resistence to, 78
management-led, 79
managers, chambers, 44
online self-branding, 79
to other Bar members, 92
proactive, 89, 90
reactions to, 79
relationship marketing, 89
research, 2
sceptics, 91
seminars to solicitors, 79
skills, 140, 154
social interaction in context of, 84
social media, 79
solicitor relationships, actively cultivating, 79
strategies, barristers improving, 104
in teams, 79, 83–85
training, 89, 105
web profiles, 79
**marketisation, Bar,** 13
**markets:**
opened up to competition, professionals, 11
*see also entries beginning with* market
**Marre Committee,** 25
**Marx, Karl,** 24
**Mason, M,** 2
**Masters degrees:**
pupillage, 64
**maternity:**
leave, women at the Bar, 143–46
policies, chambers, 46
**McGowan, Maura,** 107, 138
**MDU (Medical Defence Union),** 98
**mediation,** 33
**Medical Defence Union (MDU),** 98
**medical profession reforms,** 26
**membership, chambers,** 36, 38
**mentoring,** 35, 136
**merging sets, chambers,** 38
**merit:**
pupillage selection, 72, 73

**micro-specialist expertise,** 149–50
**Miller, P,** 13–14
**mini-pupillages,** 61, 62–63
**minimum payments:**
pupillage, 58
**Ministry of Justice (MOJ):**
Bar and, dispute between, 6
barristers' fee cuts, 30
criminal legal aid system review, 31
Very High Cost Cases (VHCC), 30
**mixed disciplinary sets, chambers,** 51
**modernisation,** 128, 150
**monopolies:**
Bar advocacy in higher courts challenged by solicitors, 25
of Bar on higher court audience rights, 9
barristers, 20–22
conveyancing, attorneys, 20
legal profession loss of, 25–26
litigation initiation, solicitors, 20
lost, Bar advocacy in higher courts, 27
opened up to competition, professionals, 11
retention, professionalism, concerns, 24
**Monopolies Commission:**
Bar Council, 24
**mooting, Inns of Court,** 132
**'more for less challenge':**
legal profession, 33
**Morison, J,** 2, 43
**multi-disciplinary practices:**
solicitor profession, 10
**multi-disciplinary sets, chambers,** 51
**Muzio, D,** 11, 12, 21, 34–35, 50, 56, 78
**MyBarrister,** 55

**narrators,** 17
**narrow specialism,** 152
**Nelken, D,** 107
**neoliberal economic policies,** 8
**neoliberal ideology,** 128
**neoliberal practices:**
professionalism, effects, 6–7
**neoliberal professions,** 10–13
**neoliberalisation:**
criminal Bar, 152
**networking:**
Inns of Court, 132
**neutrality,** 108
**new areas of work,** 149
**new commercialism, business and management, chambers,** 43–47
**new entrants:**
Inns of Court, 132
**new managerialism,** 26
**new marketeers:**
getting work, 75–93
**new practice areas:**
getting work, 85–88
**new practitioner qualifying courses:**
Inns of Court, 132
**new professionalism,** 12, 150
**new work generation,** 10
**newsletters, chambers,** 85
**non-accountability principle,** 108
**non-traditional applicants:**
pupillage selection, 60–71
**non-traditional entrants:**
research, 2
**North Eastern circuit:**
chambers, 133
**Northern circuit,** 133
**nostalgic idealisation of past,** 154

**observation research,** 5
**occupational professionalism:**
organisational logics overlapping, 12–13
**Office for Legal Complaints (OLC),** 31–32
**Office of Fair Trading (OFT),** 31
**office space:**
acquisitions, chambers, 54
**OFT (Office of Fair Trading),** 31
**OLC (Office for Legal Complaints),** 31–32
**O'Malley, L,** 78
**online branding,** 79–83
**online chambers,** 55
**online courts,** 76–77
**online dispute resolution,** 33
**online legal services,** 33
**online platforms,** 82
**online portals,** 95
**online presence, chambers,** 51
**online self-branding,** 79
**open door practice, chambers,** 43
**organisational control,** 129
**organisational culture:**
conformation to improve employability, 62
**organisational features:**
professionalism, 12
**organisational logics:**
Bar traditional characteristics reshaped by, 13
law firms becoming managerial professional businesses, 34
occupational professionalism overlapping, 12–13

**organisational management and strategy,** 154
**organisational structure:**
legal profession, 10
liberalising rules, Bar, 1
**Osiel, M,** 9, 78
**outer barristers,** 17
**outsourcers: legal process,** 33
**overcrowding, chambers,** 37
**overseas work,** 104–105
**oversight, external,** *see* **external oversight**
**Oxbridge students:**
pupillage selection, 70, 74

**packaging commercially:**
services provided by barristers, 104
**paralegals:**
chambers, alliances with, 99
**Parsons, T,** 7
**partisanship principle,** 108
**Paterson, A,** 150
**payment by results,** 1
**PCT (Price Competitive Tendering),** 115
**pedagogic role:**
Inns of Court revival, 131–32
**perfectionist approach,** 111
**performance:**
appraisals, 34
constant scrutiny, 6
measurement, 10
**peripatetic lawyers,** 17
**personal elements:**
questions containing, pupillage selection, 72
**personal goals:**
barristers coaching in achievement, 90
**personal injury:**
claims, 28
work, 98
**persuasiveness:**
pupillage applicants with, 74
**PhDs:**
pupillage, special CV-building, 61
**physical space within chambers,** 41
**Piercy, N,** 50
**plans:**
business and management, chambers, 48
**pleaders,** 17, 18
**police:**
budget cuts, 76
forces, reforms, 26
in-house lawyers, 98
**political analysis,** 2
**political life:**
Inns of Court centres of, 18
**political world:**
wider, Bar in, 6–7
**politicisation:**
professional associations, 134–35
**post-graduate degrees:**
holders, pupillage selection, 74
qualifications building, pupillage, 65
special CV-building, pupillage, 61
**post-professionalism,** 12
**potential markets:**
barristers' indifference to, 21
**power:**
balance of power shifts, 119
central to cultural evolution, 107
Foucault on, 66
professionalism, concerns, 24
**powerful clients:**
Bar culture, 118–20
influences, 129
**practice areas, new:**
getting work, 85–88
**practice development:**
chambers, 44, 47
**practice managers:**
chambers, 48
**presentation skills:**
to improve employability, 62
**pressure, external,** *see* **external pressure**
**Price Competitive Tendering (PCT),** 115
**private family work:**
direct access, 103
**privately funded Bar,** 139–142
**privately paid practitioners,** 147
**privileges, Bar,** 18–19
**pro bono services,** 126
**Pro Bono Unit, Bar,** 29, 125–26
**proactive marketing,** 89, 90
**proactive requirement:**
pupillage selection, 73–74
**proctors,** 17
**procurators,** 16–17
**procurement review:**
legal aid, 29
**profession and business:**
legal profession as, 32
**professional advancement:**
Inns of Court, 132
**professional associations,** 149
barristers, 22
politicisation, 134

unrepresentativeness, 24
*see also* specialist Bar associations
**professional autonomy,** 114, 117
**professional community,** 147
**professional conduct:**
rules, 108
standards not compromised, 151
**professional culture,** 10, 107, 154
**professional decline,** 10
**professional degradation,** 150
**professional development,** 9, 10, 134, 153
**professional expertise,** 23
**professional function, barristers,** 106
**professional identity:**
attitude to work, 110
barristers' perception, 106
commitment to work, 110
complex, deep-seated aspects of, 153
independence, feature, 109
**professional jurisdictions:**
research, 8–10
**professional life:**
attitude to work, 110
at Bar, 55–56
commercialisation, 8
commitment to work, 110
*see also* professionalism; professionals; professions
**professional practice histories,** 80
**professional profiles,** 81
**professional relationships,** 1
**professional socialisation,** 152
chambers, 37, 135, 138
Inns of Court, 131
**professional status:**
not compromised, professionalism, 151
**professional values, traditional,** 154
**professionalism,** 35
accountability, 12, 150
Anglo-American modes of, 6
cases, less autonomy in running of, 150
chambers, less autonomy in running of, 150
changing nature, 7
client at centre, 150
commercialisation, 12
commercialised, 119
competition injection reshaping, 12
under constant renegotiation, 150
constitution of, 6
consumerism legitimacy increased by critics of, 11
critics of, 11
culture developing, 6
debates about, 150
dynamic, 150
as dynamic resulting from conflict, 9
economic gains concerns, 24
external oversight, more, 150
external regulation, 12
forms adopted, 12
globalisation reshaping, 12
ideal-type, 10
as ideological concept, 150
ideology developing, 6
legal, 35
legitimacy, contingent on, 150
liberalisation reshaping, 12
managerial control, 12
managerial reforms reshaping, 12
managerialism legitimacy increased by critics of, 11
market forces, contingent on, 150
market model, enshrining key elements in, 32
monopoly retention concerns, 24
neoliberal practices effects, 6–7
new, 12, 150
occupational, 12
organisational features, 12
post-professionalism, 12
power concerns, 24
principles blurred, 12
professional conduct standards not compromised, 151
professional status not compromised, 151
pupillage selection, 74
as shifting ideological concept, 150
social service, 23, 116
standardised procedures, 12
state support, contingent on, 150
traditional, 107, 150
value-for-money services, 150
*see also* professional life; professionals; professions
**professionals:**
altruistic motives, 23
changes in working lives, emotional responses, research, 6
clients:
relationships, 10
trust, 11, 23
continuing professional development (CPD), 11
defining old problems in new ways, 9
exclusivity loss, 12

external oversight and supervision replacing self-regulation, 11
markets opened up to competition, 11
mastery in specialised fields, 23
monopolies opened up to competition, 11
as persons to trust, social and cultural assumptions surrounding, 26
professional expertise, 23
self-interested motives, 107
self-regulation, 11, 23
**professions:**
accountancy, 26
collegiate, 12, 35
commercial branch, 11
competitive approach, 8
development dependant on contingent forces, 9
disciplines growth, refinement and quality of application, 7–8
distinct areas of knowledge, creation attempts, 9
division of labour links, 7
independent, obliged to justify existence, 12
legal aid effects on, 10
legitimation recast by changing social values, 11
managerial approach, 8
market monopolies, exercise of power to obtain, 7
medical, reforms, 26
neoliberal, 10–13
neoliberal economic policies, 8
new areas of knowledge, creation attempts, 9
publicly funded branch, 11
quasi-anthropological approach, 8
self-contained areas of knowledge, creation attempts, 9
social structure links, 7
sociological conceptualisations, 7–8
structural functionalist approach, 7
teaching, reforms, 26
*see also* legal profession; professional life; professionalism; professionals; solicitors
**prosecution fees:**
Crown Prosecution Service, 31
**prosecutions, criminal,** 76
**Public Accounts Committee,** 117–18
**public awareness:**
of direct access, 103–105
**public funding,** 109
Bar, 115, 129, 139–42, 154
branch professions, 11
cuts, 150
practitioners, publicly paid, 147
sector, 128
withdrawal, Bar, 1
work, 152
**public interest:**
Bar serving, 23
as market allocation of resources, 25–26
**public law cases, legal aid,** 6
**public service:**
Bar culture, 125–26
ethos, 108, 117
**Pupil Equality Monitoring Toolkit:**
Bar Council, 67
**pupillage:**
advancement mechanisms, 61
advertising, 67
applications, 61
BAME students, 59, 73
chambers, 135–36
commercial Bar, 60
competences improvement to improve employability, 62
competition for places, 58–59, 60–61, 66
conscious bias, 73
criminal work, 60
cultural capital cultivation to improve employability, 62
CVs, 59, 61–63, 66
employability, 62, 66
family work, 60
funding, 58
further educational qualifications, 63–64
graduate degrees, 64, 65
identity work to improve employability, 62
law students' debts, 59
Masters degrees, 64
mini-pupillages, 61, 62–63
minimum payments, 58
new trends, implications, 65–66
organisational culture conformation to improve employability, 62
other work experience, 64–65
PhDs, special CV-building, 61
places, 60–61
post-graduate degrees, 61, 65
presentation skills to improve employability, 62
regulation, Bar Standards Board, 121
research, 2

selection:
academic credentials, 73
academic excellence, commercial and chancery barristers, 71
advocacy skills or potential, 72
argument skills or potential, 72
bias, 69
chambers' own criteria, 67, 68
critical thinking skills or potential, 72
cultural capital of applicants, 73
elite education focus, 69–70
enterprise requirement, 73–74
filtering criteria, 73
intellectual approach, commercial and chancery barristers, 71
intellectual rigour, 73
interview stage, 71–73
legal reasoning skills or potential, 72
merit, 73
non-traditional applicants, 60–71
objective merit, judgements based on, 72
Oxbridge students, 70, 74
personal elements, questions containing, 72
persuasiveness, applicants with, 74
postgraduate degree holders, 74
proactive requirement, 73–74
processes, 67–68
professionalism, 74
risk-takers, applicants as, 74
robustness, applicants with, 74
Russell Group university students, 69–70, 74
self-assurance, applicants with, 74
self-promotion, applicants with, 74
sifting stage, 68–71
social capital of applicants, 73
unconscious bias, 69
social capital cultivation to improve employability, 62
specialist Bar, 61
ultra-competitive entry, 60
unconscious bias, 73
uneven places, internal differentiation of, 60
unpaid, 58
work experience, 64–65
*see also* education; training
**Pupillage Gateway,** 59, 67
**pupils:**
selection, equality and diversity training, 67
supervision:
Inns of Court, 147
training courses, 121
*see also* pupillage

**QASA,** *see* **Quality Assurance Scheme for Advocates**
**qualifications:**
further educational, 63–64
legal, success qualities, 1
post-graduate degrees building, pupillage, 65
**qualities for success,** 1
**Quality Assurance Scheme for Advocates (QASA),** 115, 123–24, 135
**Quarter Sessions:**
solicitors as advocates in, 21
**quasi-anthropological approach:**
professions, 8

**reception areas, chambers,** 41
**receptionists, chambers,** 37
**recruitment:**
accountability, legal profession, 13
policies, chambers, 46
regulation, Bar Standards Board, 121
**regulation:**
accountability, 121
attorneys, 20
barristers, 22–23
code, 153
external, professionalism, 12
increased, legal profession, 13
independent, 1, 121–24
representation and, Bar Council functions separation, 32
solicitors, 20
*see also* rules
**regulator,** *see* **Bar Standards Board**
**regulatory bodies, unity,** 147
**regulatory requirements:**
compliance, chambers, 46
**relationship building:**
getting work, 88–90
**relationship marketing:**
deployment in getting work, 89
models, chambers, 79
**renegotiation:**
constant, professionalism under, 150
**rents:**
commercial, chambers, 38
**repeat clients:**
solicitors as, 77
**representation:**
advocacy function separation from, 16
barristers, 22–23

powers, Bar Council, 22
regulation and, Bar Council functions separation, 32
**representative bodies,** 147
**reputation, getting work,** 93
**research:**
advantages, 3–4
comparative study of barristers, 2
context, crisis period, 5–6
on direct access, 2
drawbacks, 4
early perspectives, 7–8
ethnographic (re)immersion, 3–4
interview extracts, 4–5
face-to-face interviews, 2–3, 155–57
family cases, 2
LBGT+ practitioners' experiences, 2
legal profession theoretical framing, 6–7
marketing, 2
neoliberal profession, 10–13
new modes of governance, 13–14
non-traditional entrants, 2
observation, 5
political analysis, 2
professional jurisdictions, 8–10
professionals' changes in working lives, emotional responses, 6
pupillage, 2
structure of book, 14–15
**residence test, legal aid,** 30
**resilience,** 153, 154
**resourcefulness,** 1
**resources, market allocation,** 25–26
**restrictive practices:**
Bar challenges, 24
breaking open, 10
legal profession, 24
**results, payment by,** 1
**risks:**
assessments:
legal profession supervision approach, 32
financial, students, 154
takers:
pupillage applicants as, 74
**ritual, symbolic,** *see* **symbolic ritual**
**robustness:**
pupillage applicants with, 74
**Rogers, J,** 2, 109, 117, 131
**rooms:**
barristers in chambers, 41
**Rose, N,** 13–14
**round table meetings,** 33
**Royal Commission on Legal Services 1979,** 24
**Royal Courts of Justice:**
Inns of Court proximity, 41
**rules:**
case management, 124–25
circuits, 131
professional conduct, 108
*see also* regulation
**Russell Group university students:**
pupillage selection, 69–70, 74

**SAHCA (Solicitors' Association of Higher Court Advocates),** 27
**sale agreements:**
auctioneers drafting, 22
**sceptics, marketing,** 91
**scriveners,** 17, 18
**scrutiny, constant,** 6
**secondments in law firms:**
getting work, 87
**selection, pupillage,** *see* **pupillage**
**self-assessment:**
Foucauldian technology of, 66
**self-assurance:**
pupillage applicants with, 74
**self-employment:**
Bar culture, 112–16
competition, 137
practitioners:
chambers, 36
employed practitioners and, barristers' dual capacity as, 32
status:
barristers retained, 151
within chambers, 137
**self-government:**
Bar, 19
indirect mechanisms of, 14
**self-improvement:**
Foucauldian technology of, 66
**self-interested motives:**
professionals, 107
**self-perpetuating oligarchies of benchers:**
Inns of Court, 22
**self-preservation, modernised,** 150
**self-promotion,** 75
barristers getting work, 78–79, 87, 90
dislike of, 79
new, younger members, 93
pupillage applicants with, 74
reactions to, 79
reluctance, 92

resistance to more enterprising ventures in, 92–93
success qualities, 1
**self-regulation:**
legal profession, 10
professionals, 23
subjects, shaping and normalising behaviour, 13–14
**selling points, barristers,** 105
**seminars:**
direct access:
human resources officers or consultants invited, 104
in family law field, 83–84
targeted at solicitors, 79, 83–84
**Senate, Bar,** 22, 25
**Serjeants-at-Law,** 17, 18
**service:**
altruistic ideal, 107
provision on basis of citizenship as universal right, 109
satisfaction and, clients in chambers, 41
**services:**
devaluation, 154
promotion of, getting work, 78
provided by barristers, 104
**sets,** *see* **chambers**
**shared interests:**
in sets in chambers, 148
**showroom common parts:**
chambers focus on, 43
**sifting stage:**
pupillage selection, 68–71
**skills:**
adaptive, 153
advocacy, *see* advocacy
analytical, 1
argument, 72
branding, 154
commercial, 149
critical thinking, 72
customer care, 105
legal reasoning, 72
marketing, 140, 154
presentation, 62
social, 89
**social assumptions:**
surrounding professionals as persons to trust, 26
**social capital:**
cultivation to improve employability, 62
of pupillage applicants, 73
**social interaction:**
in marketing context, 84
**social life:**
Inns of Court centres of, 18
**social media:**
getting work, 79–83
**social policy reforms,** 26
**social service professionalism,** 23, 116
**social skills, barristers,** 89
**social structure:**
professions links, 7
**social values:**
changing, professions legitimation recast by, 11
**socialisation:**
Inns of Court, 132, 147
new members, 154
professional, *see* professional socialisation
**Society of Gentlemen Practisers in the Courts of Law and Equity,** 20
**socio-economic factors:**
pupillage applicants' employability, 66
**sociological conceptualisations:**
professions, 7–8
**Soft Skills Development Course, Bar Council,** 89
**Solicitor Advocates,** 27
**solicitors:**
accountants, competition from, 22
advertising ban relaxed, Law Society, 25
advocacy:
criminal law work in house, 76
in higher courts, 27
specialisation, 77
work, 20, 21
advocates, training in court advocacy and, 115
Alternative Business Structures, 32
attorneys merged with, 18
auctioneers, competition from, 22
authorised bodies, 32
Bar advocacy in higher courts monopoly challenged by, 25
barristers:
cheaper than, 105
clients with little money directed to, 103
contracting services to, 113–14
cultivating relationships with, 88–90
distinguishing from, 150
patronising to and dismissive of, 77
redirecting lay clients to, 95–96
socialising with, 89

briefs, barristers' preparation delegated to, 20
challenging advocacy of Bar, 9
chambers' unsuitable direct access cases redirected to, 103
Chancery Court, 17
City of London Law Society, COMBAR standard terms for, 135
collegial governance within profession, 10
commercial approach, 10
in common law courts, 17
conferences targeted at, 83
conveyancing monopoly, 20, 24–25
CPD-accredited events, 83, 84
criminal law:
advocacy work in house, 76
financial incentive to keep in-house, 27
customer services, 10
debt collectors, competition from, 22
direct access:
clients contact and, 100–102
offending, 102–103
efficiency, 10
etiquette rules, 20
evidence, barristers' preparation delegated to, 20
fees, 30, 96–97
fragmentation, 130–31
getting work, 77–78
instructions from suddenly stopping, 78
lectures targeted at, 83
licensed conveyancers competition with, 25
litigation initiation monopoly, 20
marketing seminars to, 79
multi-disciplinary practices, 10
new work, generation, 10
performance measurement, 10
profession, 10
professional function:
distinct from barristers, 106
regulation, 20
relationships, marketing actively cultivating, 79
as repeat clients, 77
scriveners absorbed by, 18
seminars targeted at, 83–84
small firms:
chambers' alliances with, 99
specialisation, 77
training, 20
**Solicitors Regulation Authority (SRA),** 32, 27
ABS entities licensing, 52
LLP licensing, 53
seminars accredited for CPD, 83
**Solicitors' Association of Higher Court Advocates (SAHCA),** 27
**Sommerlad, H,** 73, 110
**specialism:**
advocacy, solicitors, 77
family law work, 86
getting work, 85–88
narrow, shift towards, 152
solicitors, 77
**specialist Bar,** 141–42
bespoke expert advisory and advocacy service, 153
pupillage, 61
**specialist Bar Associations:**
chambers, 40–41
educational function, 134, 147
professional development, supporting and approving, 134
represented on Bar Council, 134
training, 147
*see also* Commercial Bar Association; Criminal Bar Association
**specialists:**
advisors, barristers' independent status as, 153
barristers, 38–41, 105
chambers, *see* chambers
commercial concerns, 151
fields, professionals' mastery in, 23
Gray's Inn, 37
high-quality work ethos, 151
Lincoln's Inn, 37
marketing, chambers, 85
private/public divide and, 140–42, 147
teams, chambers, 38–41
**splintered community,** 142
**SRA,** *see* **Solicitors Regulation Authority**
**staffing:**
structures modernised, 150
**standardised procedures:**
professionalism, 12
**state funding,** 151–52, 9
*see also* legal aid
**state intervention:**
criminal Bar, 152
**state power:**
legal aid cuts threat to barristers' roles in counterbalance to, 118
**state support:**
loss, Bar culture, 116–18
professionalism contingent on, 150

**status:**
employed barristers' reduced sense of, 127
as feature of Bar, 55
**Stevens, R,** 21
**strategic overviews:**
chambers, 47, 49, 55
organisational, 154
**strike action:**
Criminal Bar Association, 30–31, 134
**structural functionalist approach, professions,** 7
**structure challenges, Bar,** 24
**students:**
financial risks and debts, 154
Inns of Court, 132, 147
training in new essential abilities, 154
*see also* pupillage; pupils
**Subconscious Bias:**
Bar Council, 67
**success fees,** 120–21
**success qualities,** 1
**super clerks, chambers,** 47–48
**supervision:**
external, *see* external oversight; external supervision
legal profession, 32
**SupplyCo,** 54
**support, chambers,** 137
**support staff, chambers,** 37, 40
**surgeries, free,** 104
**surveillance, legal profession,** 13
**Susskind, R,** 33
**Sutton Trust,** 63
**symbolic ritual:**
Inns of Court, 18

**targeting:**
international work, 104
**teaching profession, reforms,** 26
**teams:**
clerks in chambers, 48
marketing in, 79, 83–85
**technical excellence:**
getting work, 91, 93
**technological developments,** 12
**Thatcher, Margaret,** 24, 25
**Thomas of Cwmgiedd, Lord,** 138
**trade union style of leadership and representation, CBA,** 134
**traditional community:**
Inns of Court, 131
**traditional professionalism,** 107, 150
**traditional ways of working,** 151
**traditions, invented,** 138–39
**trainees:**
chambers, 48
*see also* education; pupillage; pupils; students
**training:**
accountability, legal profession, 13
advocacy, 132
attorneys, 20
chambers, 38, 135
courses, 121
in court advocacy, employed barristers and, 115
diversity, 67, 121
equality, 67, 121
ethics, 132
excellence acquired, 109
Inns of Court, 18–19, 134, 147
management, 44, 47–48, 121
marketing, 89
solicitors, 20
specialist Bar associations, 147
students:
in new essential abilities, 154
vocational, 38
***Transforming Legal Aid* consultation paper (2013),** 6, 29–31
**transparency:**
barristers, 128
chambers, 44
charging methods, 149
experience, 80
expertise, 80
legal profession, 32
**trials, fixed-term,** 124–25
**Twitter,** 81
**typing services:**
chambers, 37

**UK Statistics Authority,** 30
**ultra-competitive entry, pupillage,** 60
**unconscious bias, pupillage,** 60, 69, 73
**uneven places:**
internal differentiation of, pupillage, 60
**uneven playing field:**
pupillage applicants' employability, 66
**united community:**
Inns of Court, limitations, 133
**united profession:**
Bar Council rhetoric presenting, 138
**United States:**
corporate lawyers' independence, 118

**unity,** 134, 138, 147–48
**universal justice:**
legal aid cuts threat to barristers' roles in provision of, 118
**unpaid pupillage,** 58
**unrepresentativeness:**
professional associations, 24
**upfront information demands:**
fees, 80
**uplift fees,** 120–21
**USA,** *see* **United States**
**utter barristers,** 17

**value for money:**
focus on rather than on excellence, 128
litigation focus on, 128
services, professionalism, 150
**values:**
ethical, 107
professional, traditional, 154
**Vaughan, S,** 2
**Very High Cost Cases (VHCC),** 30
**virtual chambers,** 55
**virtual hearings,** 33
**virtual space, chambers,** 41–43
**visibility:**
high, getting work, 79–83
**visiting clients in chambers,** 43
**vocational training,** 38

**waiting areas, chambers,** 41
**web analytics, chambers,** 80
**web profiles,** 79
**Webber, J,** 108
**Weber, Max,** 24
**websites:**
branded, sets, 79
chambers, 51, 79, 103
*see also entries beginning with* online
**wellbeing:**
Bar Council survey research, 111
Bar research on, 136, 137–38, 147
**Whyte, A,** 2, 95, 96, 97, 100, 102
**wider political and economic world:**
Bar in, 6–7
**William of Orange,** 18–19
**Wilson, P,** 7
**women:**
at the Bar, *see* Bar
Australian Bar, 143, 146
**work:**
attitude to, 110
boundaries redrawn, Bar, 150
commitment to, professional life, 110
culture, shared, chambers, 38
ethos, 109, 110, 151
getting, *see* getting work
moral approach to, excellence as, 109
new areas, 149
publicly-funded, 152
unevenly or unfairly distributed within chambers, 78
**work experience:**
other, pupillage, 64–65
prerequisite to get on Bar Professional Training Course, 63
pupillage, 64–65
**working from home:**
barristers in chambers, 42
impact on chambers, 138
**workloads:**
increased, clerks in chambers, 46
**written constitutions, chambers,** 44

**Zander, M,** 24

www.ingramcontent.com/pod-product-compliance
Ingram Content Group UK Ltd.
Pitfield, Milton Keynes, MK11 3LW, UK
UKHW020817290926
15470UKWH00003B/1207

9 781509 928767

McDonald, Otis 108–9
mentioned 7, 11, 19 n.9, 84, 95, 107, 119 n.112, n.120, 120, 136, 138, 145, 147, 149–51, 153, 156, 197, 213, 221, 224–5, 244, 254, 259, 261, 280, 291, 293, 299, 303–4, 318
McReynolds, James (US Associate Justice) 61–2, 80 n.43
means-end analysis (*see also* interest-balancing) 13–15, 142, 146, 150–1, 180, 212, 224, 235, 248, 250, 254, 258, 265, 277, 292–3, 304
Menendez, Katherine (Judge) 254–8
*Merrill* (mentioned) 179, 182, 201 n.99
Militia
Act (of 1792) 99, 260
arms 47, 66, 165
English Act (of 1662) 236, 268
-linked 5–6, 48 n.31, 52, 54, 56, 58, 60, 68, 291
-restricted 48 n.31, 60
sedentary 70–1
well regulated 1, 5, 29, 36, 39, 54, 61, 63–5, 68–70, 74, 76, 78, 87, 97, 99, 102, 104–5, 115, 298
Miller (defendant, 1894) 45–6
mentioned 22, 46, 50 n.108, 88, 108–9, 291
Miller, Jack (1939) 59–60
mentioned 3, 41, 51–2, 58, 59–62, 64–72, 74–8, 80 nn.41, 44, 46, 83, 86, 89–90, 94, 98, 105–6, 109, 182, 290, 292, 297, 318
Miller, James 190
mentioned 179, 202 n.141, 293
Moore, LeRoy 129–30
mentioned 122, 129–30, 132, 158 n.38, 292
Morton Grove 52, 72–3, 75–6, 81 n.92, 108
Murphy, James (mentioned) 54, 79 n.11
Muscarello (mentioned) 101, 145, 153

Napier, Harvey 228
mentioned 93–4, 227–8, 241 n.93
Nash, Robert 150, 153–4
National Association of Gun Rights 19 n.20, 322 nn.70, 74, 323 n.88
National Firearms Act (NFA) 52, 58–60, 62–3, 66, 69, 78, 92, 94, 117 n.46, 170, 270, 306–7
National Instant Criminal Background Check System (NICS) 273–4, 276
National Rifle Association (NRA) 1, 244, 246, 250, 252–4, 283, 283 n.13, 284 n.30, 292–3
Navegar 14, 19 n.21, 179, 182–5, 201 n.99
negligence 174–8, 182–3
New York State Rifle & Pistol Association 7, 19 n.10, 121, 150, 156 n.1, 160 n.133
Newsom, Gavin (Governor) 299, 321 nn.35, 38
Norton, Elijah (Judge) 41–2
Nunn, Hawkins 29–31
mentioned 22–3, 29, 42, 48 nn.13, 41, 42, 55–6, 103, 107, 138, 145, 148, 198 n.5, 291

Oakes, Ted 71–2
mentioned 52, 66, 71–2, 75–6, 81 n.86, 292
O'Connor (petitioner) 135
mentioned 122, 132, 135, 137, 158 n.61
O'Conner, Reed (Judge) 306–7, 309
Omnibus Crime Control Act 209, 245–6
operative clause (*see also* prefatory clause) 96–8, 100–3, 255
O'Scannlain, Diarmuid (Judge) 145–9, 156

Parker, Shelly 96
mentioned 12, 19 n.19, 83–4, 95–6, 100, 118 nn.48, 49, 51, 293
Patterson, Nolon 261
mentioned 262, 264, 285 n.85
Perce (defendant) 168–9
mentioned 168, 199 n.20
permissible limitations / restrictions 2, 8–9, 32, 107, 141, 149, 291–2, 301, 318
Peruta, Edward 145, 149
mentioned 16, 20 n.26, 121–2, 136, 145, 149, 156, 159 n.107, 160 nn.119, 132, 292
Phillips, Harry (Chief Judge) 67
Prado, Edward (Judge) 247–249
Pratt, Larry 18 n.2
pre-enforcement challenge 10, 12, 14, 96

pre-existing right 152, 155, 265
prefatory clause (*see also* operative clause) 78, 90–1, 96–8, 100, 102–3, 106, 115
presumptively lawful 138, 143, 186, 192, 211, 213–14, 216, 219, 229, 231–2, 234, 248, 251, 263–4, 274–5, 277–8, 280, 282, 316
Presser, Herman 44–6
  mentioned 22, 41, 43, 50 nn.100, 101, 56, 64, 73–4, 76, 105, 108–9, 126, 130
prevailing understanding 254
Price, Randy 308, 322 n79
prohibited individuals 62, 206, 226
Protection of Lawful Commerce in Arms Act (PLCAA) 178, 182
Purdy, Ronnie (mentioned) 261, 285 n.82

Quarles, Ralph (Chief Justice) 53
Quilici, Victor 73
  mentioned 72–3, 75–6, 78, 81 n.92, 108

Ragon, H. Heartsill (Judge) 61
Rahimi, Zachey 234–7, 300–1, 303
  mentioned 18 n.5, 228, 234, 241 n.120, 260–1, 266, 293, 300, 319 n.3, 321 n.40
Range, Bryant 220, 223–7
  mentioned 220, 223, 239 n.5, 240 n.78, 259, 293
Rare Breed Triggers 307, 322 n.77
Rawle, William 87, 103, 110
reasonable regulation 2, 7, 9, 43, 55–58, 70, 73, 83–4, 121
Reconstruction Era (*see also* Founding Era) 251–4
regulation 34
Reid, defendant (Sheriff) 27–9
  mentioned 22, 26, 28, 30, 42, 48 n.19, 55, 107, 138, 145, 148
Reinhardt, Stephen (Judge) 88–92, 115–16
Rene E. 244–5
  mentioned 244, 246, 250, 283 nn. 2, 3, 4, 5, 292
Richard, Adam 262–3
  mentioned 262, 264, 285 n.86, 292–3
Ringo, Daniel (Chief Justice) 28–9, 48 n.31
Ritter, Halsted (Judge) 59–60, 79 n.33
Roberts, John (US Chief Justice) 301–3
Rohm RG-38S revolver 171–3
Roosevelt, Franklin (President) 60–1, 63–4, 78, 80 n.39
Roosevelt, Theodore (President) 289, 319 n.1
Rosenbaum, Robin (Judge) 250–4, 283
Rosenthal, Andrew 123–4
  mentioned 122, 123–4, 157 n.6, 292
Roth, Jane (Judge) 278–9
Rozier, Christopher 210–11
  mentioned 210–11, 239 n.21, 292–3

Safe Streets Act 223, 245
Saturday Night Specials (SNSs) 164, 169, 171–5, 178–9
Scalia, Antonin (US Associate Justice) 48 n.30, 78, 81 n.79, 83, 100–7, 318
Schenck, Gilbert (Justice) 130–1
Schubert, Joseph 132–3
  mentioned 132, 134, 158 n.47
Scirica, Anthony (Judge) 179–80
Seay, Andrew 263–4
  mentioned 262–3, 272, 285 n.93, 293
Second Amendment Foundation 136, 141
Seegars, Sandra 12
  mentioned 12, 14, 19 nn.16, 18, 96, 118 n.50
Settled law 4–6, 14, 115
Shelby (defendant) 42–3
  mentioned 40, 42–3, 50 n.94, 199 n.8, 291
Shepherd, Bobby (Judge) 264
Sheridan, Peter (Judge) 305–6, 310
Shettle (mentioned) 134, 158 n.57
Silberman, Laurence (Senior Judge) 95–9
Siler, Eugene (Judge) 228–9
Silveira, Sean 88
  mentioned 14, 19 n.22, 83–4, 88, 99, 115–16, 117 nn.19, 23, 196
Simpson, William 26
  mentioned 26, 48 n.15, 104, 145, 206, 239 n.3
Skoien, Steven 229–30
  mentioned 228–30, 232–3, 241 n.100
Slaughter-House Cases 108–9, 119 n.119
Smith, Jerry (Judge) 209–10, 265–29
Smith, William (Justice) 167
Stare decisis 10, 13–14, 86
Stark, Leonard (Judge) 143–4
Statute of Northampton 63, 301, 312
Stevens, Frank 66–8

mentioned 52, 66–70, 72, 75–6, 81 n.70, 93, 95, 118 n.47
Stevens, John Paul (US Associate Justice) 13, 18, 105, 113–14, 298, 321 n.26
Stevenson Dru 19 nn.23, 25
Story, Joseph (Justice) 87, 103
Stras, David (Judge) 270–3
Strickland, J. 55
mentioned 51–2, 55–6, 58, 79 n.13, 121, 157 n.3
Suarez, Julio (mentioned) 212, 214–15
Sugarmann, Josh 178, 200 n.78
Sullivan Law 122, 124, 129, 135–6
Supreme Court (US) 3–5, 16–17, 22, 31–2, 36, 41, 45, 77, 80 n.58, 83–4, 107, 121, 170, 180–1, 185, 198, 205, 207, 250, 289–90
judicial referee 289, 293–5
political entity 8, 289, 293, 295
surety laws 155, 236–7, 301–2

text, history and tradition 7, 13, 15, 19 nn.23, 24, 25, 91, 116, 180, 198, 261, 272, 309, 318
Thomas, Clarence (US Associate Justice) 121, 150–5, 319 n.3
Thomas, Peter (mentioned) 75
Toobin, Jeffery 18 n.8
Tot, Frank 63–4
mentioned 58–9, 62, 64–5, 70, 80 nn.53, 58, 292
Tucker, St. George 87, 103, 110
two-step approach 143, 150–1, 186, 191–2, 212–13, 224, 232, 234, 247–9, 254, 258, 274–5, 278, 280, 293
one step too many 151
Tyler, Clifford 273–7
mentioned 273, 277, 279–81, 286 n.137, 292–3

ultrahazardous risk theory (*see* liability theories)

Vanderstok (citation) 308, 322 n.83
Veasley, Devonte 17, 269–70, 272
mentioned 20 n.28, 262, 265, 269, 273, 286 n.124
virtuous citizenry 213, 218–20, 238, 246, 249
unvirtuous citizens 213, 218–19, 224, 238, 246, 278
Volokh, Eugene 18 n.5

Waite, Morrison (Chief Justice) 37–8
Walker, Moses (Justice) 35–6
Warin, Francis 69–71, 94–5, 117–18, n.46
mentioned 52, 66, 68–9, 71–2, 75–7, 81 n.80, 83–4, 92–5, 117 n.43, 290
Watson, John (Associate Justice) 123–4
Wesley, Richard (Judge) 136–40, 159 n.76
White, Ludivic 228–9
mentioned 211, 228–32, 241 n.94, 292
Whyte, (Justice) 26
Wiest, Howard (Justice) 127–9
Wilforth, (defendant) 41
mentioned 40–3, 50 n.88, 55, 291
Williams, Stephen (Judge) 12, 14
Wilson, Chancy 40, 165–6
mentioned 40, 47 n.1, 50, n.87, 164–5, 168, 199 n.9
Wilson, Cory (Judge) 234–7
Winkler, Adam 80 n.39
Woodbury, Peter (Judge) 64–5
Woods, William (Justice) 44–5
Woollard, Raymond 140–2
mentioned 121–2, 136, 140, 146–7, 159 n.88
Worth, Kristin 254
mentioned 244, 254, 258, 284 n.45, 293

Youth Handgun Safety Act 244–5

Zerillo, James 127
mentioned 122, 127, 157 n.27

www.ingramcontent.com/pod-product-compliance
Ingram Content Group UK Ltd.
Pitfield, Milton Keynes, MK11 3LW, UK
UKHW020221290926
15470UKWH00001B/310